Devotions for a Revolutionary Year

∞365 Days of Jesus' Radical Love for You

Lynn Cowell

Standard®
PUBLISHING

Cincinnati, Ohio

To my kids—Zach, Mariah, and Madi—my prayer is that you will hunger for God and his Word more than anything else. Always remember: "If I find in myself a desire which no experience in this world can satisfy, the most probable explanation is that I was made for another world" (C. S. Lewis, *Mere Christianity*).

Published by Standard Publishing, Cincinnati, Ohio
www.standardpub.com

Printed in: United States of America
Project editor: Laura Derico
Cover design: Entirely Creative, Scott Ryan
Interior design: Dina Sorn, Ahaa Design

While all the stories and quotations in this book are true, in some instances names and details have been changed in order to protect the identities of those involved.

All Scripture quotations, unless otherwise indicated, are taken from the *HOLY BIBLE, NEW INTERNATIONAL VERSION*®. *NIV*®. Copyright © 1973, 1978, 1984, 2011 by Biblica, Inc.™ Used by permission. All rights reserved worldwide. Scripture quotations marked (*NLT*) are taken from the Holy Bible, *New Living Translation*. Copyright © 1996, 2004. Used by permission of Tyndale House Publishers, Inc., Wheaton, Illinois 60189. All rights reserved. Scripture quotations marked (*The Message*) are taken from *The Message*. Copyright © by Eugene H. Peterson 1993, 1994, 1995, 1996, 2000, 2001, 2002. Used by permission of NavPress Publishing Group.

Published in association with the literary agency of The Blythe Daniel Agency Inc., PO Box 64197, Colorado Springs, CO 80962-4197.

ISBN 978-0-7847-3570-1

17 16 15 14 13 12   1 2 3 4 5 6 7 8 9

Contents

*I*nfatuation is a powerful thing. It has the power to make your mind, body, and heart soar. Then, faster than you can say your ex-boyfriend's name, it can drop you, leaving you sick to your stomach.

There *is* something more powerful—revolutionary love. Love that is perfect, unconditional, stable. Love that is not based on what you did for it yesterday or what you can do for it in the future. This love is unlike any you've encountered. This love forgives and forgets the past while promising an amazing future. This love is Jesus.

If you are a girl who wants more—more confidence, more security, more hope—this is the perfect book for you.

This book isn't going to radically change you. Only one book can do that—the Bible. My book simply gives you a diving board to help spring you into the pool of God's Word, where you can swim by yourself!

I hope you've already read *His Revolutionary Love: Jesus' Radical Pursuit of You*—that's what we're building on. But even if you haven't, you can dive in with us now. For the next 365 days, we're going to dig deeper into Jesus' love letters to us. Don't just read the devotions—I want you to get out your Bible; read the key verse each day, and read the verses before and after it. Take some time to figure out exactly what God is saying to you.

This year, we're going to let God **start the revolution** in our hearts, making us radical girls who can change our world for his honor.

So glad to be on this journey with you!

Jesus, thank you for choosing us. Your love is what our hearts have always craved—the only love that can fill them. Change us. Make us radical so we can share your love with others. In your powerful name, amen.

1: How Much?

This is how much God loved the world: He gave his Son, his one and only Son. And this is why: so that no one need be destroyed; by believing in him, anyone can have a whole and lasting life.
—John 3:16 (*The Message*)

••●●●••

What was at the top of your Christmas list last year? The newest boots? Apple's hottest phone?

If you could ask for something that money can't buy, what would that be? Your parents reunited? Your sister back home?

What extreme measures would you be willing to take to get your heart's desire? Move to a new city and have your family start over? Sell everything to put your sister in rehab?

Would you die?

Would you die to see their lives changed?

Jesus' answer was yes. He thought of you and what it would take for you to have new life in him. "Yes, I'll die to make that happen," was his response to his Father's request.

> **START THE REVOLUTION**
> Read John 3:16. Ask: Am I ready to say yes to God's love for me?

Talk about love! Talk about a hero!

I responded to his yes by saying yes back. Yes to receiving forgiveness and choosing his way instead of mine. Yes to having him revolutionize the way I think, act, and live.

When he died, he proved how much he wants us—me and you. The real question now is, **how much do you want him?**

Show him you want him too. Take time this year to go after him. Learn how crazy Jesus is about you. And become crazy about him!

Jesus, I am ready—ready to find out just how much you love me and to really love you in return. Help me to come to you each day. I can't wait to discover more about you! Amen.

CHAPTER ONE

2: Absolutely Beautiful

Has anyone ever seen anything like this—dawn-fresh, moon-lovely,
sun-radiant, ravishing as the night sky with its galaxies of stars?
—Song of Solomon 6:10 (*The Message*)

Have you ever heard of someone choosing his wife when he's in sixth grade? Crazy, I know! That's exactly what Greg did! He saw a girl singing a solo in church and wrote in his Bible, "I, Greg, will marry her—to be stopped by nobody!" If only he had known . . . she didn't even know his name!

Sounds like the beginning of a long romance, right? Not! Greg found her number. Called a few times. After a bit, the crush burned out . . . for *him*. Not for *her*. Why? She didn't even really know him. But she had wanted to be wanted, and he at one point wanted her. You know, it didn't even have to be Greg. She just wanted to be wanted again.

> **START THE REVOLUTION**
> Look in the mirror and say: "Jesus thinks I'm beautiful."

That girl was me, and that crush crushed me. I asked myself, "What's wrong with me? My body—my flat chest? My personality or faith?" Whatever it was, I felt ruined.

Have you ever been on the wrong end of a love equation?

Guy + Me = Value?

The fact was, and still is, there was nothing wrong with me. There is nothing wrong with you.

Jesus tells me I am beautiful . . . every part of me. Maybe at that time I wasn't Greg's type. But in Song of Solomon, a book that is often used as a metaphor for God's love for us, we read these words: "The feelings I get when I see the high mountain ranges . . . remind me of you, and I'm spoiled for anyone else! Your beauty, within and without, is absolute, dear lover, close companion" (7:5, 6, *The Message*). Jesus loves my outsides and insides! (Sounds like Greg was the one missing out!)

Don't let any guy define you. Don't let his rejection or acceptance determine whether or not you think you are beautiful. The Perfect Love says you are absolutely beautiful; listen closely to *that* truth.

Jesus, you and your love are all I want to define me. Amen.

3: Priceless

I paid a huge price for you. . . . That's how much you mean to me!
That's how much I love you! I'd sell off the whole world to
get you back, trade the creation just for you.
—Isaiah 43:3, 4 (*The Message*)

•••●●●••

When Prince William and Kate got married, it was like watching a Disney fairytale movie in real life. Except, perhaps, for all the press. Reporters commented on the price tag of everything—Kate's gown, shoes, ring, flowers, etc. Until they came to the tiara.

"Priceless."

That's how they described her gorgeous headpiece. Given to Queen Elizabeth as a gift for her eighteenth birthday, this diamond tiara was on loan to the princess-to-be. No price tag could be put on the brilliant crown; it was impossible to replace. If it should somehow disappear, Scotland Yard would be all over London in a heartbeat.

In the end though, the tiara is still just a super fancy hat. A thing that can be lost or stolen.

That's so very different from you. Why? Because **Jesus gave his everything, his very life, to make you his.**

START THE REVOLUTION
Look up the price of the biggest diamond. You're worth more than that!

The girl who understands just how much she is wanted is a girl who can be fully confident—empowered to make every decision a wise one, because she knows her decisions matter. A girl who knows that she is priceless is a girl who will never settle for anything short of the best from the one who loves her the most. A girl who is sure that she is cherished and adored is a girl who no longer worries about herself; her focus is on sharing this radical love with all those she comes in contact with. *You* can be that girl.

Jesus—help me to get this message. Help me to appreciate the price you paid for me. Amen.

4: You Belong

*And now you Gentiles have also heard the truth, the Good News
that God saves you. And when you believed in Christ, he identified
you as his own by giving you the Holy Spirit, whom he promised long
ago. The Spirit is God's guarantee that he will give us the inheritance
he promised and that he has purchased us to be his own people.
He did this so we would praise and glorify him.*

—Ephesians 1:13, 14 (*NLT*)

I couldn't care less if Greg's ring on my finger looked ridiculous. It made the statement: "I belong to him." That's what mattered.

Have you ever wanted something that said you belonged? The softball team sweatshirt? The personalized chamber music folder? Your new dad's last name?

You do belong. Just as Greg's class ring was my identity marker, the Holy Spirit *in* you can be your identity marker. His presence says you belong to the one who is perfect and who loves perfectly too!

"How does the Holy Spirit do that?" you ask.

Here's how I think it happens. Have you ever had a sense of the right thing to do? The Holy Spirit was leading. Ever had strength for something scary? The Holy Spirit brought his peace. Ever ready to explode, yet somehow you kept your cool? The Holy Spirit brought self-control.

Sometimes we don't recognize him; we think it's us. Just because we don't recognize his voice and direction, that doesn't make it any less him.

Most things in life we belong to come to an end. You and your boyfriend break up, cross-country season wraps up, and the curtains close on the play.

Not so with the Holy Spirit. He is one who never leaves, a season without end, and a play acted out eternally. Once you receive the Holy Spirit, you are forever his.

START THE REVOLUTION

Design an infinity symbol sticker with the words "Holy Spirit" in it.

Holy Spirit, today I'll need something: an answer, or hope, or direction. Help me look to you and see your presence as my identity marker. I belong to you. Amen.

5: Treasured

"On the day when I act," says the LORD Almighty, "they will be my treasured possession. I will spare them, just as a father has compassion and spares his son who serves him."
—Malachi 3:17

••●●●••

he tornado ruined *everything*. As Kim and Brenda approached the place that had once been their parents' home, nothing was there. No front door. No furniture. . . . No parents. *Everything* was destroyed.

In the days ahead, possessions of their parents began to slowly surface. Papers in a field. A quilt in a tree. Each one was a treasure to my friends because each item represented what my friends no longer had.

I wonder if God ever feels that way about his creation. When he looks at the earth where selfishness and sin rule, does he ever feel brokenhearted over the destruction that lies where beauty once was?

START THE REVOLUTION
Think of someone you treasure. Tell them about it today!

On that day when Christ returns to the earth, we, his followers, will be his treasured possession. When he returns to the earth, the sight of us will bring him joy and comfort. The *King James Version* of Malachi 3:17 calls us God's "jewels."

Does your life reflect that you are God's treasured possession? When God's eyes roam the earth, does it bring his heart so much joy to see you—the jewel among the wreckage?

Once, I would have said no. A tornado of a broken relationship left a hole in my heart. I let my problems define who I was. Learning that God treasured me brought me hope, causing me to shine like the jewel he says I am.

You are his treasured possession. Today, look at your world through the eyes of someone who is deeply cherished.

Spy on your life for the next twenty-four hours. How is God telling you "You are my treasured possession"? Make these revelations your prayer of thanks to him.

6: Real Peace

The tender mercy of our God, by which the rising sun will come to us
from heaven to shine on those living in darkness and
in the shadow of death, to guide our feet into the path of peace.
—Luke 1:78, 79

••••••

Having just left my dying father's hospital room, I searched in vain for my car in the parking deck. Twenty-four hours of visitation left me exhausted, both mentally and physically. It was my birthday, yet there wasn't anything happy about it.

There is no way I could have prepared for that day; it's a strange sensation to take care of your dad. Feelings of being robbed overwhelmed me. I was too young not to have a dad.

Climbing into my car, I felt tears streaming down my face. As soon as I turned the key, lyrics from the radio spoke of a day when going to Heaven would bring our new bodies—ultimate healing.

START THE REVOLUTION
What song brings you peace? Sing it today.

Jesus came into my car that day. He reached down into my pit of despair. He made it clear to me that he was real and Heaven is real too.

That peace stayed through the day Dad died, the day of his funeral, and every day since. **His perfect love flowing down to imperfect me quiets the fear of the future and the pain of the past.**

I know there are days when you feel that life is not fair, maybe even hopeless. At times like these, when we don't feel Jesus' love for us, our faith can be built stronger. We can learn to depend on him no matter how we feel.

Jesus, no matter how I feel, help me to remember the peace you want to give me through your perfect love. Amen.

He Wants Me

7: Eyes on You

But the eyes of the LORD are on those who fear him, on those whose hope is in his unfailing love.
—Psalm 33:18

•••●••

*I*sn't it a strange feeling when someone is staring at you? Sometimes you can't tell why. Is there something in your hair or on your shirt? You start to wonder, *What's wrong with me?*

Today, my friend was staring at my mouth. Finally she said, "You have something green in between your teeth." Ugh! How embarrassing!

Jesus stares at me too, but not like my friend! He is looking at me as one who fears him and hopes in his unfailing love. *Fear* in today's verse is a good thing; it means "worship." He looks at me because I worship him.

Verse 19 of this Psalm says his eyes are on his people "to deliver them from death and keep them alive in famine." His eyes are on me because he wants to take care of me and keep me from harm.

START THE REVOLUTION
Have a staring contest with a friend. Jesus can keep his eyes on you forever!

Jesus is looking at you today. He is fully aware of the situation you are in. He sees you feeling so alone in school. He knows you want so much to live for him. **He knows you struggle.**

But even if you completely mess up today and make everyone mad and upset, his eyes are still on you. Not eyes of disgust at your shortcomings. Not eyes rolling as he thinks, *She did it again?!* His eyes are eyes of love. He wants to help you. He wants to keep you alive, not just in body, but in mind and spirit too.

Let the truth that Jesus is looking at you with eyes of love give you strength. Thank him for having his eyes on you.

8: Perfection

There is no fear in love. But perfect love drives out fear, because fear has to do with punishment. The one who fears is not made perfect in love.
—1 John 4:18

"There is no way he could love me." Allison had done a lot of stuff—bad stuff. Stuff she had grown up learning was wrong, and yet she had done it anyway.

Now her friend Lindsay was trying to tell her that Jesus loved her and still wanted a relationship with her. Allison just couldn't believe that could be true. She knew what her parents would do if they found out; they'd kick her out. If her parents would respond that way, how could she expect anything else from a perfect God?

I'll be the first to admit it: **it's hard to understand a love that loves no matter what.** We fear coming to him in all of our mess. He is perfect and holy. We are not. It's hard to fathom that no matter what we do, he will still love us and want to have a relationship with us.

That is why his love is so revolutionary. Nothing can taint it, because it originates from the one who is perfect. Knowing he loves us this way, because of what he has done and in spite of what we have done, gives us the confidence to come to him, even when we are messed up.

It is here, living in his love, that we are forgiven, given another chance, and eventually perfected. Yes, you heard me—I said *perfected*. That is exactly what the Father wants to do with you. He doesn't want to make you just OK. He wants to take away your sin—those things that drive you *from* him—and perfect you, drawing you *to* him.

START THE REVOLUTION

Try to draw a perfect circle. Write in the circle what to do to get closer to Jesus.

Jesus, I want to be rid of _____.
(Name the thing that separates you from him.)
Please forgive me and perfect me! Amen.

9: Poor in Spirit, Rich in Love

Blessed are the poor in spirit, for theirs is the kingdom of heaven.
—Matthew 5:3

••●●••

oor in spirit. That sure doesn't sound like something I want to be! I want to be confident and have great self-esteem. I want to feel good about how I look, be proud of what I do, and be surrounded by people who like me. Doesn't everybody?

Michelle shared with me on Facebook: "Society wants us to be flawless. We compare ourselves to models. *Now* I know that Jesus thinks I am flawless. He knows me very well. . . . I don't need to try to be perfect for anybody here on earth, because my heavenly Father has an unconditional love that can forgive anything. That's what I love about Jesus. He loves me no matter what. It's hard to try to live without noticing my 'imperfections' . . . I want Jesus to be my everything."

Michelle was "poor in spirit," but this was a great place to be! Why? It caused her to reach out to Jesus. Now what does she have? Confidence and a positive outlook that cannot be taken from her. Her hope is not based on her appearance, accomplishments, or attributes. Her confidence is in Jesus' view of her as flawless (Song of Solomon 4:7).

START THE REVOLUTION
Avoid looking in the mirror today. Just be confident in Jesus' view of you!

Let's get this straight—we all have flaws. (Yes, even those supermodels in the magazines.) We all make mistakes. We all sin. But when Jesus looks at us with his kingdom perspective, **he sees who we really are and what we can be**—what we are made to be. And that is flawless.

When we are helpless to feel good about ourselves, that is the perfect time for Jesus to come in with his truth. We can move from being girls whose lives are based on this passing world to girls who are focused on what lasts forever, the kingdom of Heaven. We can go from being poor imitations to experiencing the richness Jesus has to offer. This is when we truly become radical girls!

Jesus, I struggle a lot with my self-esteem. I want to believe the truth—that you see me as flawless. Amen.

10: Near

But now in Christ Jesus you who once were far away have been brought near by the blood of Christ.
—Ephesians 2:13

••●●●••

Sad. No explanation. Just sad. There are times when I have wanted to climb back in bed, pull the covers up over my head, and just stay there. Because I have soaked my heart in God's Word, it begins to talk to me: "Why are you sad? You have so much to be thankful for!" I know this is true. Yet sometimes it's easier said than felt.

On hard days, I remind myself that although *I* change—my heart and mind swinging back and forth—Jesus' love for me doesn't. It is constant and stable.

Christ has already done all that needs to be done to draw me close to him. Whether my feelings tell me today that I am loved and Jesus is with me, or whether they lie and tell me I'm on my own and have no hope, it doesn't change Jesus' location. **My feelings cannot move him away from me.**

Paul told the Ephesians that all of us were "dead in transgressions" at one time. Another version puts it this way: "You filled your lungs with polluted unbelief, and then exhaled disobedience" (Ephesians 2:2, 3, *The Message*). But even when we were filled with sin, God took us in and, through Jesus' death and resurrection, made us alive and drew us close to him again. We didn't do anything to get God to do this for us, and nothing we do can change it. All we have to do is accept it. And if we do that, as Paul also wrote, then we are members of God's household (2:19): "You're no longer strangers or outsiders. You belong here, with as much right to the name Christian as anyone."

So on the hard days, when my emotions threaten to rock my world, I can cling to Jesus who is near and tell my feelings to quit lying. I belong with him.

START THE REVOLUTION

Use a dry-erase marker to write on your mirror: "People in this mirror may be closer to Jesus than they appear."

Jesus, no matter how I feel, please remind me that you are near. Amen.

You are altogether beautiful, my darling; there is no flaw in you.
—Song of Solomon 4:7

•••●●••

"I s it true that guys are only attracted to you because of your looks? If so, I don't have a chance." My heart breaks as I listen to Carly's words. She wants so badly to have a boyfriend, to have someone she likes, like her back.

I don't really know how to answer Carly. After all, I'm a girl too. Yes, it is common knowledge that a guy is attracted by what he sees. The question is, how's his vision? That is, is he able to see the real value of things, or does he just see what's on the surface? It takes some training and some maturity to be able to see properly.

There is a guy who sees with perfect vision.
Maybe you have never thought of Jesus in this way before, but he is a guy who sees you as you are and knows your worth.

What does he see? We're given a glimpse of this in Song of Solomon 4:7. "You are beautiful from head to toe, my dear love, beautiful beyond compare, absolutely flawless" (*The Message*). In another version, these words are "You are altogether beautiful, my darling, beautiful in every way" (*NLT*).

START THE REVOLUTION
Check your eyes today. Are you seeing beyond the surface?

When he looks at you, Jesus sees the girl he created—his work of art! He sees the girl he died for—the girl he is passionate about! You may not *feel* perfect, but Jesus says you are to die for! Speak this truth every day! I know it may not help all the time (like when that guy you like walks right by you and asks someone else to dance), but if you get used to hearing the truth about yourself, you'll believe it. And then you'll act like a person who knows she is truly valuable—and that *is* attractive.

And while we're on this topic, check your own vision. How do you look at guys? Can you see beyond face value? Practice looking at the world through Jesus' eyes.

Jesus, thank you that you saw in me a beauty that was to die for. Help me see that beauty too! Amen.

12: Let Him In

I slept but my heart was awake. Listen! My beloved is knocking:
"Open to me, my sister, my darling, my dove, my flawless one."
—Song of Solomon 5:2

•••●●•••

"I feel invisible. Like I'm walking down the hall every day, seeing all the people and potential in their lives, but does anyone see me?"

Can you relate to my friend? I know you want others to see you; you want to be wanted. I can't promise you that, someday, the group of friends you long to be a part of will let you in. I don't know if one day the guy you're crushing on will see you and text you.

What I do know is there is one who is doing all he can to get your attention. He hasn't passed you by—**he's calling you every day, sending you messages, knocking on your heart's door.**

You might wonder, *Why doesn't he just come in? He could barge right through—I mean, he's God!*

Unlike some guys you may know, Jesus is a gentleman. He doesn't barge his way into anyone's life. Forced love is not love at all. Love is only valuable when it is offered freely and accepted freely.

> **START THE REVOLUTION**
> Open the door to your room. Imagine Jesus walking right in. What do you do now?

Revelation 3:20 says, "Here I am! I stand at the door and knock. If anyone hears my voice and opens the door, I will come in and eat with him and he with me." That's pretty personal, at least at my house. We don't let just any person come in and eat with us.

There *is* someone who sees you—someone who sees all your potential, all you were created to be. Say yes to his knocking. Stop wasting your time, thoughts, and talents worrying about people who haven't noticed you. Focus your love energy on the one who loves perfectly in return.

Jesus, thank you for paying attention to me. Please come into my life and help me be all I can be. Amen.

He Wants Me

17

13: For Us

What, then, shall we say in response to these things?
If God is for us, who can be against us?
—Romans 8:31

•••●●•••

Math and I have always been archenemies. That's no surprise; writers and numbers often don't mix. The problem was, I had to have geometry to graduate. None of it made sense to me; I failed my first test. Handing me the paper with the red F, my teacher moved me to the back of the room. "Obviously you don't get it, so that is where you belong." I thought teachers were supposed to help you!

Are there days when you feel like everyone is against you? Even when you're trying your hardest?

Been there. I've felt like a Tilt-A-Whirl at the fair, always spinning, spinning, spinning—trying to make (or keep) everybody happy. It was so exhausting! And worst of all, I wasn't even sure who was the real me.

Until . . . I really got that God was for me. He wanted me, mess-ups and all. You know what happened when I got that he was for me? I stopped caring so much what others thought of me! At first, it was weird. I was so used to the anxiety of pleasing people. It didn't take long, though, for me to enjoy the new peace!

START THE REVOLUTION
Say this out loud: "If God is for me, who can be against me?"

Now, when I sense those old feelings coming up, I remind myself, "If God is for me, who can be against me?" I focus on pleasing the one who loves me perfectly, and let the Lord figure out the rest!

Thank you that YOU are for me, Jesus! Amen.

14: Ugly Words

Whoever touches you touches the apple of his eye.
—Zechariah 2:8

••●●●••

*T*he words on Facebook glared back at her. "You are so ugly! You are fat, annoying, and I hate you!"

Lindsay just sat there, staring at the screen, baffled. *What did I say? What did I do?*

Maybe this has happened to you, or in some way you've faced this same type of painful rejection. I recently spotted a T-shirt at the mall that read, "You're no one until someone talks about you." How sad! In a world where gossip fuels most of the popular TV shows, it comes as no surprise that *mean* defines many girls today.

How can we guard our hearts when someone makes us feel ugly?

Feeling unaccepted is nothing new. If you read through the whole Bible, you'll find several characters who felt un-loved or rejected. Even Jesus was "despised and rejected by mankind" (Isaiah 53:3).

> **START THE REVOLUTION**
> Print out some of the verses mentioned here or save them in your phone. Put them where you can see and read them every day.

Remembering who we are in God's eyes counteracts the poison of meanness. When I know that I am accepted by God, I can deal with insults. How do you know what God says about you? Read it in his Word:

- "My beloved is mine and I am his" (Song of Solomon 2:16).
- "You're beautiful from head to toe, my dear love, beautiful beyond compare, absolutely flawless" (Song of Solomon 4:7, *The Message*).
- "You are a chosen people, a royal priesthood, a holy nation, God's special possession" (1 Peter 2:9).

I put truth *everywhere*, so I can read it over and over again. When we feel rejected, these words remind us that we are accepted. But not just accepted—we are the "apple of his eye."

Thank you, Jesus, that you are mine and I am yours. Amen.

15: Crazy Love

"Though the mountains be shaken and the hills be removed,
yet my unfailing love for you will not be shaken nor my covenant
of peace be removed," says the LORD, *who has compassion on you.*
—Isaiah 54:10

••●●●••

"**H**urry! Hurry! You'll be too late!" I shouted at the screen. You'd think I'd never seen this movie before. In fact, I've watched it over and over. I know the hero will come right at the last second, risking his life to save hers.

Like the girl in the movie, we want to be desired, fought for, pursued. And we are. **Our Creator pursues us.** He gave up his life, paying a great price to come and rescue us.

There were times in my life when I saw Jesus as my Savior, Shepherd, and friend. But it wasn't until I read the following verses and realized the magnitude and depth of his love for me that I saw how valuable I am to him:

> Don't be afraid, I've redeemed you. I've called your name. You're mine. When you're in over your head, I'll be there with you. When you're in rough waters, you will not go down. When you're between a rock and a hard place, it won't be a dead end—Because I am God, your personal God, The Holy of Israel, your Savior. I paid a huge price for you. . . . That's how much you mean to me! That's how much I love you! I'd sell off the whole world to get you back, trade the creation just for you. (Isaiah 43:1-4, *The Message*)

He'd give up everything just for me? The whole world? That's crazy! This truth satisfied a deep longing in my heart, a longing I didn't even know I had. This is the love that fills the love gaps in my wanting heart and answers the question: Am I valuable enough to be pursued?

Yes, I am. And so are you, my friend.

START THE REVOLUTION
Watch your favorite romantic movie and remember that Jesus is pursuing you too!

Jesus, thank you for giving up everything for me! Amen.

16: Wild

Be here—the king is wild for you. Since he's your lord, adore him.
—Psalm 45:11 (*The Message*)

••●●●••

"**H**e loved me; but did he like me?" I grew up learning about salvation and Jesus dying for my sins, so I got that he loved me. Did he like me, though? When he looked at me, was he disappointed in me? What could I do to get him to like me more?

I wish I could understand where such warped thinking came from. Maybe it's the fake society we live in. We have "friends" who "like" us in front of us, but behind us, they are quick to tell all the ways we annoy them. Could the same be true of Jesus?

Then I discovered the truth. Even knowing my deepest thoughts, my darkest deeds, and my disappointing attitudes didn't change his loving thoughts toward me.

He didn't die for me because he had to; he did it because he wanted to! He did it because he is wild about me! He was on the day he died; he is still today.

In the *New International Version*, our verse today says, "Let the king be enthralled by your beauty." *Enthralled* means to be captivated or charmed. When he looks at you, not only does he like you, not only does he love you, he's captivated by you! **He can't take his eyes off you.** He's crazy about you!

START THE REVOLUTION
How do you feel about your most favorite things in the whole world? Jesus loves you like that!

Think of one thing that you think Jesus likes about you. Now think of one thing you like about him. Make these into your prayer today.

He Wants Me

21

17: Chosen

For he chose us in him before the creation of the world to be holy and blameless in his sight. In love he predestined us for adoption to sonship through Jesus Christ, in accordance with his pleasure and will.
—Ephesians 1:4, 5

•••●••

"If I had known she was going to tell my secrets, I would have never become friends with her!" "If I had known he was going to dump me, I would have never gone out with him!" "If I had known that this was the way it was going to turn out, I would have never _____ !" (Fill in the blank.) Ever have these thoughts?

Just think of this: God *did* know exactly the way everything was going to turn out when it came to his relationship with us—and he still created us! He knew some would reject him: "I don't want that!" He knew others would say "Not now. Maybe after college." He knew some would break his heart.

He also knew some would love him deeply. This is why he still chooses to put his heart out there and risk rejection. He does it again and again because he wants close, intimate relationship with us. He is willing to go through the pain of rejection from some in order to experience the joy of chosen love from others.

> **START THE REVOLUTION**
> Make an invitation from God to you. Be sure to spend some extra time with him this week.

Why would he go through this? Because **love is only valuable when love is chosen.**

Jesus doesn't need love from us; he is already complete in the relationship he has with the Father and the Holy Spirit. He does, however, want a relationship with us.

Don't take this invitation lightly, friend. The Creator of the universe wants to interact daily and relate with you. Don't let this opportunity for real love pass you by. Choose his deep love.

Jesus, may I never say no, or later, to what you offer me. Today I am saying yes to you! Amen.

18: Lenses

For now we see only a reflection as in a mirror;
then we shall see face to face.
—1 Corinthians 13:12

••●●••

Ever seen a girl who had no idea that a certain guy was crazy about her? Let me tell you about Abby and John.

Abby is an absolutely adorable girl. One of Abby's best friends is John. Abby and John do *everything* together. One day when I was hanging out with their friend Megan, she said, "I wish I had a best friend like John."

I thought, *Best friends? No way. John has it bad for Abby.*

Several months later, I was with Megan when she said, "Guess what? John told Abby he's liked her this whole time!"

"*Really?!*" I replied with a grin.

Abby didn't see herself as a girl who was wanted. When she looked in the mirror, she saw a skinny girl with braces. But that isn't what John saw at all!

A lot of us are just like Abby. When we look at ourselves, we don't see what *Jesus* sees. **Mirrors can distort our vision.** But someday when we see him face-to-face, we'll see in his eyes a true reflection. Until then we need to remind ourselves of the truth that Jesus sees us as beautiful and is crazy about us. Then our confidence will be built on something that can never be taken from us.

Today, look at your life as the girl in the know, like I was in the know about John and Abby. Look through the lenses of a girl who is being pursued and fought over. What does your world really look like through the lenses of one who is wanted?

> **START THE REVOLUTION**
> Look through a magnifying glass. Remember: Jesus' vision magnifies all the best in you.

Give me your lenses, Jesus. Amen.

19: How You're Made

I praise you because I am fearfully and wonderfully made;
your words are wonderful, I know that full well.
—Psalm 139:14

• • ● ● ● • •

I hate the number, the one staring back at me on the scale today. I try not to care, to not let that number have power over how I feel.

But it's hard.

I feel pressure to fit into skinny jeans, to avoid at all costs having a muffin top or flabby legs. Some of the pressure comes from society: commercials, magazines, movies, and TV shows. Hollywood makes it hard on us girls! Perfect bodies, hair, and teeth—it's exhausting to even think of keeping up with it all.

Other days, **the pressure comes from within.** I look in the mirror; I see the teeth that never had braces. *Would that have made me feel more beautiful? Is it too late?*

It's not just the teeth; my chest could really use some help too. And so on and so on . . .

This is where our battles take place: on the scale, in front of the mirror, in the closet. And this is where we need to fight back!

Stand on your battleground and ask Jesus for help.

Consider the beauty of our Lord and Savior, and let him define for you what true beauty is. Repeat today's verse: "I am wonderfully made!"

> **START THE REVOLUTION**
> Arm yourself for battle. Use the sword of the Spirit—God's Word—as you face your battle today.

Jesus, I don't want to offend you and criticize the way you made me, but I could really use some help here. Open my eyes to show me what you see. Amen.

20: Everlasting

The LORD appeared to us in the past, saying: "I have loved you with an everlasting love; I have drawn you with unfailing kindness."
—Jeremiah 31:3

•••●•••

*N*ame some things in your life that are eternal. Things that never end. Pretty short list, isn't it?

One thing on your list should be the love of God. He's been loving you and will love you forever: before he created you, in this short gap called life, and when you leave this earth. How incredible! You would think that, since we have this kind of unending love from God, it would be a no-brainer to invest in loving him back. Even though we receive this perfect love, though, sometimes we fail. **We spend much of our efforts on things that are not eternal.** And so little energy returning the love that is.

In most relationships, when we don't call or reach out and show we care, those relationships falter or even fall apart. Ever have a best friend move away or go to a different school? Relationships that are not convenient are often hard to keep.

God's love is not like that! He keeps reaching out to us with his everlasting love, no matter what! His is not a love we should take for granted; we need to meet with him, loving him back, every day!

It can be easy to forget God in the day-to-day details of our busy lives. We allow things, both good and bad, to crowd him out. But even then his response is to draw us back; he wants us so much!

START THE REVOLUTION
What will you do today to put energy back into your relationship with him?

Thank you, Jesus, for such a perfect, everlasting love. Amen.

21: Lavish

*See what great love the Father has lavished on us, that we should be
called children of God! And that is what we are! The reason the world
does not know us is that it did not know him.*

—1 John 3:1

•••●●••

Whenever I read my Bible and see the word *love,* I just have to start digging. I guess I must be one desperate girl, because I just can't seem to get enough.

Today's key verse tells us that the Father has lavished his great love on us. *Lavished* isn't a word in my everyday vocabulary. Dictionary.com says it means: "to expend or give in great amounts or without limit."

Have you ever been squeezing someone in a giant bear hug and they squeak out "Stop!"? Maybe their love language isn't physical touch! Possibly you've had a friend wish you didn't call so much, or a guy who thought you were spending too much time with each other.

Not so with God! There is no point at which God says "OK, that's enough," when it comes to his love. It's impossible for him to spoil you, so **he just keeps giving and giving.**

One of the ways he expresses this crazy, luxurious love is by calling us his children. YOU are the child of God! You belong to the one who owns and created everything.

START THE REVOLUTION

Are you proud of the name "Christian"? What does it mean to you?

*Thank you for calling me your child. Thank you for
adopting me and making me your own. Amen.*

22: Wanted

It's in Christ that we find out who we are and what we are living for.
Long before we first heard of Christ and got our hopes up, he had his
eye on us, had designs on us for glorious living, part of the overall
purpose he is working out in everything and everyone.
—Ephesians 1:11, 12 (*The Message*)

•• • ◉ •• •

If you read *His Revolutionary Love,* you know I was a stalker-type girl at one point. I schemed and planned about how I could spend the rest of my life with Greg. Here's an example of how over the top I was. In my sophomore year I didn't buy my yearbook. I figured that, since Greg was a senior at the same school, we would already have his copy when we someday got married! Can you even believe me? (Seriously, I either needed help or I had really crazy faith! Maybe both?)

This type of thinking can really tank a girl in the pit of self-pity. Daydreaming to the point of obsession can end up being just another reminder that you aren't wanted!

I am so glad that Jesus took care of all that! **Talk about feeling wanted!** Today's verse says that before I even heard of Christ, he had chosen me. He already had a plan in place for us to be together. He worked out all the details for how he was going to bring my life and his incredible plan together!

> ### START THE REVOLUTION
> Be a Jesus stalker today. Read his messages over and over again. Find out where he's working, and join him!

When we focus on this reality, that Jesus wants us and has an amazing future for us, it builds confidence in our hearts. This kind of confidence empowers us to be joyful—with or without that guy we've been stalking!

Find out whose you are and what you're living for. Become a Jesus stalker! You know all that time you spend (or waste) thinking about that guy, cruising his Facebook page, reading his tweets? Just think how much more amazing you would become if you took this same time and energy and stalked Jesus! That wouldn't be time wasted; it would be time invested!

Jesus, help me to become a Jesus stalker! Amen.

He Wants Me

> *It wasn't so long ago that you were mired in that old stagnant life of sin. . . . It's a wonder God didn't lose his temper and do away with the whole lot of us. Instead, immense in mercy and with an incredible love, he embraced us. He took our sin-dead lives and made us alive in Christ. He did all this on his own, with no help from us!*
> —Ephesians 2:1-5 (*The Message*)

•••●••

Ever have someone be kind to you when you deserved the worst? I was in a hurry. (Then again, when am I not? I think I was just born stuck in high gear.) I hopped into my little black car, shoved my gearshift into reverse, floored the gas—and slammed right into a huge mulch pile. There, for the entire world to see, shone a new crack in my bumper.

You know what worried me most? Not the cost of the repair. Not the expense of my newly increased insurance bill. What really concerned me was my husband's reaction. I just knew that he was going to be sooooo mad. If not that, he'd be really disappointed in me. I hated to have to deliver the bad news!

But when I finally did tell Greg, do you know what he did? **He forgave me.** He looked at the crack and said, "I know you didn't mean to."

I really didn't see that coming! I thought I'd get what I deserved—yelled at! Greg had every reason to lose his temper, but he didn't. Instead, he totally demonstrated the love of Jesus.

I deserve to be yelled at—and a lot more—by God. For the sins I've committed, I deserve death. But instead, Jesus forgives me and gives me a new life. He shows me mercy—a gift of love I will never deserve.

START THE REVOLUTION

Who in your life needs love they don't deserve? Spill out some mercy on those around you today.

Show me who needs your love today, Jesus, and let it pour out through me. Amen.

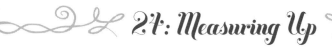

24: Measuring Up

I pray that you, being rooted and established in love, may have power,
together with all the Lord's holy people, to grasp how wide and long and
high and deep is the love of Christ, and to know this love that surpasses
knowledge—that you may be filled to the measure of all the fullness of God.
—Ephesians 3:17-19

•••••••

What rattles your confidence and pushes your insecurity buttons? My thing is being around success. Somehow, I breathe in the lie that all people are created in the same way, so we should all be able to do the same things.

I can't stand the insecurity coming up inside me. It's like the last time I got the flu.

What does it for you? The look and giggle as you walk down the hall. Striking out—for the third time in a row? Having a teacher read test scores out loud? All these events have something in common: **comparison**. We feel as if our best is being compared to another's, and we just don't measure up.

This shifty thing called self-esteem can create trouble, even for the most secure. It's a trial that won't go away, no matter what your age. So what's a girl to do?

Base your esteem on the one constant: Christ's love for and in you. His perfect love never changes. Here, rooted in this solid love, we can rest secure. The more we understand how endless his love truly is, the more stable we will be—inside and out.

When bad things happen—and they will, over and over again—we can keep going back to his unshakable devotion. We can return to the truth of his radical love and have it fill our aching hearts again and again.

START THE REVOLUTION
Read today's passage again. Allow the truth of the depth of his love to fill your heart's gap.

Jesus, help me remember that whatever happens today,
it isn't anything that your powerful love and I
cannot handle together! Amen.

He Wants Me

29

25: Sing It

By day the LORD directs his love, at night his song is with me—
a prayer to the God of my life.

—Psalm 42:8

•••●•••

*D*on't you love when you feel strong? There have been different seasons in my life when I have been very fit. When I was fifteen, I ran my first half marathon. I loved the ability to go out and just run and run and run. It made me feel powerful—free.

There is another time when I feel strong: in the morning. During my favorite time of the day, I spend quiet moments with Jesus. Filling my heart and mind with just what I need to make it through the day— love and hope. Seriously, sometimes I actually giggle when I'm gathering my Bible and journal. I just love it.

Nighttime, though, can be really hard. As I lie in bed, my mind swirls, pulling me into a spiral focus on my troubles. **Inside my heart, a war goes on between faith and fear.**

Do you ever struggle at night? Maybe you have thoughts like these: "Nobody else is home alone. Other people are out together, having fun, while I'm here alone."

We can take a cue from David. During the day, he allowed the Lord's love for him to give him direction. Knowing he was loved gave him the strength to make the hard choices that were the best choices. Then at night he put away all the words and hard thinking and just sang praise to God.

START THE REVOLUTION

Choose a song to sing—a song that thanks him for his deep love for you! Sing this song tonight as you lie in bed.

Today, make your prayer a song to him—
even if it isn't night.

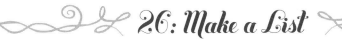

26: Make a List

How beautiful you are, my darling! Oh, how beautiful!
Your eyes behind your veil are doves. Your hair is like a flock of goats
descending from the hills of Gilead.
—Song of Solomon 4:1

• • ● ● ● • •

"**I** am in love!" she tells you. Then she begins to tell you everything that is so wonderful about her guy:

- His smile when I walk into the room.
- His manners. He even opens my door!
- He only has eyes for me.
- He's a guy's guy, totally manly!
- I feel beautiful when I am with him.

At this point, you've probably heard enough and are trying to figure out some way to get her to stop.

There is one who does the same about you; he goes on and on. Throughout the Bible, God expresses his love for us. And one book in particular is said to reflect the love of God for his creation: Song of Solomon. It's not hard to see just how wild about you he is. Here are some descriptions from Song of Solomon 4 (*The Message*):

- You're so beautiful.
- Your smile is generous and full.
- You've captured my heart, dear friend.
- How beautiful your love, dear, dear friend.

He goes on and on, saying: "**You're beautiful from head to toe**, my dear love, beautiful beyond compare, absolutely flawless" (v. 7).

Radical girl, if he has filled a whole book on how crazy he is about you, how about starting a journal about why you are wild about him? You'll need a lot of pages to describe your amazing Lord.

START THE REVOLUTION

Start a journal. Here's a first line: I'm crazy about him because he's crazy about me!

Jesus, I can't wait to dive into your Word and learn just how amazing you are! Amen.

27 : Hopefully in Love

You've captured my heart, dear friend. You looked at me, and I fell in love. One look my way and I was hopelessly in love!"
—Song of Solomon 4:9 (*The Message*)

••●●●••

maybe you're still having a hard time believing that Jesus is in love with you. Does your mind think *Why? What's so great about me?* Possibly a lack of a boyfriend is what makes it hard for you to believe that *you* could capture the heart of anyone!

But you have. The picture painted in Song of Solomon is one of a King utterly in love with the object of his devotion. Let's consider the image of two guys. First, there's the typical guy at your school: young, immature, still trying to figure life out, insecure, selfish . . . need we go on? Contrast him to Jesus: perfect, all-knowing, and unconditionally loving—the very definition of unselfish.

START THE REVOLUTION
If you're stuck thinking you are unlovable—look again, through the eyes of Jesus.

Now who are you going to believe when it comes to your lovability level? That crush who is crushing you or the one who is flipped-out, madly in love with you?

Since you can *see and hear* your crush, it makes it easier to believe him. Seeing all the couples at school holding hands, going out, texting, tweeting . . . it makes it hard not to view that picture as the only kind of love. But if you'll take some time to **look a little deeper**, you can see the shallowness of this type of relationship. Often it is filled with the "what can you do for me" mentality. Rarely is it unselfish and about the benefit of the other person.

The love that loves no matter what you do, the love that only wants to know you—*that* is real love.

Jesus, please fill that gap in my heart that wants a crush I can touch. You are all I need! Amen.

28: Unselfish Love

I have made you known to them, and will continue to make you known
in order that the love you have for me may be in them
and that I myself may be in them.

—John 17:26

••●●●••

*J*esus, speaking to his Father God in this verse, says he is going to continue what he started: sharing with everyone he can about his Father. Jesus wants us to get the depth of love that exists between himself and God.

It's unfortunate that in the English language we have only one word for *love*. Love can have so many different meanings! You can love your parents, love the beach, and love going to church—all completely different kinds of love.

In the study notes of my Bible, it says that the word for *love* in this verse is *agape*. Agape love is so different from the types of love we usually live out. **Agape isn't just a feeling; it's a choice** that is made to value and treat as precious the one it loves. It's isn't about what's in it for me; it's all about how the one loving can benefit the one loved.

This is the perfect love that Jesus has for us. It's rooted in unselfishness and is pure. Agape love is the love that Jesus wants us to have in us, so that his love can live out of us.

START THE REVOLUTION

Choose to show love today— especially to someone not easy for you to love.

Jesus, the "love" I know depends on feelings. Fill me with your perfect agape love and give me the strength to pour out your love on others. Amen.

29: He Fought for You

My Father, who has given them to me, is greater than all;
no one can snatch them out of my Father's hand.
—John 10:29

••●●●••

I have never been fought over. Never. Not for a team on the playground. Not between two girls who wanted to be my best friend. For sure not between two guys. Unless you count that dream I had after watching the first *Pirates of the Caribbean* movie. Seriously though, I don't think that counts.

There was a side of me, like Elizabeth in that movie, that wanted to be fought over! Part of me just wanted to know that someone was so crazy about me, he'd do anything for me.

When I read today's verse, I heard Jesus saying, "That's me, Lynn!" Nothing is going to take me away from him, and he will always rescue me. His love compels him to do anything and everything to protect me.

Read today's verse out loud. When I read it, I picture Jesus, on the day I gave him my life, standing up and shouting for all to hear:  **"This one is mine!"**

I don't have to wish that someone would fight over me, and neither do you. Jesus already did, on the cross. This was more than just a few thrown punches. Jesus fought to the death and beat Satan by a long shot!

START THE REVOLUTION

Read today's verse out loud, shouting it out! Put your name in place of "them."

Jesus, you are my rescuer! Thank you for fighting for me then, and every day since! Amen.

30: He Got There First

We love because he first loved us.
—1 John 4:19

••○●○••

*T*here is something very powerful about our first crush. I should know; mine lasted seven years . . . and then I married him!

You know, when I first fell for Greg, it was kind of weird. I mean, I didn't even know him. That first time he called, I couldn't put his face and name together in my mind. One thing I did know. Someone—a *boy* someone—was calling me, and I liked it!

I hate to admit that being wanted was my reason for letting this crush even begin. But it's the truth. There is something almost riveting about having someone like you first.

I'm sure that is what first got me about Jesus too. As embarrassed as I am to admit that, it helps knowing that I am not the only one! When John wrote a letter to the churches in Asia, he made this statement: "We love be-cause he first loved us."

I guess it's just human nature: **when we are loved, we find it a lot easier to return love.**

So now that you know he loves you, and loves you greatly, it's time to spread it around. Spread it first back to Jesus and then on to all those around you. Let this love fill your heart until it can't help but spill out. Get so full with his love, there is nothing that can hold it back. Love because he first loved you.

> **START THE REVOLUTION**
> Love someone today, because Jesus loved you first.

Jesus, you loved me before I even knew about you. Fill me up so I can pour you out! Amen.

31: Refuge

The LORD is good, a strong refuge when trouble comes.
He is close to those who trust in him.
—Nahum 1:7 (*NLT*)

•••●•••

There's not a ton of hugs or snuggling going on around here; I live in a house of people whose love language is not physical touch. In fact, we just might ask you to move over if you get too close on the couch. We all love each other; we just don't show it with slobbery kisses and bear crushes.

One of the many things I love about God is that every language is his love language. Words of affirmation, quality time, gifts, acts of service—he loves them all. And it is absolutely impossible to get too close to this one who loves you so much.

Love is vulnerable; love is open. In fact, those qualities are exactly what it takes to let this radical love of Jesus revolutionize your life. Today's verse says he is close to those who trust in him. When you know that you are loved, it is not hard to trust. You know that the person has your best at heart each time, every time.

START THE REVOLUTION
Memorize Nahum 1:7.

When we make a choice to depend on his love in our hard situations, it will cause us to draw closer to him than we were before, and he wants that! The confidence we gain from giving our troubles to the one who can be trusted will be a confidence we can rely on again and again.

I want you close to me, Jesus! I want to run to your
strength and love again and again! Amen.

32: Rescue

Who is this, robed in splendor, striding forward in the greatness of his strength? "It is I, proclaiming victory, mighty to save."
—Isaiah 63:1

•••●●••

*A*nyone who knows me knows I am crazy about movies set back in time, such as *A Little Princess* and *Braveheart*. Throw a little romance in there, and I am hooked!

Today's verse reminds me of a time gone by. I picture Aragorn from *Lord of the Rings*, riding on a horse, rescuing those he loved from evil.

There are some days when I need someone who loves me to come to my rescue. Pressures around me threaten to pull me under. My own dumb mistakes leave my relationships in a mess. My own thoughts make me feel sad and dejected.

We don't have to wish that we lived in a different time, with knights coming to our rescue. We live in a time when a Prince has come to our rescue, and his name is Jesus. There is no reason for us to try to pull ourselves out of our sticky situations we can't repair. Jesus, who has all power and strength, is ready to come to our rescue. It is so simple; it just takes calling one word: *Jesus*.

Simply saying his name brings power into our lives. I really don't understand it. I just know that when I feel like I can't take any more, whispering his name brings his peace.

> **START THE REVOLUTION**
> Say his name: *Jesus.* Experience the peace of the one who rescues you.

Jesus, I can't ever repay you for rescuing me. Thank you for giving me your strength. Amen.

33: He Bends

I led them with cords of human kindness, with ties of love.
To them I was like one who lifts a little child to the cheek,
and I bent down to feed them.

—Hosea 11:4

•••●●●•••

*H*ow could I have messed up . . . again? Falling for that same old trap? I didn't mean to. It wasn't like I was purposefully trying to make her look bad.

I feel awful; the weight of sin is pulling me under. *I'll just never be who I want to be.* Seeking relief, I begin to pray.

Truth comes to my rescue. Coming alongside the mud pit of discouragement that I have thrown myself into, Jesus leads me. He picks me up, whispering, "I forgive you." He opens his arms of love wide, inviting me to come and accept his forgiveness. Yes, his heart for me is obedience, but right now, he just reminds me his care isn't based on my being perfect.

Even as we are learning just how crazy Jesus is about us, some days our own inability to get things right drags us under. God stoops to us, loving us in a way we can understand and receive. He bends down to meet me so I can accept his perfect love.

Can you picture it? Ever see a father swing his little girl up high? In Daddy's arms she feels both thrilled with and safe in his strength. Ever watch a father feed his child, bending to give her one bite at a time? She depends on him for food, and she trusts that what he gives her will be good. We have a perfect Father, who wants to protect and nourish us, just as we are. We don't have to become lovable; we just have to let his love in. Jesus takes care of the changing.

START THE REVOLUTION

When you are feeling down, run to him. Tell him how you feel, then rest quietly, allowing him to tell you how much he adores you.

Jesus, I need to know your love, especially on the days when I feel down about myself. I just can't get enough of you or your love. Amen.

34: Different

You will be a crown of splendor in the LORD's hand,
a royal diadem in the hand of your God.
—Isaiah 62:3

···●●●···

"I can't stop thinking about my weight," Mandy confessed. "Every time I eat, I feel guilty. Even the parts of my body that I know I shouldn't worry about, I do. I feel trapped. I wish I had long skinny legs like other girls at school."

My friend Mandy is slipping down the mountain of comparison and is about to hit bottom. If you looked at her, this conversation would make no sense. She is a gorgeous girl, but that is not what Mandy sees. She sees *different*. Different from the girls at school. Different from the girls on TV. She doesn't like different.

I, too, have gotten caught by comparison. Friendships. Outfits. Success. I know that feeling of being trapped; maybe you do too.

I've found only one escape from the comparison prison: looking to Jesus. When I stop my mind from comparing myself to others and instead look to my Jesus, I am set free from jealousy jail.

God calls his people a crown of splendor in his hand. When I read this verse, I picture a royal crown, like the one worn by Princess Kate at the royal wedding. Full of diamonds, brilliant and gorgeous. Dictionary.com defines *splendor* as: grandeur, glory, and brilliant distinction. How's that for different?

Friend, **God does want you to see yourself as *different*—a brilliant distinction** from every other girl on the earth. It's up to you to replace the lies in your mind with the truth of who you are.

> **START THE REVOLUTION**
> Today, remind yourself: "I am a crown of splendor in God's hand."

Lord, thank you for making me different.
Help me to see my value as you see it. Amen.

35: Between Us

Who shall separate us from the love of Christ? . . . I am convinced
that neither death nor life, neither angels nor demons, neither the
present nor the future, nor any powers, neither height nor depth,
nor anything else in all creation, will be able to separate us
from the love of God that is in Christ Jesus our Lord.
—Romans 8:35, 38, 39

hy didn't she like me? I had only dated her son a couple of times. But she let him know often how she felt—he told me! Maybe it was one of those "no one is good enough for my boy" deals. I would analyze myself. When I was around her, I tried not to be loud, used my best manners, and made conversation politely.

None of it worked. Her dislike of me caused us to break up. (That's probably what she was hoping for!)

I am so glad Jesus' love for us is so powerful—**nothing can come between us—nothing!** No trouble or hardship can separate us from his love. No mother, or any other person, for that matter!

There may be times when you don't *feel* his love; in fact, you may feel just the opposite. Make up your mind today that you will believe this truth: nothing can separate you from Jesus' love. When the time comes that you feel he's as far away as he can be, you can go back to this day, when you planted deep in your heart this seed of truth.

START THE REVOLUTION

Your bond with God is not like other relationships—*nothing* can separate you from his love.

Jesus, there are so many things I can't count on.
Thank you that you and your love can be counted on.
Amen.

36: Surprises

It is the glory of God to conceal a matter;
to search out a matter is the glory of kings.
—Proverbs 25:2

•••●••

Have you ever had someone completely surprise you with a gift? One year for my birthday, Greg planned the *perfect* surprise! Without my knowing, he had my best friends flown to our town, hid them in a hotel, and then had them sit at our table in a restaurant before we arrived for dinner. When the restaurant hostess asked us if we would mind sharing a table with another couple, I was so mad! This was my birthday! I didn't want to share this special day with people I didn't know.

As we approached the table, the couple's backs were to us. I was still fuming. When I turned to sit down, I was completely blown away! There were two of the people who meant the most to me! The fact that Greg would work so hard to surprise me was really the best gift of all! It was no easy task to keep this a secret from me. He really wanted me to know that he loved me so much!

> **START THE REVOLUTION**
> Look out for God's surprises in your day today.

Sometimes I feel like God does the same thing; he creates surprises just to tell me how much he loves me. Since I am a nature freak, that is where I've discovered a lot of my surprises. **A purple and peach sunset.** Fog-cloaked mountains. A turquoise-covered ocean. The first time I went snorkeling I was blown away by the gorgeous treasures hidden under the ocean's surface. Talk about God hiding a surprise!

He wants to show you just how much he loves you too! Today, keep your eyes open for God to love on you in the most unexpected ways. Remember, nothing is a coincidence! God is speaking his love to you.

Lord, I've got my eyes open. Show me your love! Amen.

He Wants Me

*We remember before our God and Father your work produced by faith,
your labor prompted by love, and your endurance inspired by hope in
our Lord Jesus Christ. For we know, brothers and sisters loved by God,
that he has chosen you, because our gospel came to you not simply with
words but also with power, with the Holy Spirit and deep conviction.*

—1 Thessalonians 1:3-5

I hated Valentine's Day. Most of all, I hated the annual flower fund-raiser. When that day started though, I was hopeful. Maybe there *was* someone who would use this day to express how he really felt about me. First block of classes, second block, lunch. Nothing. Fourth block. . . . Then the "flower girl" glided into our room.

She called my name! I saw it—the pink flower. My heart began to flutter. Then I saw who it was from. *Really? Him?*

For a brief second, I allowed myself to get excited.

Then reality kicked in. *There's no way this can be true.* He was popular; I was not. There's no way he would want me. I shoved the flower down in my backpack. I feared it wasn't real, so I acted like it never happened. Never knowing the truth was better than finding out it was a joke.

START THE REVOLUTION

Find out more about God's chosen people in the Bible.

Since then I have discovered Jesus has chosen me—chosen a life for me. He has work for me to do, through faith and love and endurance. You too are chosen! You are not an accident, nor a mistake. **You are a person of worth and purpose** created by God, and through him you can have power and conviction.

*Lord, I'm trying to get it: you have chosen me and my
value comes from you. Thank you! Amen.*

38: Return to Me

"Return to me, and I will return to you," says the LORD Almighty.
—Malachi 3:7

··●●●··

Your weekend with the girls got out of control, and you found yourself in the center of the gossip storm. The small disagreement with your parents escalated, ending in a grounding because you became disrespectful. That peck on the cheek became so much more, and now you feel shame.

Sin. It leaves us feeling awful—embarrassed and shameful.

When you sin, does God say "I can't believe you! I'm so disappointed"? Does he turn away from us? His Word doesn't lead me to believe that. In fact, he tells us exactly what to do when we are in this place: "Return to me, and I will return to you."

In this passage, God's people had been ripping him off. He was blessing them, and they were keeping it all to themselves, not giving any back to him. He instructs them on how to **get back to serving him**. "Return to me and I'll return to you. Start bringing your tithe into the temple; do what is right. You take the first step toward me, and I'll take the next step toward you."

If you need to return to him, start by asking for forgiveness. Then do the right thing. Admit to your friends you were wrong to gossip. Ask your parents to forgive your disrespect. Break up with the boy. Return to Jesus. You'll find he is right there, ready to have you back.

> ### START THE REVOLUTION
> Have you turned away from God? What steps do you need to take now?

Jesus, it is so easy to mess up. Thank you for making it simple, through forgiveness, to come back. Amen.

39: On Fire

Place me like a seal over your heart, like a seal on your arm;
for love is as strong as death, its jealousy unyielding as the grave.
It burns like blazing fire, like a mighty flame. Many waters cannot
quench love; rivers cannot sweep it away. If one were to give all the
wealth of one's house for love, it would be utterly scorned.

—Song of Solomon 8:6, 7

*L*ove is very powerful. Wars have been started for love. Families have been betrayed for love. People have died for love. That's the power of human love.

Multiply that by a number bigger than we can conceive, and that would represent the power of God's love for us. Love of this kind is not hot today and moved on to somewhere else by tomorrow. It has the ability to stay no matter what comes; there is no trouble that can cause God to run.

When his love becomes the thing we live for, it creates a fire in our lives—**a passion that gives our lives purpose and meaning**. He becomes the reason for the decisions we make.

Radical girl, you need more to live for than the next boyfriend, the next party, or the next weekend. Jesus is that thing.

START THE REVOLUTION

Look at the images of God's love in these verses. Paint your own word pictures. How do you describe his love?

Jesus, set your love for me as a seal over my heart.
May you be the one thing I live for. Amen.

40: His Ideas

No eye has seen, no ear has heard, and no mind has imagined what God has prepared for those who love him.
—1 Corinthians 2:9 (*NLT*)

••●●●••

*H*ave you ever prepared a surprise for someone you loved? Weren't you just so excited to see them completely blown away by your gift?

I knew she would love it! Her favorite band was in America—all the way from England. It might possibly be a once-in-a-lifetime opportunity; so I bought her the concert tickets.

It was all I could do to keep it a secret! I told her sister, making her take a vow of silence. (I had to tell at least one person!)

Her birthday finally came. When she opened her gift, she let out a scream! She was completely shocked! (You know, it's possible to get someone something they want, and it's possible to get someone a surprise, but to surprise them with something they want is a huge feat!)

Those concert tickets were nothing compared to what God says he has conceived for you! The God who has access to the best of the best prepared a plan for you, and he is just waiting to bring it all together. **Our lives are like puzzle pieces,** and at just the right time, God brings another piece in to create the whole picture. Our part? Just keep loving and obeying him.

START THE REVOLUTION

Give a small gift to someone just because. Think about the joy God has in store for each of us.

Jesus, all I can say is, bring it on! I can't wait to see the amazing love you have prepared for me. Empower me to stay close to you so that you can bring all the puzzle pieces together. Amen.

He Wants Me

41: Because

But because of his great love for us, God, who is rich in mercy, made us
alive with Christ even when we were dead in transgressions—
it is by grace you have been saved.

—Ephesians 2:4, 5

ecause. There's a word we use all the time. "I can't pick up my bedroom, because I am doing my homework!" "I ate the last piece of cake because I wanted to!" *Because.*

A lot of the time when we use that word, it's pretty empty. It's a signal of an excuse coming up—and usually an illegitimate excuse. Or maybe just a reason without any explanation: "Because I said so."

But in this verse, *because* isn't empty. It's full of purpose, of meaning, and of love.

Because of love. Because of love, when God looked at us, he chose to make us alive. Because of love, he chose to send Jesus. **Because of love, he gave us new life.** Even though there was no reason in us to do it.

It's your turn now. Your turn to say *because.* Because he first loved me, I live my life for him. Because he first loved me, I choose to honor him. Because he first loved me, I choose his way and not my own.

START THE REVOLUTION

How do you use the word *because?* What will you do because of God's love for you?

Jesus, you offer me everything.
Help me to give you my everything in return. Amen.

CHAPTER TWO

42: Tears

Jesus wept.
—John 11:35

•••●••••

We sat on the floor in the empty house. Why did we have to go? We loved our church, our house, our town. Just two days ago, the now empty house had been filled with people and laughter, Christmas decorations and tasty treats. Now our home was an empty shell.

As we wept together, my family knew it was time to begin our move. Our broken hearts and bloodshot eyes wouldn't change the fact that we had to go.

Tears. They come like a flood bursting a dam. They may spill out of our eyes, but they begin in our hearts. Hurting friendships, broken families, disappointing outcomes. All result in tears.

Jesus wept too. His dear friend Lazarus had died, and Jesus' heart had crumbled.

Maybe it's a bit twisted to think this way, but **I'm glad Jesus felt this loss.** I'm glad, because it makes me feel less alone when I'm hurting. Knowing he felt the same pain I feel comforts me; it helps me to know he gets me.

You'll feel sad sometime in the not-too-distant future. You may be at school, on the ball field, or in your room. When those tears well up and course down your cheeks, shut your eyes. Picture yourself crawling up onto Jesus' lap. He's stroking your hair and whispering in your ear, "I've been there. Just let me hold you." You'll be amazed at the comfort he will bring.

START THE REVOLUTION

Jesus had compassion for his friends. Show compassion to the people you interact with today.

Jesus, I am sorry that you experienced loss when you were here, but I am glad that, even in sorrow, you get me. Amen.

43: Revealing

If our hearts condemn us, we know that God is greater than our hearts,
and he knows everything.

—1 John 3:20

•••●●•••

*E*verything. He knows stuff about me that I don't know about myself. When others ask, "What's wrong?" and I sincerely don't know, he does. He can help. Jesus can reveal to us exactly what we need.

Is unforgiveness festering in your heart? Has that insecure spot been poked by a rude comment? Could it be that you're not really over a broken relationship?

Jesus knows. He can and wants to help you know what's wrong too. He wants to identify the hole in your heart. When you see it for what it is, **he'll fill the hole** so that you can be whole again.

Paul talked about dealing with troubles and this space inside of us when he wrote in 2 Corinthians 4:8-10: "We are hard pressed on every side, but not crushed; perplexed, but not in despair; persecuted, but not abandoned; struck down, but not destroyed. We always carry around in our body the death of Jesus, so that the life of Jesus may also be revealed in our body."

START THE REVOLUTION

Look at troubles you've had. Can you see how they led you on the path to Jesus?

Each one of us was created with a space—a space that only Jesus can fill. So don't resent this space. You may wish that you didn't have any problems, but God can use your problems. Your troubles may be exactly what you need to drive you to Jesus, and *that* is a very good thing!

Jesus, my problems drive me crazy! Help me to see
what you know and to allow my troubles
to steer me closer to you!

44: Freedom

I will walk about in freedom, for I have sought out your precepts.
—Psalm 119:45

•••●●••

loved being busy! Being overwhelmed made me feel important. I loved nothing more than creating a to-do list, simply for the happiness of checking it off. Telling a friend about my busy life made it sound so important!

Busyness quieted the voices of insignificance that screamed inside my head. But it wore me down. I sensed God asking me to **let some stuff go**, but I didn't want to. When I didn't, he started removing things . . . one by one. That's when I began to experience freedom and peace from simply being me. I found my completion in being his girl.

Freedom is a word I want to fully understand. I define freedom as: unconfined by my human limitations; free to be an expression of my amazing God and his revolutionary love.

David must have been a bit like me, a person who had to preach to himself on occasion. He told himself, "I will walk about in freedom, for I have sought out your precepts" (Psalm 119:45).

David was saying that he could have freedom because he was seeking God's commands. Most non-Christians don't think of Christians as being free—especially Christians who try to live under God's law. But lawless living leads to all kinds of spiritual, physical, and emotional imprisonment.

Since God is not a God of chaos or confinement, when I follow *his* ways, he brings freedom. He causes the things he has not called me to do, or to be a part of, to fade into the background.

Maybe like me, you are addicted to frenzy and you don't want to exchange crazy for calm. Ask the Lord to give you a desire to experience his peace.

> **START THE REVOLUTION**
> Think about it. What would your life look like without God's law?

Father, I need to live without being driven by compulsion or emotions. Help me find your freedom. Amen.

45: Image

From heaven the LORD looks down and sees all mankind;
from his dwelling place he watches all who live on earth—
he who forms the hearts of all, who considers everything they do.
—Psalm 33:13-15

•••●●•

"What was your biggest struggle in high school?" It had been a few years since Katelyn graduated, and I wanted to see how she saw things now that she was out. Her reply: "All the energy I spent, and sometimes still do, trying to project and keep up my image."

Facebook, Twitter, texting, outfits, hairstyles, room decorations, cell phones. They all say something. So with careful planning, you can create the image of who you want to be, whether that image is true or not.

There is a reason God made you the way he did. He liked what he created. He didn't create you to have another girl's laugh, her sense of humor, her accent. He created you to be you!

So often **we spend a lot of energy trying to be *like* someone else**. Is each outfit, each stray hair put in place to make sure that others will want to hang out with you?

START THE REVOLUTION

Name five things you like about yourself. Thank God for those things.

What if you spent that energy *liking* yourself? I think you would be one happy girl and a blast to be around! You wouldn't have to think so hard about what you would say next, wear next, or do next, because you would just be you!

Today, if you find yourself envying another girl's smile or walk or anything, speak to yourself and say: "God made me just the way he wanted to, and he likes me as I am. And I like me too!" You'll see . . . soon you'll be liking yourself a whole lot more!

Jesus, this may be hard to say, but thank you for making me me! Teach me to like me exactly the way you made me! Amen.

46: Be a Servant

Everything they do is done for people to see.
—Matthew 23:5

• • ● • ● • •

have this icky need: the need to be thanked. Every time I do anything for anyone, I always announce it.

"I folded your clean clothes for you."

"I picked up the shoes you left out."

"I volunteered at church today . . . for four hours."

I'm waiting for someone to say thank you. That's the least I deserve for what I did, right?

At least that is what I thought until I read Jesus' words. Jesus railed on those who only did things for people to see. In Matthew 23, further down in verses 11 and 12, he said, "Do you want to stand out? Then step down. Be a servant. **If you puff yourself up, you'll get the wind knocked out of you.** But if you're content to simply be yourself, your life will count for plenty" (*The Message*).

START THE REVOLUTION

Do an anonymous good deed today. Don't let anyone know about it.

Jesus sees right through my actions; he knows me. This need to be thanked is really a gross cover-up for pride; I just want others to see how great I am.

When our motivations for the things we do are not pure, when they are for us to be noticed and not to serve another, Jesus sees right through them. If I don't change my heart, then I can expect Jesus to send something to change it for me! He loves me too much to leave me the way I am.

Jesus, strip me of my pride. I know it's nasty. I just want to be your girl. Amen.

47: Cover-Up

*Live as free people, but do not use your freedom
as a cover-up for evil; live as God's slaves.*
—1 Peter 2:16

•••●••••

Tyra was dragging it all out in the open as she interviewed a panel of teen girls. The topic: sexting. The surprise guests: their mothers. I watched as fifteen-, fourteen-, and thirteen-year-old girls talked frankly of the explicit language and nude pictures they regularly exchange with their friends. Their mothers had no idea it was happening. The girl on the phone was a totally different girl than the daughter at home.

What about you? Who are you really? **What image are you portraying?** Is the girl at the supper table each evening the same girl on Facebook, or is it all fake? Are you one girl when you pray to the Lord at night and a different one when you are texting in the dark?

In Acts 5, Peter was being pushed and pulled by those around him who called the shots, the guys who determined who was in, and who was out. (They had so much power, they could determine who would live and who would die!) Peter's answer to these dudes was "It's better to obey God rather than men."

START THE REVOLUTION

Be honest about the real you and the image you project. Are they the same?

Does your life reflect Peter's statement? Are you embarrassed about your faith? Would you rather do what it takes to fit in than stand up and stand out?

Standing for something when everyone else is falling for everything is beyond hard. Yet in 2 Timothy 1:12, Paul challenged Timothy, "Yet I am not ashamed, because I know whom I have believed, and am convinced that he is able to guard what I have entrusted to him for that day."

It's time to decide. Who are you going to be, and what are you going to stand for?

*Jesus, I want to stand up for you. It's so hard.
Holy Spirit, whisper to me when I am being fake and
empower me to be real. Amen.*

48: Delighted in You

He will take great delight in you; in his love
he will no longer rebuke you, but will rejoice over you with singing.
—Zephaniah 3:17

I have heard it said that the way you see your dad is the way that you see God. So, how do you see your dad?

Fun, easy to please, protective? A perfectionist, uptight, never available?

My dad always worked. It wasn't that he didn't love me; he was just always busy. In order to get his attention, I had to be doing something. Running cross-country. Performing in a school concert. **When I performed, Dad came.**

Somehow I transferred this to God; to get his attention and approval, I must have to do something.

It was so freeing when I found out that wasn't true! He loves me just the way I am. Yes, he wants me to grow and become more like him. But whether I do or don't, it doesn't change his *love* for me.

> ## START THE REVOLUTION
> When you picture God as your Father, what kind of father do you see?

When he looks at me, he doesn't see the flaws I see; he sees the finished product. He sees the one that is so in love with him, my desire is to become like him. He doesn't see a hopeless cause—someone unlovable or beyond his reach.

Jesus knows my deepest thoughts, my darkest deeds, and my disappointing attitudes, and none of that changes his loving thoughts toward me. Knowing that gives me the courage to keep coming back for his love and forgiveness, even when I mess up.

This is the truth that I want you to grab hold of too! We will make mistakes; it's inevitable, because we are human. But no mistake is ever too big to make him quit loving us and drawing us in.

Jesus, forgive me for failing you when I _____. (Fill in the blank.) Thank you for loving me in spite of my failing, and thank you for giving me the power to change. Amen.

49: Searched

You have searched me, LORD, and you know me.
—Psalm 139:1

•••●•••

he vase on my counter is really weird; it was formed by a method called *raku*. After this vase was pulled from the kiln where it had baked, it was set in sawdust to smolder. It continued to burn even though it had been removed from the kiln. This caused the insides to turn *black*.

I think at one point, I resembled the pot; the inside was not as pretty as the outside. Black even. I was prideful, judgmental, and yet at the same time, insecure. It's weird that two things so different—pride and insecurity—could be side by side in my heart.

Every few weeks, I would tell Jesus he could have complete control of my life, again. I felt sure that when Jesus looked at me, he was disappointed in me.

Maybe on the outside you too appear to have it all together, but things aren't so together on the inside. Do you find yourself every day performing a certain way, **trying to keep up with the expectations** of everyone? Maybe you feel no one really gets you; no one knows the "real" you.

God isn't disappointed in you. He knows everything—the stuff others see, and the stuff they don't—and he still loves you. Even when you make bad decisions, shameful decisions you would be mortified if your parents knew, it doesn't change the way he feels about you. It doesn't alter or erase his love. You are his treasure!

START THE REVOLUTION

Practice seeing yourself as his treasure. When you think negative thoughts about yourself, say "Jesus says I am flawless to him."

Jesus, help me to be the same girl, inside and out:
yours. Amen.

50: Critical

But doom to you who fight your Maker—you're a pot at odds
with the potter! Does clay talk back to the potter:
"What are you doing? What clumsy fingers!"
—Isaiah 45:9 (*The Message*)

•••●●••

"I wish I wasn't so short!" "I wish I wasn't so tall!" Stand inside the hall of a dressing room in any mall in America and you're sure to hear plenty of comments! I'm pretty sure I have never heard anyone say "I absolutely love my body! It is so great!" It's too bad, because that is exactly what the Potter who formed you wants you to think!

So, when God hears us criticize *his* creation, how does he feel?

I think he's offended. That's how I would feel if someone called my painting in my family room ugly. **Terribly offended!**

Do we see our vicious comments about ourselves as offensive to our Creator? When we look in the mirror and cut ourselves down, when we look at another girl and wish we could wear her skinny jeans, when we criticize the way that we were made—we are criticizing God! We are telling him, "You didn't do a good job!"

What part of yourself do you like the least? When God made that part, he knew exactly what he was doing, and he did it well! Right now, I want you to say to God, "Thank you, God, for _____." (Fill in the blank with that part of yourself you like the least.) If you want to see real change in your life in the way you see yourself, I want you to do this each and every time you have a harsh thought about this area. Exchange a critical heart for a thankful heart. That's how you become a revolutionary girl!

START THE REVOLUTION

List the body parts you like the best. Ask God to use all of you to do his work.

Thank you, God, for _____. Amen.

51: Clean Record

*For as high as the heavens are above the earth, so great is his love for
those who fear him; as far as the east is from the west,
so far has he removed our transgressions from us.*
—Psalm 103:11, 12

•••●•••

What does Jesus see when he looks at you? Some days, he sees a heart that pleases him. Other days . . . well, let's just say he doesn't.

Like an irate parent, does he rant and rave in Heaven and say "That girl will never change! She always will _____!" (You can fill in the blank with your unique set of issues.)

God's Word tells us no. Today's verse uses a word we don't really use in our vocabulary: *transgressions*. Transgressions are actions that offend God's character and go against his will. For example, you really want to go to a party. Your parents say no, because they don't know the girl giving the party (or her parents). You choose to go anyway.

The Bible says to honor and obey our parents, so when we don't, it's sin. We not only offend our parents, we offend God. We may suffer consequences for our actions, such as punishment from our parents and damaging the trust our parents have in us. But when we ask for forgiveness from God, we are saved from his punishment and **receive his mercy instead**. He wipes our records clean; it is as if those offenses never occurred.

So how can Jesus wipe our records clean? He is perfect and died for imperfect us. Only one who is perfect can do that.

START THE REVOLUTION

Write one of your "issues" on a sheet of paper with a pencil. Ask Jesus to forgive you. Now erase what you wrote. Jesus can do that for you. Let him!

*Jesus, help me to forgive myself as
easily as you forgive me. Amen.*

52: God Is Good

The LORD is good to those whose hope
is in him, to the one who seeks him.
—Lamentations 3:25

•••●••

She knows she's created for the stage. Inspired by success stories on TV, she knows she has what it takes to make it big. I don't doubt she does. Whenever I hear her sing, tears come to my eyes. I wonder though, has Shannon sought Jesus out to learn what he wants for her life?

Shannon loves Jesus. I just don't know if her dream is his dream. Is her definition of success identical to his? Jesus promises he is good to those whose hope is in him; is that where Shannon's hope lies?

Good and God are not always the same.

They can be, but sometimes Jesus' way and our way may be different ways. The one thing I do know: his way is always best.

I found this out. I had a plan to be a pastor's wife; spending my life supporting a man who shared Jesus.

God completely ruined those plans. As I went after him, through reading his Word and prayer, he changed up my plans for Bible college and any chance I had of meeting a preacher man. I was quite upset. But I finally decided to put my hope in the one who loved me most.

Where did I end up? You could say I became the "preacher." Never would I have dreamt that *I* would be the one speaking and writing. Thinking that big wasn't on my radar. While I dreamed of being the cheerleader, Jesus had me as quarterback.

I'm not sure what God's plan is for Shannon. The big stage might be the exact spot where his good comes about. I do know his good is exactly what he wants most for her; I hope that's what Shannon wants too. He promises that he is good to those whose hope is in him, and his good is always the best!

START THE REVOLUTION

Look at your to-do list for the day. Does God show up on your list?

Lord, open my heart and mind to
want your best for my life. Amen.

53: Feeling Like Dirt

As parents feel for their children, God feels for those who fear him.
He knows us inside and out, keeps in mind that we're made of mud.
—Psalm 103:13, 14 *(The Message)*

••••••

There are days when I don't understand myself. Yelling at a person I love, saying a sharp comment that hurts a friend, or forgetting something really important. At these times, I feel terrible—like dirt. How can I expect other people to understand me, when I don't even understand myself?

Do you have someone in your life who really understands you?

I hope one of the people is your mom or dad. Parents can provide a hug when the tears won't stop flowing. They can be an ear when your mind won't stop swirling. Parents can be just the source of love you need when you're having trouble even loving yourself.

You may or may not have an earthly parent like that, but you do have a heavenly parent like that! God, your heavenly Father, created you, so he gets you! He knows you better than you know yourself.

For those of us who worship Jesus and accept him as being in control of our lives, he is quick to show mercy. He holds back from pouring out on me what I deserve for all those times I have sinned against him. He is compassionate, remembering my particular weak spots and looking forward to the day when those places will no longer be a part of who I am.

START THE REVOLUTION

Tell your parent something about yourself—maybe something you've never told them before!

Jesus, thank you for your compassion.
Help me to have it for myself and others. Amen.

54: Solid

And he brought him to Jesus. Jesus looked at him and said,
"You are Simon son of John. You will be called Cephas"
(which, when translated, is Peter).

—John 1:42

••●●●••

When you see the guy who talks too much in class, what do you think? *Wow, is he ever annoying.* What crosses your mind when the girl at your lunch table is showing too much cleavage? *She is trying way too hard.*

Did Jesus ever get annoyed? Well, I think he did, but not about the petty things that bother us. When he got annoyed with the Pharisees and teachers of the law, he spoke truth to them. He could speak that way because he knew everything about them. He knew what they needed to hear. After all, he's God!

How much do we know about those we find annoying?

When Jesus called Simon, he was just an average fisherman. Yet Jesus gave him the new name, Peter, meaning "rock." Jesus saw the solid man that Peter would become. He saw past the fisherman and past the guy who would deny him. He saw the Peter who would one day spread the news of Jesus all over Asia and become a pillar of the church.

START THE REVOLUTION

Jesus sees you as you will be one day. Learn to see others in the same way.

His love does the same in you. He sees the girl you are becoming each day; he sees you choosing his way over your own. He sees the confident girl, sharing her faith with her actions of love. He believes in the unselfish girl to come, making his name famous by putting others before herself. **He looks to the best of who you will become** as you allow him to revolutionize your life with his love.

Jesus wants to empower you with this same love to see others the way that he sees them. Envision that chatterbox boy as self-assured—knowing he's wanted. See the immodest girl as a girl no longer needing attention—Jesus fills her need. Who else do you see?

Jesus, help me see _____ the way you see them.
Use me to love them. Amen.

55: Masterpiece

For we are God's masterpiece. He has created us anew in Christ Jesus,
so we can do the good things he planned for us long ago.
—Ephesians 2:10 (*NLT*)

• • ● ● • •

The Art Institute of Chicago was an amazing place to visit. Works of art by artists I had only ever heard of hung everywhere. Not being an artist myself, I am sometimes blown away by the beautiful creations others are able to come up with. These pieces of work are the best of the best—masterpieces.

Dictionary.com says a *masterpiece* means: a person's greatest piece of work, done with masterly skill, or a consummate example of skill or excellence of any kind.

Insert your name and that definition into today's verse.

I am part of God's greatest piece of work, one that God made with masterly skills—an example of his excellence. Wow. That's a lot to take in.

Is that what I think when I look in the mirror? Some days I listen to girls criticize the smallest flaws in each other. Quietly, I analyze and see the same flaws in myself—I'm hardly a masterpiece by those standards. Other days, when I fill up my heart with the truth of how he sees me, I feel like I can see what he sees.

START THE REVOLUTION

What do you see in you that was created by the masterful hand of God?

He alone knows the good things you were created to do. Believe that you are his masterpiece. Then you will be equipped for what he has for you to do.

Jesus, open my eyes to see myself as you do. Amen.

56: One Purpose

Then all your people will be righteous and they will possess the land forever. They are the shoot I have planted, the work of my hands, for the display of my splendor.
—Isaiah 60:21

• • • ● • • •

"I don't know my purpose." With a somber face, Karen made this statement. I could see she was really torn up about it. "I don't know my purpose," she repeated.

There has been a lot of talk over the past few years about "our purpose"—that thing we were created to do. While I think it has been good for some, this emphasis has created a lot of pressure for others. If we don't know exactly what God has for us to do, anxiety can take control, causing us to worry on overdrive.

To be honest, I'm just not sure it's that difficult to figure out. We were all created for one purpose, and today's verse spells that out: to display God's glory. Plain and simple. So whether you are going to school, doing a job, helping out at home—whatever it is, you were made to **reflect the life-changing love that is inside you**.

Yes, I believe that God knows more specifics about your purpose, but when you don't know what those are, always start with the foundation. Make God famous wherever you are, and let him take care of the details.

START THE REVOLUTION

Look at your plan for today. Is there room in it to display his splendor?

Jesus, may my life be all about making you famous. Amen.

57: Potential

Brothers and sisters, I do not consider myself yet to have taken hold of it. But one thing I do: Forgetting what is behind and straining toward what is ahead, I press on toward the goal to win the prize for which God has called me heavenward in Christ Jesus.

—Philippians 3:13, 14

••●●●••

*B*efore Paul was an amazing follower of God, he *thought* he was an amazing follower of God. That was before God knocked him around a bit. No joking.

Jesus had come and changed up the way that many people thought about God and the laws of the Bible; Paul (then called Saul) didn't like it. In fact, he believed that Jesus and everyone who followed him were wrong and going against God.

START THE REVOLUTION

Do you know what goal you are pressing toward? If not, find out today!

Paul couldn't just watch that happen. He got permission to put in jail those who believed in Jesus. He thought he was the best thing God had going for him, until God got his attention.

In Acts 9, Paul was on a mission when a light from Heaven shone so brightly, he was thrown to the ground. Jesus asked him, "Why are you doing this to me?" Paul was stunned! After that experience, he completely turned his life around and became a real follower of God by loving his Son, Jesus.

God knows the things that you have done in your past that have been against him. He also knows all the potential that lies within you to bring him glory.

Do not let what you have done in your past define who you are today. This is who you are: one who is madly loved by the King and made new in him. It's time to forget who you were before and **grasp the new you of today.**

Lord, help me forget what's old and grab the me who's new in you. Amen.

58: Trouble

You are my hiding place; you will protect me from trouble and surround me with songs of deliverance.

—Psalm 32:7

·•◦●◉●◦•·

Trouble. When I say the word *trouble*, what comes to your mind? Here are just a few of my answers: food issues, impatience, lack of compassion, scatterbrained, clumsy, overcommitted, nervous, uptight . . . OK, I think that is enough for now. These "troubles" cause me trouble—just about every day. Sometimes, they even like to work together against me!

When I am overcommitted, I become scatterbrained. Being scatterbrained makes me nervous and uptight. When I feel nervous and uptight, I am very impatient and I lack compassion for others. When I am impatient and lack compassion, I move too fast and get mean. Trouble!

START THE REVOLUTION
Who do you go to first when you feel trouble coming on?

On days when all these weaknesses work together against me, I can really feel rotten about myself. I begin to think that I am a loser. How can God really use a girl like me? I can become frustrated with my lack of growth and say to myself, "I can't believe you did that—again!"

Thankfully, the more I pour God's truth from the Bible into my heart, the less frustrated I get. In his Word, I'm surrounded by "songs of deliverance." Jesus has an answer for those areas I need to grow. He wants every area of my life to point to him. **He offers me a safe place** to get back on my feet through his limitless forgiveness. He is a source of constant help, where I can find protection again and again.

He makes the same offers to you: forgiveness, deliverance, and protection. As he extends his helping hand to you, grab hold of it in prayer and receive his help that's always there.

Jesus, I want to grow. Forgive me for where I fail and give me grace to keep going. Amen.

59: Jealous Much?

But the LORD said to Samuel, "Do not consider his appearance or his height, for I have rejected him. The LORD does not look at the things people look at. People look at the outward appearance, but the LORD looks at the heart."
—1 Samuel 16:7

Packed in like gummy bears left in a hot car, Greg and I waited in the lobby for the concert to start. Out of nowhere he asked, "When a girl walks in a room, why do girls size her up?" I was so embarrassed! We were even in church! Was the judgment that girls silently pass on each other so obvious that even a guy noticed it?

What causes us to scrutinize each other so? Curiosity? Sometimes. Insecurity? Often. Jealousy? Bingo. Powerful jealousy.

In 1 Samuel 1, we meet two girls. Peninnah had plenty of children; Hannah had none. Peninnah rubbed it in, getting under Hannah's skin. Why was she so mean? Jealousy. Peninnah knew Elkanah, their joint husband, loved Hannah more. She let jealousy brew in her heart, eventually spilling over, dumping its toxin on Hannah.

Void of security in the radical love of Jesus, empty hearts are made vulnerable to jealous thoughts. **Jealousy poisons our words.**

Jesus desires us to be so filled by his revolutionary love, there will be no room for jealousy. He wants us to overflow with this love toward others. The only way we can experience this supernatural overflow is when hearts are full. When we sense jealousy's tentacles trying to grasp our hearts, we can say through the power of the Holy Spirit, "God's plan for her life is not God's plan for my life. I am filled by Jesus, and I will choose to thank him for my blessings."

> **START THE REVOLUTION**
> Think of someone you've been jealous of before. Thank God for that person's abilities.

Father, I struggle. Empower me to embrace your plan and your blessings in my life and to choose to be happy for others as well. Amen.

He Knows Me

60: Complete

*May you experience the love of Christ, though it is too great
to understand fully. Then you will be made complete
with all the fullness of life and power that comes from God.*
—Ephesians 3:19 (*NLT*)

••●●●••

ave you ever felt like you had to perform a certain way for acceptance, approval, or affirmation? I have. Acting good for parents, coaches, teachers, or pastors made them happy with me. But *I* wasn't happy with me. I just couldn't keep up with trying to be perfect; at times I felt like performing would swallow me whole.

This insecurity bled into my relationship with the Lord. I felt sure that when Jesus looked *at* me, he was disappointed *in* me too. Was what I did *ever* enough?

Jesus wasn't disappointed in me. In fact, I already had his approval, and it had nothing to do with me, and everything to do with Jesus' death on the cross.

Does your sometimes wobbly heart just want to be accepted, approved, and affirmed too?

Jesus sees. **He knows us inside and out**—the good, the bad, and the ugly. His desire is for us to grow, to become holy and more like him every day, but our *performance* doesn't change the way he feels about us.

START THE REVOLUTION

Read all of Ephesians 3. What do these verses say to you?

Jesus' love is everlasting. He never takes it away based on my performance. His love is unfailing. He never quits accepting me because of what I fail to do. And all the while, he is drawing me to himself. You know what this does? It makes me want to be like him!

Dear Lord, knowing you love all of me brings so much relief to my heart. Help me to truly grab hold of this truth. May your revolutionary love completely transform every part of me. Amen.

61: Good Gifts

Which of you, if your son asks for bread, will give him a stone?
Or if he asks for a fish, will give him a snake? If you, then, though you
are evil, know how to give good gifts to your children, how much more
will your Father in heaven give good gifts to those who ask him!
—Matthew 7:9-11

•••●••

O n my sweet-sixteen birthday, my parents gave me a unique keychain with a key to their car. I loved it! That key represented freedom and independence. Exactly what I was craving. It was the right gift at the right time.

If my parents had given me that exact same gift when I was six, it would have been very strange! At six I wouldn't have even known how to use it! My parents knew what to give and when to give it.

In Matthew 7, we see Jesus talking about a similar thing. Most parents know what their kids want. Most parents also want to give their kids good gifts—things they know will make their sons or daughters happy, or things that will be useful to them, or both.

If we know most earthly and imperfect moms and dads want to do this for their kids, how come we sometimes seem unsure that our heavenly and perfect Father knows what we want or need? Sometimes we just grow impatient with God's timing. We want the gift and we want it now. But then real problems start when we try to get the gift on our own.

There are times, with all our prayers, when God seems to be saying no or at least not now. It is here, in the place where our desires intersect his will, that we have to **trust that Father knows best**—that he knows exactly what we need and he wants nothing more than to give us good gifts. Every time, in his time, the gift is good and it is perfect.

> **START THE REVOLUTION**
> Remember today that "good" and what you want are not always the same.

Dear Lord, waiting on you is so hard!
Help me bring my desires to you, knowing you have my
best interests at heart. Amen.

He Knows Me

62: He Knows

Before a word is on my tongue you, LORD, know it completely.
—Psalm 139:4

••●●●••

gh. I didn't want to. I just didn't want to. It wasn't my responsibility. I shouldn't have to do it. Hadn't I done enough already today, this week, this year? I was tired. Why couldn't someone else do it?

Wow. You can hear the whining coming off the page, can't you? Hurts my ears even to write those words. But those were my thoughts. And they were almost my spoken words. It wouldn't have been so tragic if I had said them. Probably would've just hurt someone's feelings a little. But would it have been worth even that? Just because I was grumpy and didn't want to get off my couch and do a simple little task?

As I finally hauled myself up off the couch, my friend asked, "What's wrong?" It felt as though God was asking me. Or maybe telling me. However you look at it, it was just enough of a warning to make me hold my tongue and get a grip.

God knows our words before we even say them. He knows them completely. To me that means he knows not just the particular set of letters that I want to speak, he knows exactly my intention in saying them.

And that's not always good. Like when I'm grumpy and want to say things I don't really mean.

But it is good that **God knows me so well.** And for that reason, it's good when I take the time to listen to what he has to say to me. How many stupid things I would be saved from saying, if I would only listen to him!

START THE REVOLUTION

Read all of Psalm 139 out loud. God knows us so well, and still loves us so much!

Jesus, you know me so well. Help me learn to listen to you more. Amen.

 # 63: Overcomer

I have told you these things, so that in me you may have peace.
In this world you will have trouble.
But take heart! I have overcome the world.
—John 16:33

• • ● ● • •

*H*ave you ever wished you could know the future? Why doesn't God just go ahead and tell you? If you could just know where you're going to college *now,* you could complete the requirements for that school. If you knew where you were going to work *now,* you wouldn't waste time learning about other careers. If you could only know who you'll marry, you could spend time learning more about his personality type. Seems to me that this knowing the future thing might be a really good idea!

But what about the things that are not going to be so great?

God knows his plans for you and he knows you. He knows what is best for you, and what you need to know today to prepare for tomorrow.

Life isn't going to be perfect. John tells us that Jesus told his disciples, "In this world you will have trouble. But **take heart!** I have overcome the world." You will have trouble; it's part of the package. But no matter what that trouble is, there isn't any trouble that he can't overcome and bring his peace into.

Someday, maybe today, you're going to need the reassurance that God knows you, knows what is going on with you, and can bring peace to your trouble. Take heart; he has overcome the world.

START THE REVOLUTION
Write a description of where you think you'll be in five years. Plan to check in five years and see what God has done!

Jesus, thank you that you have the future under control! Amen.

Trust in him at all times, you people;
pour out your hearts to him, for God is our refuge.
—Psalm 62:8

•••●•••

*D*o you have times when you say, "Why waste my breath explaining how I feel? They won't understand, or even worse, they'll still take it the wrong way." When my brain says these things, my heart feels so alone. I long for someone who can crawl inside my mind and understand me without me saying a word.

I've heard people say that there's a person out there who can know you that well—**a soul mate**. Really I just think that's wishful thinking. Everyone wants to be understood, to be known completely and to be loved still. But no one can read my mind 24/7.

Except Jesus. He gets me . . . all the time. He understands why that comment hurt—the one others think was just silly. When others think I'm weird to fear the things I do, he understands what triggers my heart. And it's for this reason that I pour out my heart to him.

Like David said in today's verse, I can trust in God at all times. And because I can trust in him at all times, I can pour out my heart to him. Day or night. In school or in my room. On my knees or on the court. Wherever I need him, he's there. He is my refuge.

START THE REVOLUTION

What's weighing on your mind? Find Scripture to help you see your worries through God's perspective.

Jesus, thank you that I do have a soul mate in you.
I can pour out my heart to you; you will be my
protection. Amen.

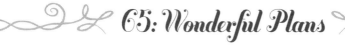

65: Wonderful Plans

Many, LORD my God, are the wonders you have done,
the things you planned for us. None can compare with you;
were I to speak and tell of your deeds, they would be too many to declare.
—Psalm 40:5

• • ● ● ● • •

*H*ow does your school choose leaders? the best player? the most popular or prettiest?

David was the youngest in his family, with the most menial job, yet God worked wonders in his life. First Samuel 16 tells his story. The country of Israel, God's chosen people, had a king named Saul, who thought he could make the calls and decisions—instead of God. So God took him out.

He told Samuel the prophet to go to Jesse's family. All Jesse's sons lined up. Samuel saw the first one and thought, *This must be the one.* But the Lord said, "Don't look at what's outside; look at the heart." All seven of the sons passed by, and God said no each time. Samuel asked if Jesse had any more sons. Jesse said, "Yes, but he's out taking care of the sheep." Samuel wanted to see him.

> **START THE REVOLUTION**
> Read the story of David in 1 Samuel 16. What might God have in store for you?

David was the one. God changed David from sheepherder to king!

Do you sometimes feel like a nobody? Invisible? Every day, you're going to school, doing homework, helping around the house, and nobody knows you or sees you.

God sees you, and he has a plan for you! A plan that if he were to tell you now, **it might just floor you!** It doesn't matter to God how popular you are, who knows you, or what you've been given to do in this world. He has chosen you to be a girl who is going to show off his wonders.

You just concern yourself with being where he wants you to be, when you are supposed to be there, and let him take care of the rest!

Jesus, thank you for choosing me to show off your wonders! Amen.

66: Needing Him

A woman in that town who lived a sinful life learned that Jesus was
eating at the Pharisee's house, so she came there with an alabaster jar
of perfume. As she stood behind him at his feet weeping,
she began to wet his feet with her tears. Then she wiped them
with her hair, kissed them and poured perfume on them.

—Luke 7:37, 38

••●●●••

Have you ever had one of those days when, as soon as you opened your eyes, you knew it wasn't going to be a good day? On this Saturday, I knew it was a bummer. For starters, I woke up early!

Then negative thoughts began to roll through my head, and the tears rolled down my face. *I have no purpose. I'm not beautiful.* These feelings were not new to me; I had struggled with them for a really long time. I hate when I feel this way—so needy.

START THE REVOLUTION
Read Luke 7:36-50. What do you get from this story?

My neediness—my cravings for affirmation, approval, and affection, sometimes feel like slime in my heart, having the capability of leaking into and around everything in my life. It really doesn't take much for it to ooze out. Someone does "it" again, and my mind and heart are transported back to a time when the same hurt happened, but with another person. **I feel needy.**

I love this story in Luke. I encourage you to read the whole thing for yourself. Here is this really needy woman, and you know what I learn from her? It's OK to be needy. Her craving for love, affection, and attention drove her to exactly what she needed—Jesus.

Today, you might find yourself feeling needy. A friend will let you down. Your boyfriend might break up with you. Your parent may yell at you for no reason. When this happens, breathe the simple prayer below.

Jesus, I need you. Amen.

67: Just Like Us

For we do not have a high priest who is unable to empathize with our weaknesses, but we have one who has been tempted in every way, just as we are—yet he did not sin.

—Hebrews 4:15

Ever notice how there is this strange side of us that likes pain? We pick at our scabs and run our tongue over our toothaches. Weird, isn't it?

Those are both examples of physical pain, but what about emotional pain? Ever indulge in the pain of self-pity? Feeling sorry for ourselves actually feels good at times.

When we are feeling sorry for ourselves, we may be saying something like this to God: "You don't know what you are doing. Don't you see me suffering like this? Aren't you going to *do* something?"

Self-pity has a way of making us single ourselves out from others. Surely our pain is so much worse than anyone else's.

But it doesn't take long to come up with an example of someone who suffered far more than we can ever imagine. **He knows what we are going through**, and he knows what we can handle.

So, let's stop lounging in the pity party and, as the writer of Hebrews said, "approach God's throne of grace with confidence, so that we may receive mercy and find grace to help us in our time of need" (4:16).

START THE REVOLUTION

Remember: nothing is going to happen today that Jesus didn't already know you could handle ... with him.

Jesus, thank you that I can approach you, knowing for sure that you know exactly what I'm going through. Thank you for your mercy and grace. Amen.

He Knows Me

73

68: Comparisons

For you will be treated as you treat others. The standard you use in judging is the standard by which you will be judged.
—Matthew 7:2 (*NLT*)

•••●••

Why do girls compare and compete with each other? What is it that causes us to look at another girl—especially a pretty or popular one—and feel the need to find *something* wrong? We look at her—her hair, her skin, her body, her bag. We look for *anything* that isn't right. Somehow, we think it will make us feel better if we can just find one area where we are better than her.

In her book *A Confident Heart*, my friend Renee Swope says, "We compare our insides to her outsides and that just isn't right."

God knows us; he knows that we compare because our own self-esteem and confidence is so low. But does he excuse it?

No, in fact, he tells us that whatever and however we dish it out, it will come right back at us. Read today's verse again.

Listen to your thoughts today. When you catch yourself criticizing another girl, stop. Whether it is in your head or with your mouth, stop. Then say a prayer for her. Watch God; he'll **switch your comparison to compassion**.

START THE REVOLUTION

Instead of comparing with and criticizing someone else today, compare yourself to God.

Jesus, I want to hate comparison. Make that happen in me. Amen.

69: To the Very End

And teaching them to obey everything I have commanded you. And surely I am with you always, to the very end of the age.
—Matthew 28:20

••••••

*N*othing bugs me more than when someone says, "God is just too busy for the small things."

What? If that is the case, then why did he so clearly say, "I am with you always"? He makes it very clear that he is there; in the big stuff and in the little stuff. To the very end. He has to be! What you might find big, I might find small. But the things that I find big, you think are nothing at all!

He knows how we each see things and are affected by things differently. **Each thing, each detail, is never missed by him.** And he is there with us, in every moment of every day of our lives, no matter how significant or meaningless that moment might seem to us at the time.

So, if he never misses one thing about you, why would you ever ignore him all day? If it was your best friend who was paying attention to every detail of your life, you wouldn't ignore her all day, would you?

> **START THE REVOLUTION**
> Write down three details of your life. How do you see God using those details?

Thank you, Jesus, for caring for every part of my life—from the small details to the big moments. Amen.

70: No Stress

You will keep in perfect peace all who trust in you,
all whose thoughts are fixed on you!
—Isaiah 26:3 (*NLT*)

••●●●••

ou know how you struggle with those anxious thoughts each day? Worrying about your grades—how are you ever going to pass calculus? Anxious about your group and the drama over who's going to prom with whom. Stressing about your guy (or lack of!)?

God sees your anxiety and longs to take it from you. He knows the things that disturb you; that's why he made this promise in today's verse. But we have to do something too—we have to keep our thoughts fixed on him.

That's the hard part. Switching our attention **from the hard things to the heart thing**—Jesus.

My friend Caleigh has on her dresser a plaque that says "Good Morning, this is God. I'll be taking over all your problems from here." Love it! She needs this reminder, first thing in the morning, to unload her problems on Jesus.

START THE REVOLUTION

Pretend your heart is your backpack. What's in it? Name three things on your back that cause anxiety.

Hand your anxious thoughts to Jesus in prayer today and then ask for the courage to not take them back!

71: Take a Step

*The LORD is my strength and my shield; my heart trusts in him,
and he helps me. My heart leaps for joy, and with my song I praise him.*
—Psalm 28:7

••●●●••

What's your cycle? On my washer, I have several cycles: delicates, cottons, permanent press. If I don't choose one, the washer will pick automatic. What's your cycle? Do you pick one, or does life choose one for you?

One common cycle we use is the cycle of surviving:

- We worry. "How will I pass chemistry? What if I don't get into college?"
- We feel helpless. "I have to find a way to get in. I've got to get some help!"
- We feel defeated. "I can't afford SAT prep. I'm discouraged. I don't even care!"
- We feel abandoned. "Why aren't you helping me, God?"
- We worry.

God knows your cycle. But if he didn't make it, then he wants you to break it!

He wants you on the cycle of trust:

- I trust God. "Lord, I'm yours. Help me; give me your wisdom."
- I am helped. Trust opened the door for him to work in me.
- I experience joy. Seeing God help me brings joy!
- I am thankful! I can't help but be grateful!
- I choose to trust. Seeing his faithfulness helps me trust again!

God isn't going to break us out of our cycles automatically; we have to take the first steps. We choose to see that he is our strength, asking and trusting for help. We choose to leave worry behind as we trust Jesus.

START THE REVOLUTION
Where do you need to take a step of trust and ask for help today?

Lord, today I trust you for _____. Every time I want to worry, I will choose to trust in you. Amen.

72: Battle Help

In your strength I can crush an army;
with my God I can scale any wall.
—Psalm 18:29 (*NLT*)

•••●●•••

Aren't you glad that you are not like David, the guy who wrote this psalm? (Psalms is a book found in the middle of the Old Testament.) He wrote Psalm 18 to thank God for helping him when King Saul was trying to kill him. He was literally being chased by guys who wanted to murder him!

Vicki's troubles aren't murders, but they're still troubles! When I asked her how I could pray for her, she gave me a list:

START THE REVOLUTION

Ask a friend to give you a list of her prayer requests. Pray for her.

- Pray I get over him. (The guy she's been crushing on for months!)
- Pray I figure out algebra. (Sometimes she just doesn't get it.)
- Pray I get more sleep. (Homework, sports, youth group—it all takes time.)
- Pray I get rid of my zits. (A clear face would be nice!)

Vicki's list is a lot different from David's. To some, her prayer requests might seem insignificant, but to Vicki, these things are **a big deal**. In her world, they are her battles.

I'm so glad Jesus knows these things that cause us concern. Though they are nothing he can't handle, we need to be reminded that with his help we can do the hard stuff.

Lord, today I don't have to crush an army or scale a wall
like David, but I do need your help with _____.
(Fill in the blank with your personal battle.) Thank you
that with your strength, I can do it! Amen.

73: Protection

I sought the LORD, and he answered me; he delivered me from all my fears. Those who look to him are radiant; their faces are never covered with shame. . . . The angel of the LORD encamps around those who fear him, and he delivers them.

—Psalm 34:4-7

••••••

What do you fear? Chemistry. Play tryouts. Speech class. The dark. College. Violence. Big cities. Driver's Ed. Gym. Guys. Zits.

So many people, places, and things to fear.

I sometimes fear the future. What will it hold? Can I handle it? Will I have what it takes when I get there?

It's good to know I am not alone. David had fears too, and he was a king, with armies! In Psalm 34 he wrote that God delivered him from "all [his] fears." Not just the big ones, not just certain kinds. But ALL. I guess if God can handle king-sized fears, he can handle mine too.

David also said "the angel of the LORD encamps around those who fear him, and he delivers them."

An angel. Camping out around us to protect us. How cool is that? Even though I've never seen one (I would love to!), I know God has sent them to help me. I can't count the number of times I've escaped, when I should have been creamed by another car. I know it was his angels guarding me.

It's no wonder that David said those who look to God are "radiant" and "their faces are never covered with shame." When you're on God's side, he makes sure you win in the end—you never have to be embarrassed or humiliated. He will never let you down.

START THE REVOLUTION

Write your king-sized fears on a sheet of paper. Draw a circle around them. Pray and imagine an angel surrounding you.

What do you fear? Pray today, "Lord, because you love me, you will rescue me from _____." (Plug your fear in here.) "Thank you for protecting me, because I am proud to be your girl. Amen."

74: By Faith

We live by faith, not by sight.
—2 Corinthians 5:7

••●●••

*H*ow *could God pull this one off?* I wondered. I wanted to get into a school, and I felt like God was telling me to go to *that* school. But when the letter came, one word gave me the answer: *full.* As in, no room for me.

But I knew God was speaking to me to go to that school! How could it be full?

So what's a girl to do? When you've read your Bible, prayed, received good counsel from someone who's tight with Jesus . . . but the road ahead has a huge "DO NOT ENTER" sign—what do you do?

You believe. You live by faith and not by sight. You say to Jesus, "I have no idea how you are going to pull this off, but I trust you, even though it looks impossible."

Yes, those around you may think you're crazy. That's OK. People thought Noah was crazy when he was building the ark, but when it started to pour, they all wanted on!

That school did contact me—two days before school was going to start. You know what? I wasn't ready! Since I wasn't walking by faith, **I let the practical get in front of me.** "I just can't get ready and move 1,000 miles away in two days." Yep, that's what I told them. See, I prayed and asked Jesus to open the doors, and when he did, I wasn't ready. Bad move. I've always regretted that decision.

He knows you. He knows the plans he has for you; for good and not for evil (Jeremiah 29:11). Your job is to believe and prepare. When the answer comes, you'll be ready.

> **START THE REVOLUTION**
> Memorize 2 Corinthians 5:7. Try not to get blinded by practicalities.

Jesus, help me to turn my eyes from the obstacles around me and look only to you. Amen.

75: Nothing to Hide

The light shines in the darkness, and the darkness has not overcome it.
—John 1:5

••••◉••

*J*ulie felt like she couldn't get away with anything. No matter what it was or how sneaky her plan, her parents *always* found out. Every time. This time they found out about the guy she had been texting—the guy who contacted her randomly while she was playing a game on her iPhone. It wasn't a big deal! It's not like she had planned to meet him or anything. They were just getting to know each other.

Jesus loves you so much, radical girl, and it's his love that causes your parents to find out when you try to hide things. His love protects. His love knows where you need some advice, and so he's planted advice givers in your life. **He'll blow your cover every time,** because he loves you so!

START THE REVOLUTION

Get under the covers with a flashlight and read John 1:1-18.

I don't know if you can relate to Julie or not, but I'm sure it's no news to you that your Father God really does know about everything. For the radical girl who is more concerned about following Jesus than anything else, she has nothing to worry about. She doesn't have anything in her life to hide.

My advice is to remember the line spoken by Pius Thicknesse in *Harry Potter and the Deathly Hallows*: "You have nothing to fear, if you have nothing to hide." Live a life of peace and freedom, nothing in the dark, and you'll live without fear.

Jesus, I know you already see that thing I'm trying to hide. I need courage to tell my parents about it. Give me the words to tell them. Amen.

He Knows Me

76: Hemmed In

You hem me in behind and before, and you lay your hand upon me.
—Psalm 139:5

•••●••

Have you ever felt alone? Truly alone? Abbey has. The night her parents were fighting—ending in their decision to get a divorce. When she came over, I didn't really know what to say. In fact, all I could do was hold her and pray for her.

In today's verse, the words *behind and before* refer to time—as in what is in the past behind and what is forthcoming in the time to come. Jesus has always been "behind" what is going on in your world and he will always be "before" in your future. **You are never truly alone.**

I wish I could say that this will be true with the people you depend on—your family or best friends—but I can't. People are imperfect humans, so they do let us down. But that is not true with Jesus. He is perfect. He will never let you down. He will surround you with his love.

> **START THE REVOLUTION**
> Hems keep cloth from unraveling. How is that like your relationship with Jesus?

Jesus, I needed to know today that you are with me, no matter what. Thanks! Amen.

77: Uniquely You

*Before I formed you in the womb I knew you, before you were born
I set you apart; I appointed you as a prophet to the nations.*

—Jeremiah 1:5

• • ● ● • •

Is it weird for you to think that before you were even formed, God knew you? Before you were born, he set you apart with a plan for your life?

He knew you and he knows you. He knows what gifts and talents he gave you so that you would have everything you need to do the work he has created you to do.

I really stink at math. You know what? That's OK! Because for the work God has called me to do, I don't need math. As a speaker and writer, I needed to do well in English (and I did!) God knew what he wanted me to do and **he gave me what I needed to do it!**

He knows you too! He knows what makes the unique parts of you. Even if you feel that others miss what makes you special, your unique talents will grow and become refined as you grow closer and closer to him!

START THE REVOLUTION

List all the things you can do for God right now. Look up in the Bible what other young people did for God.

When God told Jeremiah he would be his prophet to the nations, Jeremiah protested: "I do not know how to speak; I am too young" (v. 6). But God told Jeremiah not to say that, because God would be with him and rescue him. And I know God is telling you the same thing: you're not too young to do what God has made you to do. And you're not too young to tell others about the love of your life!

Choose one thing that is unique about you. Thank God that he gave you that gift and keep your eyes open for how he might use your uniqueness soon!

78: Keep Calm

When anxiety was great within me, your consolation brought me joy.
—Psalm 94:19

•••●●•••

After basketball practice, Haley's chest felt constricted, like nothing she had ever experienced before. She thought she was getting a cold. Giving her the standard remedy—"You just need some rest and to slow down"—her mom sent her to bed early. It seemed to help some, but still, she just didn't feel right.

The next night, on her way home from practice, it hit her like a train wreck. Her chest began to heave; she couldn't breathe. Haley's doctor said she was having a panic attack. She was taking all her stress at home directly to heart and it was making her feel like she was having a heart attack!

It would be so great if we could avoid all anxiety in life, wouldn't it? If life would go so smoothly that we could just enjoy the good parts?

Unfortunately it doesn't work that way! Jesus promised us in John 16:33 that in this life we would have many troubles. He also said, "But take heart! I have overcome the world."

START THE REVOLUTION

Name your number one anxiety. Turn it over to Jesus.

Jesus doesn't promise to make life easy or to remove our problems, but he does promise to bring us comfort, right in the middle of our anxiety. **His comfort brings joy!**

Jesus, when my heart wants to freak out, remind me to run to you for comfort. Amen.

79: Perfect Timing

Every good and perfect gift is from above, coming down from the Father of the heavenly lights, who does not change like shifting shadows.

—James 1:17

••●●●••

*J*ennifer on Facebook said about this verse: "This is my life verse; it fits perfectly with what God has done in my life. I have tried and tried to make things happen my way, but God pulled me back. When I finally let him take over, he blessed me like crazy. He has always known what is best for me—he longs to give us perfect gifts . . . in his time. He never changes and never fails."

Jennifer has found the secret: God gives us what is best for us, **when it's best for us**. He knows you, and what is best for your best friend may not be what is best for you. What may be best for the neighbor, the girl next to you in chorus, or the third-base player may not be what is best for you.

That's where trust comes in! We trust that God is the giver of all good gifts, and that if and when the time is perfect, he will bring that good gift.

START THE REVOLUTION

What are you pining for? Trusting God is the mark of a revolutionary girl!

Jesus, I hate to wait. But I know your best is worth waiting for. Help me! Amen.

80: More Than We Imagine

Now to him who is able to do immeasurably more than all we ask or imagine, according to his power that is at work within us, to him be glory in the church and in Christ Jesus throughout all generations, for ever and ever! Amen.
—Ephesians 3:20, 21

•••●••

re you a dreamer? When you think of the future, do you have big plans or do you simply want to survive? Sometimes when an author writes a book, she'll write the ending first, and then write the rest. She knows exactly the way that she wants the story to end, so once that is crafted, she will write the rest of the plot to lead up to that ending.

Jesus also writes the ending first—the ending of our lives. He knows what he has planned for us, good and not evil, to give us a hope and a future (Jeremiah 29:11). His ending is for us to give him glory, shining the light of his goodness to the world.

When you think of your book of life, **how do you picture the ending?** However big (or small) you think of it, God tells us that his plans for us are "immeasurably more than all we ask or imagine." *How?* you might think. *I am average; there is nothing special about me!*

START THE REVOLUTION
Write out Ephesians 3:20, 21, then draw a picture of what God might do with you.

He creates these plans not based on you, but based on him and his power at work within you. I challenge you to begin to ask God to help you to dream, and dream big! Pastor Rich Nightingale, my youth pastor, used to tell us, "Dream something so big that unless God intervenes, it is bound to fail."

He knows you and he knows who you will be when you are completely surrendered to him and his plans for you. Don't miss it, radical girl. Don't choose a mediocre story when God is trying to write a *New York Times* best seller!

Take a few minutes for a "daydream" prayer. Think of the best possible ending to your story. Ask God to intervene—giving you the faith to dream his type of ending.

81: He Knows You by Name

But now, this is what the LORD says—he who created you, Jacob,
he who formed you, Israel: "Do not fear, for I have redeemed you;
I have summoned you by name; you are mine."
—Isaiah 43:1

•••●●●••

Sitting at the table during lunch during a conference, I look around and see several class rings. Only these class rings are way too big to belong to these girls. They *must* belong to their boyfriends. Girls have always longed to have something that says, "I belong to him." A sweatshirt, a jersey, a ring . . .

Jesus knows that **you long to belong**. That is why he made sure to let you know that you do belong—to him.

What do you have that announces to others that you are his? Is it your kind heart that is like his? Is it your love for the unlovable? How about your purity? A girl who is his is proud to announce it to the world. She has finally found "the one."

Jesus doesn't give you his ring, sweatshirt, or jersey. He gives you something permanent and forever—his unconditional love.

If you want to be really bold about telling the world who you belong to, you could get a ring or shirt or something else you could wear every day that makes the announcement! It will be a reminder to you, but it could also be a great conversation starter with someone who needs to belong too!

> **START THE REVOLUTION**
> What do you have that says you belong to Jesus? Wear it, share it. Be proud!

Thank you, Jesus, that even though I may not belong anywhere else, I do belong to you! Amen.

CHAPTER THREE

He Speaks to Me

82: Repent

From that time on Jesus began to preach, "Repent,
for the kingdom of heaven has come near."
—Matthew 4:17

•••••••

ouldn't it have been amazing to have been in on Jesus' very first sermon? We're too late for that, but Matthew penned his first words for us to read: "Repent, for the kingdom of heaven has come near."

Of all the things Jesus could have said, why did he start with that? Why didn't he start with "Love one another"—something a bit more warm and fuzzy?

Jesus started with step one: repentance. This means to feel sorry for sin and to *change* for the better.

I grew up hearing: **"Say you're sorry!"** Maybe your mom does the same thing. I know her intentions were good, but I was almost never sorry! *Sorry* to me meant:

- Sorry you caught me.
- Whatever it takes to get you to stop yelling.
- Maybe this will make you feel better about what I have done.

Rarely did it mean: "I'll change."

START THE REVOLUTION

Say you are sorry today to someone you've hurt . . . and mean it.

These definitions of sorry are nowhere close to what Jesus commands. We need sorrow that brings change. If there's no change, the words are empty. As long as we're still calling the shots in our lives, the words are pointless. When we decide what we'll do, where we'll go, and who we'll do it with, we're in charge. As long as we're in charge, Jesus isn't. Jesus says it is time for that to end; he's the master.

Once he's master, *then* we can hear him speak.

Jesus, help me to be aware of my sins and to be
truly sorry for what I've done. Amen.

83: Whose Voice?

My sheep listen to my voice; I know them, and they follow me.
—John 10:27

••●●●••

*D*eciphering who to listen to can be really hard. "Sports are important; be well-rounded." "Take AP classes; get college credits early." "Don't fill your calendar; you're going to burn out!"

It's enough to make a girl's head spin! During her junior year, Jo became so over-whelmed, her relationship with Christ was set aside. The pressure caused her to become very depressed.

I've always struggled with being a people pleaser. I hate to let other people down—I want them to be happy with me. Often, though, keeping everyone happy keeps me miserable! It's like trying to keep up a schedule for someone with a split personality. **I can't be every-thing to everyone**.

You know what? That's OK! Jesus says he's the one I have to please. He puts me at peace, "Listen to *my* voice. I know you. Follow me."

Here's where the struggle comes in: How do I hear *his* voice when there are so many other voices?

START THE REVOLUTION

Here's a reading project. Read all the words spoken by Jesus in the book of John.

That's the mark of the truly mature girl. She learns to pray and listen for his answer. When she needs to make a decision, the radical girl reads God's Word, expecting the Holy Spirit to speak to her through it. She turns to Jesus instead of peers, knowing that, even if he is silent for a while, he knows her and has her best in mind at all times.

Learning to hear God speak is not easy. It's not quick, which can be oh-so-hard for the "get it to me now" girl. It requires diligence to read and study his Word, even when I don't feel like it. Yet the result brings with it peace and purpose like no other.

Jesus, I want to hear and recognize you.
Help me to be disciplined. Amen.

84: Trust

*Because of my integrity you uphold me and
set me in your presence forever.*
Psalm 41:12

•••●••

I couldn't believe Jesus would ask me *not* to go to college. Yet when I read the ad in the magazine, I knew it was God: "If you want to be the servant of all, come and serve with us." He had been whispering to me all week.

Days before, I had read an article on serving God. I wanted to serve God; that's why I had been planning to go to Christian college. But this ministry said that serving was doing for others when no one knew about it; giving to those who couldn't repay. Shaken to my core, I was forced to look at my reasons for pursuing ministry.

Next came a sermon one night later: **"To be used of God, you have to become a servant of God."** God was serious about this servant thing!

When I read the magazine, I sensed the Holy Spirit saying, "This is what I want you to do." Even though I was scared, in a strange way, I was peaceful.

Was it easy? No! Yet I knew I needed to trust God with this new direction, even though I was scared.

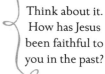

START THE REVOLUTION

Think about it. How has Jesus been faithful to you in the past?

That decision to trust God was the first of many; I learned God had my best interests in mind. I have never regretted my decision to trust and obey.

When stepping out of what is comfortable and choosing to obey, go back and revisit Jesus' faithfulness to you. A history of trust can compel you to trust again.

In the next twenty-four hours, you'll probably have something to trust Jesus with: a fight with your parents, a test in school, or a decision. Pray and tell Jesus you will trust him when it comes.

85: Don't Run

But Jonah ran away from the LORD and headed for Tarshish.
—Jonah 1:3

•••••••

Sometimes I don't want to hear God speak. What if it is one of those times when he points something out I don't want to see? He might ask me to do something I don't want to do. I know I'm not alone. Tammy feels this way too: "I am restless when God speaks to me because sometimes I don't want to hear the Holy Spirit prompting me. 'Tell that girl she looks nice today and her speech was really inspiring' or 'Tell her she has great character.' I have excuses: I don't feel like it; it's not convenient; **I won't look cool**.

"When I don't listen, I miss the opportunity to speak his truth into someone's life. This girl, who may not be able to hear him, can hear me. Jesus knows girls are insecure about how they look, what they wear, what their body shape is, and if they are accepted."

When God speaks to us, sometimes it's not for us or about us; it's about them.

Don't miss your opportunity to encourage another girl, even if she is a stranger. Who knows? Your words might be the only kind words she hears all day!

START THE REVOLUTION

Listen to the Holy Spirit and make someone feel great today!

Jesus, you know this makes me nervous! Give me courage today to find someone to speak kind words to! Amen.

86: Wash Up

To make her holy, cleansing her by the washing with water
through the word, and to present her to himself as a radiant church,
without stain or wrinkle or any other blemish, but holy and blameless.
—Ephesians 5:26, 27

•••●•••

I'm a freak about being clean—especially when it's hot. If I'm working in the sun, I get dirty, sweaty, stinky! When I'm done, water is the first thing I seek. Water cleanses, refreshes. It is not unusual for me to shower twice a day in the hot months. I've got to be clean; sweat is not my friend!

The question is, do I feel that strongly about washing my heart several times a day?

Our world exposes us to all kinds of messes: media, relationships, work, school. **Sometimes we get dirty—filthy even**. Stinky attitudes, smelly viewpoints. We've got to shower! We have to set aside time, in the middle of it all, to be washed and refreshed by God's Word. It may be a note card in your agenda. Perhaps carry your Bible in your backpack for a sneak peak. What about "bookending your day" as author Ann Voskamp calls it—beginning and ending your day in God's Word?

START THE REVOLUTION
Take God's Word with you today and "wash up" as needed.

We have to continually wash ourselves in his Word, cleansing our hearts. We can do this through conversations about what he's doing in our lives, reading his truth, and through prayer. His Word will make us more like him.

Lord, help me to smell me when I stink!
Then help me to run to you. Amen.

87: War Zone

Though an army besiege me, my heart will not fear;
though war break out against me, even then I will be confident.
—Psalm 27:3

•••●•••

Nothing else could go wrong, Alexandra felt confident of that. She didn't like her school; there was no one there like her. Her passions were singing, dancing, acting. Those around her were only interested in softball. She'd survived her parents' divorce, which happened a few years ago. Her dad even had a girlfriend Alexandra liked, but now she was moving. She just hoped it wouldn't get any worse; that was her worst fear.

I'm sure you've had days when it feels like everything and everyone is against you. Your friends talk about you, school is nothing but a struggle, and your parents seem to constantly be on your case. It feels like your life is a war zone. **You wish you could just hide your head** under your pillow and stay there.

START THE REVOLUTION

Who do you run to when you are afraid? Jesus will always be there for you.

Even here, in this place where it seems there is no hope, Jesus speaks to you. "Do not fear, I am with you always," he whispers. Just his presence brings peace to a desperate situation. His love brings light and hope where there seems to be only fear.

When the cyclone of worry is swirling in your mind, threatening to take over, allow the perfect and peaceful love of Jesus to push fear from your trembling heart.

Make this your prayer: "I will not fear. I will be confident in the Lord's love for me."

88: Mirror Image

So God created mankind in his own image, in the image of God
he created them; male and female he created them.

—Genesis 1:27

•••●●•••

S he had heard this voice before; it was her own. It spoke to her often and to-night was no exception. Preparing for church, Bridgette found herself saying, "I should wear makeup so I can be just as pretty as the other girls." The real thoughts that scrolled across her mind whispered, *I am not good enough.* She knew she needed truth to come against this lie. Opening her devotional, she read, "We please him most, not by frantically trying to make our-selves good, but by throwing ourselves into his arms with all our imperfections, and believing that he understands everything and loves us still" (A. W. Tozer, *The Root of the Righteous*).

What a boost to her self-confidence were these words! Bridgette knew that God loves her even when she pretends to be someone she's not.

Bridgette washed all the makeup off and looked in the mirror. Her biggest surprise: she actually liked what she saw! She saw the image of a girl who was created by a perfect God; a girl he said was beautiful. She didn't wash her face because she was against makeup; Bridgette just wanted to be more worried about what God thought of her, not the world. She reminded herself of the Scripture which says, "A friend of the world becomes an enemy of God" (James 4:4).

The mirror may seem harmless, but for many it's a major battleground. Comparing ourselves to others, picking at ourselves, we forget we are made in the image of the perfect one.

START THE REVOLUTION
Don't go to the mirror unprepared. Write verses and post them where you will see them each day.

Pray that you know the truth in today's verse:
"So God created mankind in his own image."

89: Follow Me

The next day Jesus decided to leave for Galilee.
Finding Philip, he said to him, "Follow me."
—John 1:43

"*F*ollow me." Jesus spoke to the disciples as he called them. He didn't reveal what the next three years held. They would be overwhelmed; they might have even turned around. "Follow me" was all he said.

I wanted to know my future. *What college will I attend? Will I work in a church or marry a pastor?* Jesus knew I wouldn't go to college, work in a church, or marry a pastor. He chose to reveal only enough for me to take the next step.

Do you find yourself worrying about your next step? Asking questions about tomorrow, next month, next year? Spinning around issues that don't have anything to do with today?

Jesus knows which answers to your questions are yes and which ones are no. He knows when and where to reveal them to you. Your part is to **take the next step in obedience**.

> ### START THE REVOLUTION
> Are there questions you want answers to? Jesus says, "Follow me."

I've learned each no from God is a stepping stone to his amazing yes when I obey. I learned in the dark that when I step forward in trust and obedience, blessing is down the path. Even those paths that hold pain can be part of the process—teaching me obedience over worry, fear, and control.

Now, when fear and doubt surface in the dark, I silence the what-ifs. I ask him what I need to do *today*. Walking away from worry, I express my concerns to Jesus and trust his ability to take care of what's next.

Dear Lord, the dark can be frightening. Help me trust you over and over again. I want that. Amen.

90: Staying True

We are not trying to please people but God, who tests our hearts.
—1 Thessalonians 2:4

••••••

How do we know when it's the Holy Spirit speaking to us, or just what we want? First, we see what the Bible has to say about what we want.

My mother once told me, "If God wants you to know, he loves you enough to tell you himself." She gave me this advice during a time when **I was confused**. My parents had just switched churches. Church was my life; I was devastated. Together, we made the decision I would continue to go to the old church, while my parents went to the new.

One Sunday evening I attended church with my parents. A woman approached and said she had something to tell me that God wanted me to know. She told me I was supposed to stop attending the old church and begin coming with my parents. She said I was rebellious.

START THE REVOLUTION
Memorize 1 Thessalonians 2:4.

Rebellious? Really? My parents and I were in agreement!

So what was her real story? She also had a child in the same position, and she wanted her child to attend church with her. Her thinking was that, if I began going to the new church, her child would come too. She claimed to be "hearing from God," when really she was trying to manipulate me for her own means.

I am so glad I had Mom, who helped me to see God's heart. I was, in fact, honoring my father and mother as his Word says.

Listen for God. Listen for him and remember what he says will always line up with his Word.

Jesus, I want to learn to hear from you. Help me to be consistent about reading your Word. Open my eyes to expect to see you in my everyday life. Amen.

He Speaks to Me

91: My Turn

I say to myself, "The LORD is my portion; therefore I will wait for him.
The LORD is good to those whose hope is in him,
to the one who seeks him."

—Lamentations 3:24, 25

•••◉••

It's my turn. Who hasn't had that thought? It's my turn to be chosen. My turn to make the play. My turn for a date for prom.

It's my turn is a flashing red warning sign. Something's wrong. **It's a signal that we are empty**; looking to something or someone else to fill our hearts.

Each one of us has come into this earth with a heart waiting to be filled. When we are young, there are those who nurture and care for us, such as family, teachers, and coaches. They pour into us for a while, but their real job is to point us to Jesus.

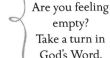

START THE REVOLUTION
Are you feeling empty?
Take a turn in God's Word.

Then there comes the time when it's our turn. No longer are we dependent on someone to pour into us. It's our turn to run to Jesus ourselves.

Our verse today starts out with "I say to myself." *We* are the ones who have to teach ourselves the truth of God's Word. It isn't the responsibility of our pastor, youth worker, or parents. It's ours.

Next time you hear your thoughts tell you it's your turn, take a look at your heart. Have you been neglecting to fill it up with God's truth?

Jesus, I need to hear you speak to me every day.
I need to remember it is my turn—my turn to take in
your truth through your Word! Amen.

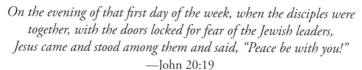

92: Be with You

On the evening of that first day of the week, when the disciples were together, with the doors locked for fear of the Jewish leaders, Jesus came and stood among them and said, "Peace be with you!"
—John 20:19

••●●●••

What keeps your stomach in knots? What are the things, in the dark of your room, that swirl in your mind? When worrisome thoughts come in my head, if I don't stop them, my mind will drag my heart to a place of despair. **Anxiety takes control.** I am caught between easy emotions and disciplined faith.

There was a time when Jesus' disciples knew great anxiety. They had given up everything to follow Jesus, and now he was dead.

If you have ever had someone close to you die, you've tasted the pain of saying good-bye. But this was no ordinary death. Jesus had been murdered. The disciples were disillusioned and shattered.

Suddenly Jesus stood among them, dispelling their despair with these words: "Peace be with you!"

Anxiety can be such a powerful force in our lives. When coupled with fear, it will try to leash us like its dog, dragging us wherever it wants us to go. Jesus is aware of the war spinning in your heart and mind. Just as he came to the disciples when they were hiding in fear, he enters your life as well. Through the power of his Word, he says, "Peace be with you."

START THE REVOLUTION

Practice this anxiety release: make tight fists, count to ten, then open your hands. As you do, imagine Jesus lifting your burden out of your hands.

If you feel anxious, pray this prayer: "Peace be with me." Open your Bible and invite the Holy Spirit's presence into your situation.

93: In the Dark

*"But the people who live there are powerful, and the cities are fortified
and very large. We even saw descendants of Anak there." . . .
But the men who had gone up with him said,
"We can't attack those people; they are stronger than we are."*
—Numbers 13:28, 31

••●●●••

In Numbers 13, Moses had sent spies from the camp of the Israelites to check out the new land God had given them. When they returned home, they announced, "There is no way we can take over the land God promised; it is full of people too powerful for us!"

The spies were looking at the situation "in the dark." **They were scared of what they saw** and let this fear determine their words. They didn't ask God what he had to say about it. Anxiety was going to call all the shots on what they would do next.

START THE REVOLUTION

Be courageous, like Caleb. Allow your eyes of faith to adjust in the dark, so you can see tomorrow as God sees.

That is, until Caleb stepped in. Verse 30 says he "silenced the people before Moses and said, 'We should go up and take possession of the land, for we can certainly do it.'" Caleb wanted to allow faith to call the shots on what they would do next. He allowed his eyes of faith to adjust to the dark situation, so he could see it through God's eyes and hear what God would want to say.

Your life may seem pitch-black. Like the spies, you might only see the worst of your circumstances. Choose to be like Caleb. Ask God to help you see things the way he sees them—with hope of what the future can hold and what he can do. He wants to speak to you, bringing confidence in his power to your trouble.

Jesus, teach me to see as you do. Amen.

94: Pause

*For to us a child is born, to us a son is given,
and the government will be on his shoulders. And he will be called
Wonderful Counselor, Mighty God, Everlasting Father, Prince of Peace.*
—Isaiah 9:6

•••••••

rapped. No matter which choice I made, someone would be let down. Do I choose the expected thing—the thing I don't want to do? Do I go with the option that will make those closest to me happy with me? The turmoil in my mind brought tears to my eyes.

I prayed, but **the one thing I failed to do was wait**. I failed to wait for an answer.

When we ask the Wonderful Counselor for clarity and direction, we must be willing to pause to hear him speak. This waiting may be for a few quiet moments. Other times it may be days, months . . . even years.

This day, I prayed and then chose the path that offered the least amount of pain at the moment. The next day, however, when I sat down to spend time with Jesus, I felt the weight of my wrong decision.

Jesus is the Wonderful Counselor. He can and is willing to provide us each and every day with astounding wisdom for the decisions we face. The question is, am I willing to get quiet and slow down to hear?

START THE REVOLUTION

Write a letter. Paint a picture. Read all of Isaiah 9. Pray and wait. Practice the art of pausing.

I want to hear, Jesus, but my brain is always in high gear. Teach me to slow down and listen. Amen.

95: Connect

Remain in me, as I also remain in you.
No branch can bear fruit by itself; it must remain in the vine.
Neither can you bear fruit unless you remain in me.
—John 15:4

••●●●••

After every Thanksgiving, my family heads out for our favorite annual holiday tradition—going to the mountains to cut down our Christmas tree. Full of excitement, we strap it to the top of our truck and haul it home. Twinkling lights, beautiful ornaments, and colorful ribbons make it sparkle as it adorns our living room. For a whole month we enjoy its beauty.

But as the new year comes around, all the little needles begin to fall. **No longer connected to the roots**, our beautiful tree has been cut off from its source of life. Though it sparkles for a season, in time the branches become brittle. We have no choice but to throw it out.

Unfortunately, we can become like a Christmas tree. Jesus says that unless we remain connected to him, with our roots dug down deep in the soil of his Word, we won't live. Sure, like the Christmas tree, we'll look beautiful for a season. The water of going to church or youth group will keep our hearts looking good for a while, but if we are not daily connected to him, through reading his Word and prayer, we'll eventually dry up too. Jesus goes on to lay out the future for the one who is not in daily relationship with him (v. 6): "If you do not remain in me, you are like a branch that is thrown away and withers; such branches are picked up, thrown into the fire and burned."

> **START THE REVOLUTION**
> Get alone with Jesus— no distractions— and soak up the life-giving truth of his Word.

Jesus, I choose to be connected to you today so I can bear fruit in my life. Amen.

96: Renew

Don't copy the behavior and customs of this world, but let God transform you into a new person by changing the way you think. Then you will learn to know God's will for you, which is good and pleasing and perfect.
—Romans 12:2 (*NLT*)

•••●•••

It sounds so mysterious, doesn't it? Knowing the will of God? Just the thought of the Creator of the universe communicating with puny little me is overwhelming. Why would—or maybe the question is how could—God speak to me?

You are so right, friend. It is an incredible privilege and honor for us to hear from God about his plan for our lives. The way to begin hearing him speak is by preparing a place for him to speak.

Our minds can be scary places! Filled with memories, things we've been taught, stuff we watch and see each day—there is a lot of space that has been used up. But are our minds filled with things that will help us to hear God speak to us? Things such as:

- his Word
- worship songs
- books we have read from those who have studied him

Or is it filled with:

- movies we've watched
- pop music
- books by those who don't know him

If it's the latter, when God speaks to us, we might miss it, because we are not used to hearing from him.

We need to be careful what goes into our minds. This is not going to be an easy thing to do! It will take a lot of maturity. But the more we let God transform our thinking, the more we will know his good and pleasing and perfect will.

START THE REVOLUTION

Pick one thing you will do today to prepare your mind to hear from him.

Jesus, help me to prepare a place where I can hear you speak. Amen.

97: Learn a Language

Why is my language not clear to you?
Because you are unable to hear what I say.
—John 8:43

•••••••

My family is really weird; we have a language of our own. Sometimes it is not too hard to figure out. Other times, though, it's more difficult. You have to hang around us for a while to know that when someone asks for "spook john gawdy" for supper, they want spaghetti. It's not hard for me to follow—I get them. After all, I live with them!

This quirky form of communication is one way we love each other. We communicate in a way that is uniquely "Cowell." But we're not exclusive. Anyone who wants to understand us can. Our "language" is not a secret language. When you come around for a while, you'll learn it, and if you're not careful, you'll start talking strange too!

Jesus told the Pharisees that they were unable to hear him. It wasn't that Jesus wasn't speaking their language— it was that they weren't trying to understand him.

Like the Cowell speech, **the way Jesus talks is not a secret**; in fact, he wants everyone to learn his language. The more you are in his presence, the more you will recognize the things he says that are uniquely "Jesus." When you begin to recognize him speaking to you throughout your day, you can follow him. For instance, I recently had a thought that I should buy my friend a certain devotional book. The day I gave it to her, she called me crying. What she had read that day was exactly what she needed to hear. That thought I had to give her the book wasn't my own; it was Jesus speaking to me to give my friend exactly what she needed.

> **START THE REVOLUTION**
> Read God's Word and watch for messages that are uniquely "Jesus."

Jesus, I want to learn your language. Teach me to discern when you speak to me. Amen.

16: Magic Erasing

How can a young person stay on the path of purity?
By living according to your word.
—Psalm 119:9

••●●●••

Every year I ask God to give me a word for the year; a word that will define my relationship with him. My word this year is ***purity***. Desperate to leave behind ugly attitudes and thoughts not like those of Jesus, I want to be made pure. I am asking him to cleanse away anything in my life that doesn't reflect his life in me.

Jesus paid a huge price for my forgiveness; to make me clean. But that death wasn't for a one-time cleansing, leaving me free to go about doing things as I want to now. A pure heart and mind is what he wants for me each day and here is how to get it: my heart and mind are cleansed when I read and soak in his Word.

START THE REVOLUTION

Read Psalm 119. Imagine Jesus cleaning your heart and mind as you read.

Mr. Clean's Magic Erasers are just that. Magical! White sponges filled with cleaners, they get grit out like nothing else. There is one problem though; the erasers crumble to bits as I scrub the grout on my floor. Every time I clean, I have to use a new one.

Every day, I have to scrub my sin and the natural tendencies of my human heart. Once isn't enough; I have to keep applying God's truth day after day, bringing my heart to a place of purity. Reading just any book won't do it. Going to church or youth group isn't the magic formula either. It's me reading his Word for myself.

When he speaks to you his words of truth, your heart will be clean too. But only you can apply this magic eraser!

Jesus, thank you for your "magic eraser."
Make me clean today! Amen.

99: Breathe

Look to the LORD and his strength; seek his face always.
—Psalm 105:4

•••◦•••

As Amy's alarm clock went off, she groaned, "Nooooo!" Monday again! The thought of another school week started her spiraling down a dark tunnel. She couldn't keep going: 5:30 a.m. wake-up calls, 11:00 p.m. bedtimes. She felt that if she didn't get a break soon, she was going to lose it!

Deadlines, exams, chores, work, SATs, college applications, sports, piano, drama, youth group, homework, voice lessons, working out, church—when does the list ever end!

> **START THE REVOLUTION**
> Breathe in deeply, and as you exhale, whisper "Jesus."

The weight of all of our responsibilities can be crushing, like the fifty-pound backpack you lug around school. Each activity feels like another brick in your load of life. Everyone expects you to give your all to each one, but you feel completely fried. Where's a girl to find relief?

David speaks truth to our worn-out hearts, "Look to the LORD and his strength; seek his face always." Maybe that's all you can do—turn your heart to Jesus. That may be the only thing you need!

Right now, stop rushing. Turn your phone to silent. Now, breathe deeply. As you exhale, whisper his name: "Jesus." Do it again.

When you feel crushed by life, do this again and again. Give him the opportunity to speak his strength into your life and give you direction to move you from stressed out to strengthened within.

Pray: "You are my strength; I seek your face."
Give him a chance to respond. Just sit still,
eyes shut, and let him speak.

100: New

He who was seated on the throne said, "I am making everything new!"
Then he said, "Write this down, for these words are trustworthy and true."
—Revelation 21:5

•••●•••

eturning from breakfast with a friend, my mind is swirling. *I really wish I wouldn't have said that. Why didn't I just listen? You can't say anything wrong if you just listen! I wonder what she thinks about what I said. Oh, why did I say that!* I'm wishing so badly this morning for do-overs.

I'm guessing you have wished for do-overs before. Words you would take back. Places you wouldn't go. Things you wished you hadn't done. It seems to just come with the package of being human. It's part of the package I don't like so well.

START THE REVOLUTION

Think about yesterday. What do you want to do over? Don't dwell on it. Do something about it!

I could sit here and replay over and over again what I said. Recreating the conversation in my mind, I could pretend to change it all; say this and not say that. I could berate myself, telling me just how dumb I am for opening my mouth . . . again. The choice is mine: spiral down further and further to a place where I feel terrible about myself or . . . **I could listen to Jesus speaking to me.**

I could pick up my Bible and replace the thoughts in my head with the thoughts in his: "I make all things new! I want to bring glory to me through the remainder of this day; it's not over! I am able. Are you willing?"

I am! I see that there are still many more hours today to tap into his wisdom and strength. Not just for the remainder of this day, but for days to come. Let's have do-overs, and let's begin them with Jesus!

Jesus, today, I am desperate for this immeasurable power to work and flow through me. You are able; I am willing. Together, let's make a great pair!

101: Dreaming

For nothing is impossible with God.
—Luke 1:37 (*NLT*)

•••••••

*A*re you a dreamer? I can be. I like to think of what I'll do "when I grow up." Where I'll live, work I'll do, places I'll go, people I'll help, and messages I'll share.

When I was younger, I dreamt; just not dreams that required a miracle to make them come true. That was all before God started messing with me. He had a different plan.

Jesus had a plan that I couldn't work out on my own. He had a purpose for me that would require me to fully depend on him, because I wouldn't be able to make it happen alone. He didn't want me to just read books to my teens about Jesus; he wanted me to write books to teens about Jesus. With my experience and my education, or should I say the lack of it, **he wanted to do the impossible**.

He wants to do the same in you. Not the same plan, of course! But he wants to speak to you a plan and a purpose that is impossible for you; impossible for you to do unless you are completely dependent on him and his power. He has a purpose for you to make a difference in the lives of others.

START THE REVOLUTION

Ask God to invade your dreams. Ask him to give you creative ideas for ways to serve him.

Pray: tell God that you want him to do the impossible in you. Then, through his Word and spending time in prayer, keep your eyes open for him to do just that!

102: Set Apart

While they were worshiping the Lord and fasting,
the Holy Spirit said, "Set apart for me Barnabas and Saul
for the work to which I have called them."
—Acts 13:2

••●●●••

*I*f you're like me, there are times when you just need God to tell you what to do! You have so many decisions to make—some small, others monumental. I've made some bad decisions in the past; I don't want to make them again! Sometimes I get desperate to hear from God.

When you've prayed and prayed, and all you feel is confusion, frustration, and fear—what do you do?

I found the answer in the book of Acts. "While they were worshiping the Lord and fasting, the Holy Spirit said." The Holy Spirit gave them direction. What were they doing? Worshiping and fasting.

When we worship and fast, we get *us* out of the picture.

Sometimes our prayers become completely one-sided. "Lord, tell me." "Lord, give me." These can be very good prayers, but sometimes we need to take our question, problem, or issue, give it to Jesus, and trust he'll answer. Then we need to get on with it. Get on with worshiping him as the Master and Lord of our lives. Praise him, in advance, for the answer that is already on the way.

START THE REVOLUTION
Spend the rest of this day worshiping and possibly fasting (if your parents are OK with this), and getting as close to Jesus as you can.

Fasting is not something we do to force God to move. It's a move we make to get closer to him. Based on the clear direction that the disciples received in today's verse, worship and fasting got the disciples close enough to hear their next step.

Today, pray about the answer you need and leave the problem there with Jesus.

103: Going Without

A hand touched me and set me trembling on my hands and knees. He said, "Daniel, you who are highly esteemed, consider carefully the words I am about to speak to you, and stand up, for I have now been sent to you."
—Daniel 10:10, 11

•••●••

*F*asting is when you go without food or certain foods for a period of time for the sole purpose of drawing closer to God. It's not to lose weight or get attention. It can help us draw closer to God when we set aside something we need for something we need more—him.

Daniel needed to hear from God. Daniel 10:3 says for three weeks he ate no "choice foods." "Choice" foods on my list include: ice cream, Reese's Cups, and frozen yogurt! Daniel gave up yummy things to hear from God.

His result? He heard from God. God sent "a man dressed in linen, with a belt of the finest gold" to give Daniel what he needed.

I'm not saying if you fast from tasty foods for twenty-one days God will send an angel or Jesus to speak to you! But if we look at the radical way Daniel pursued God, we see the radical way he heard from him!

START THE REVOLUTION
Read his Word. Spend time in prayer and worship. Get ready to do radical things for God.

Is there any part of your life that is blocking you from hearing from Jesus? If you want a revolution in your life, you've got to take radical steps to get there. Experiencing his best doesn't just happen; he reveals himself to those who run hard after him!

Jesus, being radical takes guts. Please give me some! Amen.

104: Open My Mind

Then he opened their minds so they could understand the Scriptures.
—Luke 24:45

• • ● • • •

I have a confession. **Sometimes when I read the Bible, I don't get it.** I might read the same verse three times and still struggle to understand what it means. This used to make me feel dumb; like there was something wrong with me. When I listened to other Christians speak, they seemed to get it all right. What was my problem?

Nothing. There was nothing wrong with me, I just needed and still need a little help from Jesus. Some parts of Scripture are really difficult. For these tricky spots, it can be useful to get some help from those who have studied it and can explain it to me. But what I really need most is to create a prayer from today's verse: "He opened their minds so they could understand the Scriptures." Jesus wants us to understand our manual for navigating our way through this life. Every part of it can help us as we live out our lives here.

START THE REVOLUTION

Put as much work (more!) into trying to understand God's Word as you do any other subject you study.

When you come across a verse you don't get, slow down. Breathe deeply and ask Jesus, "Will you open my mind and help me to understand what you are saying?" Read the Scripture again. Sit quiet for a moment and wait for him to help you to understand what he is trying to say. Read the verses before and the ones after, looking for clues to his meaning. If you have a study Bible, check out the other verses that go along with the passage you are reading.

Remember, it does neither of you any good for you to be in the dark. Ask for understanding and expect him to answer!

I want to understand your Word, Lord. Open my mind to understand your Scriptures. Amen.

105: Consumed

*Jesus answered, "It is written: 'Man shall not live on bread alone,
but on every word that comes from the mouth of God.'"*
—Matthew 4:4

•••●•••

Living on the words of God? What could Jesus possibly mean?

Last year, I decided to follow Jesus' words literally. I started the new year with fasting. There is power in fasting, and I needed a big dose of power.

The first three days were really hard. I was seriously hungry, and my brain screamed, "Hey, where's the food?" In reality, it wasn't too hard on my body. I had plenty of reserves for it to pull from!

After day three, I experienced a visible lack of energy. But by day seven the strangest thing happened—I didn't feel hungry anymore! My body stopped yelling, and I was fine.

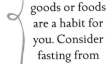

START THE REVOLUTION

Think about what material goods or foods are a habit for you. Consider fasting from those things for a time.

You know the great thing? **I was no longer consumed with food.** My mind and focus switched to what I needed—Jesus.

I saw amazing things happen as I began to pray new prayers. People I love were set free from addictions. A dear friend became passionate about Jesus.

Some people may feel that fasting is not for teens. For the girl who wants to truly be radical and have Jesus revolutionize her life, I believe fasting can be a means for that. Maybe you will fast from sugar or soda. Some fast from meat for a season and only eat fruits and vegetables. Ask Jesus what he wants you to fast from and take it from there.

I can't say I really understand how the whole thing about fasting works, but I did learn this: fasting clears away the clutter so I can clearly hear the King.

*Jesus, I want to be clutter-free.
Show me if fasting is for me. Amen.*

106: Hidden Messages

The secret things belong to the LORD our God,
but the things revealed belong to us and to our children forever,
that we may follow all the words of this law.
—Deuteronomy 29:29

•••●••••

Do you tend to gravitate toward certain books of the Bible, while avoiding others? I did, until I discovered I was missing some of the best parts about knowing God. You see, sometimes his love notes to us are hidden.

A friend helped me find these hidden love notes by looking at the Bible from a different perspective. Rather than seeing it as a book about God speaking only to the Israelites or other people, she encouraged me to put myself into the verses.

You try! Put your name into this passage: "The LORD your God has chosen you out of all the peoples on the face of the earth to be his people, his treasured possession" (Deuteronomy 7:6). When I did this, **it felt like God was whispering directly to me!**

I've branched into other books of the Bible since then, and have personalized many passages. I'm finding his love notes hidden all throughout the Bible. Hosea, Zechariah, Habakkuk—books packed with personal messages for us to enjoy. Besides reading through the Bible, doing a key-word search on a topic I am struggling with has also helped me to find new verses I had not seen before.

Do you usually avoid reading the Old Testament? Are there books of the Bible that you've never read? Approach these parts of the Bible in a new way. Look for God's words of love toward you. You may just stumble across a little love note from God, tucked away for you to find!

> **START THE REVOLUTION**
> Are there books of the Bible that you've never read? Start exploring them today!

Jesus, I'm ready to check out new books! Let's go! Amen.

107: Choose Your Weapon

For the word of God is alive and active. Sharper than any double-edged sword, it penetrates even to dividing soul and spirit, joints and marrow; it judges the thoughts and attitudes of the heart.
—Hebrews 4:12

•••●••••

*B*ehind the plate, Madi's great. Her arm gets the best of them out at second base. She moves from catcher to first base with ease; she's flexible in the outfield. Yet her batting's been weak. Her coach's diagnosis: her bat. Madi grew, and so she needed a longer, heavier, stronger bat.

After days of investigating, Madi got a new "weapon." The instructions said she needed at least fifty good hits until she would be comfortable with the new feel. She didn't like it at first. It was uncomfortable and heavy. But she kept on using it. In the yard and in batting cages, she put in time and effort to be sure she would be well adjusted before a real game.

START THE REVOLUTION

Post about a favorite verse on Facebook or Twitter or on your blog.

She's now batting at the top of the order! Doubles, triples, even home runs are her norm. She wields that bat, smacks the ball, and racks up points for her team.

As we grow in our faith, we need to look for passages in God's Word that empower us. We should **ask Jesus what he sees that needs to change**. When fear, doubt, anger, or pride are thrown our way, we can swing back with memorized verses of the Word. Instead of allowing complaining, grumbling, and discouragement, we can strike them with prayer.

The Word is called a double-edged sword, but unless we practice applying it to our lives, it does no good. Unless we invest time to use the Word and prayer as our "weapons," we will never know what it is like to bat at the top of the order! Unless we have his Word where and when we need it, we'll not know what it's like to win!

Lord, I need you today. Show me where I need to use the weapons you've given us—your Word and prayer—in my life. Amen.

108: First Steps

Invite Jesse to the sacrifice, and I will show you what to do.
—1 Samuel 16:3

•••●•••

Ever have the feeling you were supposed to do something, but you really didn't want to do it? Maria knows that feeling. The special services were more than amazing. She had been asking the Lord all week to speak to her; she really wanted to learn to hear his voice every single day.

The next day, Maria felt certain Jesus wanted her to invite Steven to tomorrow night's service . . . but she really didn't want to. She didn't even know Steven; they just sat next to each other in class. Yet Maria knew that if she wanted to hear God speak again, she needed to obey when he was speaking now.

So, before her mind could talk her heart out of it, she shot off a text. "Will you come with me to church tomorrow night?" He said yes! She was so excited to see what Jesus was going to do next.

The next night, as she headed out the door, he bailed. *Why did God ask her to be bold if Steven wasn't even going to come?* She felt stupid. Maybe it wasn't even God who had spoken to her anyway.

> **START THE REVOLUTION**
> Take the first step toward something God wants you to do today.

But I believe it was God, and she obeyed like she was supposed to. Just because another person doesn't respond to the message, it doesn't mean it wasn't from God.

God told Samuel to anoint a new king for Israel. Samuel freaked out: "**How can I go?** The current king will hear and kill me!" (1 Samuel 16:2). God gave Samuel a promise: take this first step; I'll show you what to do next.

That's what Maria did. Who knows what's next? God hasn't given Maria that direction yet. But she can have peace that she obeyed God, and because she did, her heart is wide open to hear his voice again.

Lord, help me obey before my mind can talk my heart out of it. Amen.

109: Scared

So I was afraid and went out and hid your gold in the ground.
See, here is what belongs to you.
—Matthew 25:25

•••●●•••

Cammie let her insecurity hold her back from things she secretly wanted to do. Fear of what others thought handcuffed her, causing her to stick with her comfortable group, who spent every day after school "chilling." They were all scared—together. Nobody would admit it.

Fear is a very powerful force: **the more attention you give it, the bigger it grows**. Courage is the same way: the more you're brave, the more courage you have.

This is especially true when it comes to the things of God. You may have heard this saying before: "God does not call the qualified; he qualifies the called."

START THE REVOLUTION
God has called you to do something for his glory—he will equip you to do it. Be bold and step out!

Take a few minutes and read Jesus' story of the three guys and the bags of gold; it's found in Matthew 25:14-30. Three guys each received bags of gold from their boss. One got five, one got two, and one received one. The first two invested so that they gave their boss even more money when he returned from out of town. The third guy freaked, burying his money. Check out verse 26 and see just how happy his boss was! Think about what meaning this story has for you. What do you need to be doing with what God has given you?

Lord, help me to use the gifts you've given to me.
Amen.

110: Not Yet

*If you belonged to the world, it would love you as its own. As it is,
you do not belong to the world, but I have chosen you out of the world.*
—John 15:19

•••●●•••

"Why is it that there are days when I really feel like I don't fit in? It's more than not being popular; I really feel different, like I'm not supposed to be here." This world can be a difficult place, as my friend described. Have you ever felt like you didn't belong? I have.

In his book *Mere Christianity*, C. S. Lewis talks about this. He says the reason for our dissatisfaction here is most likely that we are simply "made for another world." It is no wonder that we sometimes feel like nothing can make us feel truly comfortable here; we were made for Heaven.

In today's verse, Jesus tells us straight up: "you do not belong to the world." When we choose to follow him, we choose to no longer belong to the world we live in. I think everybody feels mixed up about life on this earth—people are constantly trying to fit in. They do it in more healthy ways—like nature adventures or exercise programs—and in unhealthy ways—like becoming addicted to drugs or having plastic surgery to become "perfect." But in the end, nothing satisfies. **Nobody fits.** To be Jesus' follower means that you recognize this, and you don't try to fit into a worldly pattern anymore. You look forward instead to living with God and being restored to him.

My friend Jeff described this as the "now and the not yet." We're stuck between where we are and the place we were made to live one day. While we're here, we are to love, honor, and follow Jesus. He'll give us instructions through his Word and the Holy Spirit. Just knowing he's with me and speaks to me gives me the peace I need.

START THE REVOLUTION

Have you been trying to fit in? Stop it today! Get comfortable with being different.

Look up the chorus from Building 429's song "Where I Belong" and make those words your prayer: "All I know is I'm not home yet. This is not where I belong. . . ."

111: Step by Step

You provide a broad path for my feet, so that my ankles do not give way.
—Psalm 18:36

••●●●••

Cutting through a jungle, saber in hand, fighting just to find my way. Do you feel like this some days? Like you don't really know what you are doing, but you sure are struggling?

Each day is filled with many decisions. Piano, softball, or both? How's a girl to know what to do?

I love today's verse. If you've ever run, you might too. When I was running cross-country, there were plenty of opportunities to twist my ankle. Trip in a hidden hole on a course. Hit a patch of ice in the winter. Miss the curb when switching from street to sidewalk. Yep—those are all ways I have wiped out while running.

> **START THE REVOLUTION**
> Get some exercise. As you run/jog/walk, thank God for every step.

When it comes to walking with Jesus, tripping up is one thing I definitely don't want to do. When running, if I twist my ankle, I stay off it for a few days and let it get back to normal. If I trip by making an unwise decision in my life though, **it can change the course of my entire life.**

If we focus on the path that God is creating for our feet, he will make clear our next step. He doesn't say he'll show us the path for the next month or year. He says he'll take care of the one beneath us, the one we need to walk on today.

Radical girl, listen for his quiet voice today, especially as you read his Word. He'll tell you which way to go—your part is to listen and obey.

Jesus, open my ears and lead the way. Amen.

112: Bad News Days

They will have no fear of bad news;
their hearts are steadfast, trusting in the LORD.
—Psalm 112:7

•• ● ●••

She had done EVERYTHING to get into her favorite college. She'd gone through an SAT prep course and had taken the test three times. She'd volunteered like crazy and had taken on leadership roles. She had done all she knew to do.

When I asked P. J. how she was doing while she waited to hear from the college, she said, "I've decided that if I don't get in, I'm going to take a year off and do missions work." I loved P. J.'s answer! Did she want to get in more than anything? Yeah! But P. J. was trusting Jesus; if he wanted her to get in, she would. If he didn't, he had a plan that was better, and she was ready to look for that better plan.

David tells us that when we are listening to Jesus, we don't have to fear bad news. Our hearts can trust that whatever the news is, our Jesus already knew it, and knew that he would be with us in it. **He already has set into motion our good, so we can trust in him.**

I was so excited when the text from P. J. came saying, "In!" But what excites me even more is her heart that learned to trust him while she waited.

START THE REVOLUTION
Look at a newspaper. Pick a "bad news" story and pray for the people involved.

Lord, sometimes I am on edge, just knowing bad news might come. Instead, I want to trust. Teach me! Amen.

113: God Says What?

The fear of the LORD is the beginning of wisdom,
and knowledge of the Holy One is understanding.
—Proverbs 9:10

Have you ever heard someone say, "God told me _____," and then they went on to fill in that blank with something that is totally against what God says in his Word?

I recently read a tweet that said, "God doesn't say anything in the Bible that says you can't party, so I wish people would just get off my case." She obviously doesn't know what the Bible says clearly in Ephesians 5:18: "Don't be drunk with wine, because that will ruin your life. Instead, be filled with the Holy Spirit" *(NLT)*.

You know what is even scarier than the fact that she doesn't know what the Bible says? Her lack of reverence for God. Today's verse tells us that the *fear* of the Lord is the beginning of wisdom. If you want to **be a wise girl** (the opposite of dumb), you will fear God. You will have reverence for his holiness. Then you'll get smart and find out what he really says in his Word. Read it and find out!

And I'm just saying . . . if you don't know what the Bible says, don't tweet it!

START THE REVOLUTION

Tweet an actual Bible verse, and just leave it at that.

Jesus, you are way more than my buddy, you are God. When I read your Word, help me to hear not only your words of love, but your words of holiness too! Amen.

114: Which Way?

Whether you turn to the right or to the left, your ears will hear a voice behind you, saying, "This is the way; walk in it."
—Isaiah 30:21

•••●•••

When someone asks me, "How do you hear God's voice when you need to make a decision?" I answer: "Slowly."

There is a reason that people call our relationship with God "walking with Jesus." The journey we're on doesn't happen in leaps or sprints. I mean, when you want to get from your couch to your kitchen, how do you get there?

One step at a time.

That's how we walk with Christ as well. One step at a time.

Say you have a decision to make: to go to Christian high school or public school. Start out praying, asking the Lord to give you wisdom. He promises he will (James 1:5). Then, take one step in the direction you think you want to go (as long as you know it's not one that would dishonor God). As you step in that direction, for example, you might go and tour the school you think you want to go to. Look for what I call yellow or red lights—indicators that this would not be God's

START THE REVOLUTION

Memorize today's Scripture. Take a pen and write "Isaiah 30:21" in your right and left hands.

best for you. These might be things you hear or see that seem not quite right or just plain bad for you. All the while you are considering your options, keep praying and reading your Bible, asking God for his wisdom. If you receive no yellow (warning) or red (stop) lights, take another step. Apply or register for the school—again, keeping your ears and heart open for God to tell you through the Bible, wise counsel, or in your heart what is to be your next step.

The more you read his Word, the more you will just know which direction God will have you take. Reading his Word teaches you to hear his voice. So dig in and learn the voice of your love!

Jesus, hearing your voice sounds so mysterious. I know you want to speak to me. Teach me to listen. Amen.

115: Open Ears

The Sovereign LORD has given me a well-instructed tongue, to know the word that sustains the weary. He wakens me morning by morning, wakens my ear to listen like one being instructed. The Sovereign LORD has opened my ears; I have not been rebellious, I have not turned away.
—Isaiah 50:4, 5

•••●••••

"**I** can't hear God speak to me." I've heard that many times and said that many times. When I finished my training at Bible School, I had no idea what was next. Get more schooling? Move back home? I felt lost.

My counselor said, "Get with God and find out what he wants." Her instruction frustrated me! **I already asked God what he wanted, and he wasn't talking.** When I told her this, she said, "Maybe God isn't answering because your answer is maybe. Tell God no matter what he wants, you'll do it, and I bet you'll get your answer."

I grabbed my Bible, headed out to a field behind school, and curled up next to a huge toilet paper roll (hay bale). I read my Bible and prayed. I can't say I really got an answer, but the story of Timothy apprenticing with Paul resonated with me. I did tell God that, no matter what, my answer is yes—and I meant it.

> **START THE REVOLUTION**
> Write down one area in your life where you are "holding out" on God. Pray about it.

The next day, I received a letter. My brother-in-law and sister were moving to start a church—would I come? Never did I see that coming! But God did. When I was willing and read his Word to seek him, he set me up to receive that letter with an open heart; I was open to apprenticing with my brother-in-law and sister. I made plans to move.

I'm not saying hearing God's voice is going to work like this every time; it doesn't. But if you are willing and do not turn your heart away, you'll eventually hear his.

Read the "Start the Revolution" challenge. Pray "I'm willing." Just see what God's going to do!

116: Get Away

But Jesus often withdrew to lonely places and prayed.
Luke 5:16

••●●••

When you have eight kids, you become an amazing multitasker; at least my mom was. I, on the other hand, just never got the hang of it. Attempting to rinse out my swimsuit while starting my shower water, I forget the sink water is on and run water on the floor! If I answer my cell phone while still in the driveway, I hit a mailbox. (True stories!)

My inability to multitask is actually good when it comes to spending time with Jesus. He doesn't want us to multitask when it comes to him. He wants us all to himself. See, when it came to his relationship with his Father while he was on earth, the Bible tells us that he would get away to pray.

Jesus wants you to get away too! **Get away from your "noise."** Sometimes you may even need to get away from home to really get quiet.

START THE REVOLUTION
Find a getaway place for you and God.

We've got to get quiet if we want to get God's heart. The radical girl is serious about hearing God's voice. Because you are a radical girl, you'll put other stuff aside to hear God and him alone.

When can you get away today? In the morning, when no one's stirring? At night, in your room? Pick a time today to get away and get quiet. Take your Bible, choose a verse to think on, and get quiet. You may not experience any huge revelation today, but as you keep on investing, you will learn to hear his voice.

Lord, help me to want to get your heart so much, I'm willing to get quiet. Amen.

117: The Great Outdoors

*For I am the LORD your God, who stirs up the sea
so that its waves roar—the LORD Almighty is his name.*
—Isaiah 51:15

•••●•••

Although the Bible is the primary way that God speaks to us, it is not the only way. One of my favorite ways is through nature; I'm a nature freak! My favorite thing is to spend a day stomping around the mountains. I love gurgling streams, patches of moss, delicate ferns, and piles of pinecones. *Crunching* leaves under my brown, scuffed-up boots is a sound that soothes my heart.

Being in God's creation draws me close to his heart. I can see things that I miss in the city: his creativity and peace. I hear what is drowned out by town noise: hawks whistling, squirrels scurrying, and turkeys gobbling. The quiet of the pre-dawn sky becomes the quiet in my heart as I whisper prayers to my Jesus, and I sense him whispering back to me. He reminds me what this life is really about— relationship with him. His majesty reminds me how big and powerful he is.

START THE REVOLUTION
Get outside today!

But you don't have to get to the mountains to hear God in nature.

You could sing his praise lying on the grass or gazing at the sky. Trying to see the farthest star with your naked eye. A single flower can speak of his attention to detail as you take in color, smell, and beauty.

When can you get outside today? Get alone, get quiet, and get with the one who made all things beautiful, including you.

God, you didn't have to make the planet so pretty, but thank you that you did. Help me to see you in this world more often. Amen.

118: Store It Up

My son, if you accept my words and store up my commands with you. . . .
Then you will understand what is right and just and fair—
every good path.
—Proverbs 2:1, 9

•••●••

Have you ever had just the right thing at the right time? GPS on your phone when lost? Blanket in the back of your car for a cold football game? A spare set of gym clothes in your friend's locker when you forgot yours? Wasn't it so good to have just what you needed when you needed it?

That is what it is like when you need an answer—wisdom—and God's Word comes to mind.

I opened the door to find my dear friend in tears. She walked in, not saying a word, hugging me as her body shook. Life was rocking her family and she didn't know what to do.

We made our way to the couch where she began to unload all the troubles of the past few days. As I listened, God's Word came to my mind. "Share this verse." "Speak that truth." After she was all poured out, I began to pour in God's truth over her broken heart. **His words were exactly what she needed** for her next step.

When we study and memorize God's Word, it's stored up in our hearts. We may not need what we read that day, next week, or next month. But if we will continue to add his words to our hearts, his truth will be there right when we need it.

START THE REVOLUTION
Pack up some emergency Bible verses. What ones do you need to memorize?

Jesus, help me to be disciplined to study and memorize your Word so that it will be in my heart and mind when I need it. Amen.

119: Answers

Suddenly an angel of the Lord appeared and a light shone in the cell.
He struck Peter on the side and woke him up.
"Quick, get up!" he said, and the chains fell off Peter's wrists.

—Acts 12:7

••●●•••

eter was stuck . . . in prison. King Herod was none too thrilled with the good news of Jesus that Peter was spreading around. Planning to persecute him, Herod threw him into prison. Peter was counting on the prayers of the church for a rescue.

So there is Peter, sleeping chained to two guards, with another guard at the door, when an angel shows up. The angel smacks Peter on the side and says, "Get up!" The chains fall off Peter's wrists.

How's that for answering a prayer? Peter was so stunned, he wasn't sure if it was real or a dream!

Sometimes **God will speak and show up in ways we are not looking for.** We may be asking God to help us and answer our prayers, and when he does, we don't even recognize him!

My friend really needed a car; hers was just about dead. A couple she didn't even know offered to give her one. She called me, asking, "Do you think this could be God?" Of course it was! When she prayed, she just never expected him to *give* her a car . . . especially from complete strangers. That's just how cool God is!

When you pray, don't rule out anything. God is God! He can and will deliver your answer any way he wants. In fact, the more bizarre the response, the more we can say it was his doing and not ours!

START THE REVOLUTION

Ask some faithful people you know to tell you about a time they were surprised by God.

Praise Jesus right now for the times he has answered your prayers, especially when you were shocked by his answer!

 # 120: Sit or Spin

She had a sister called Mary,
who sat at the Lord's feet listening to what he said.
But Martha was distracted by all the preparations that had to be made.
—Luke 10:39, 40

••●●••

"Hurry up! You'll miss the bus!" "Make your bed before you come down to breakfast. Do it fast; there's not much time!" "Quickly brush your teeth, then we've got to go!"

Hurry, faster, quickly. Ever walk into a room and can't remember why you went there? I have. Often, in fact! My brain spins so fast that, when I finally get to the place I was supposed to be, I can't remember why I went there!

Here's a secret: **Jesus rarely speaks in our spinning.** I can't think of one place in the Bible where Jesus is sharing truth while multitasking. Instead, he was sitting on a hill. Standing in a boat. Having dinner with friends.

START THE REVOLUTION

Set aside ten minutes today to sit and listen to God.

Martha was a spinner—trying to get everything all done. Mary was a sitter—taking in Jesus' truth. Are you a spinner or a sitter?

Choose to slow down so you can hear him speak. He's waiting to talk to you!

There is so much going on, Jesus. It's hard to imagine how I can sit. Show me where I can make time. Amen.

121: Wait a Minute

In the morning, LORD, you hear my voice;
in the morning I lay my requests before you and wait expectantly.
—Psalm 5:3

Karley was so frustrated! At her small group, they're learning to hear God, and she's trying. She really is! Pen and paper in hand, Karley read a few verses and got quiet. "God, I want to hear from you. Please speak. I'm ready." She waited and waited and waited. Five minutes. (That might not sound like very long to you, but have *you* ever waited in silence for five whole minutes for God to speak? It's really hard!)

Here's the thing about God: he's not in a hurry. Never has been, never will be. He knows his timing is always perfect, because he sees everything. He sees what needs to happen exactly when and where.

God's not in a hurry to speak because he wants to teach you. Teach you how to wait and wait patiently, with your ears open and your heart ready to obey. If he just started gushing each time you said, "Go God!" then he would just be another thing on your list of lists that happen when you demand. Microwave snacks. Google answers. God speaking.

If you choose to forgo the waiting, you might just miss out on what he has to offer you. Let's not go there!

Choose to be a girl who leaves impatience behind and learns to wait on God. You will hear him, in his time.

START THE REVOLUTION

Paint something (your nails, a picture, your favorite chair). Wait for it to dry. Don't do anything else, just practice waiting.

God, this is really hard. To be honest, I just don't get this waiting business. I want to get you, though. Teach me to wait and hear you. Amen.

So do not throw away your confidence; it will be richly rewarded.
You need to persevere so that when you have done the will of God,
you will receive what he has promised.

—Hebrews 10:35, 36

I'm hoping that you are digging into your Bible each and every day and learning all kinds of new stuff that is in there. Now that we have spent 120 days soaking in the truth that Jesus wants us, knows us, and speaks to us, I hope you are full of confidence in Christ and his radical love for you.

Have the last 120 days impacted you in a positive way? The everyday, living-with-your-family, going-to-school you? Have any lies you believed about yourself before been replaced now with truth? **Are you able to hear God speak to you more than you did before?** Do you shine out confidence and self-esteem, because you are the one Jesus is crazy about?

I hope your answer to all these questions is yes!

If not, you might want to go back to the beginning and soak your heart in these truths a bit more. For some of us, the lies that we have believed are especially hard to shake. Don't give up; just feed your heart more truth. Persevere, as the Hebrews passage says, and you will be "richly rewarded."

If you are getting the messages God is sending you, then let's go! We're going to spend the next 120 days learning what we can do to return this amazing love back to our Jesus!

START THE REVOLUTION

Make a list of your thoughts and ideas inspired by the past 120 days of devotions.

Jesus, I get it! I understand that the depth of your love is exactly what I need to fill my heart. I believe that in you I am a confident girl, and I am ready to love you back like you love me. Let's go, Lord! Amen.

CHAPTER FOUR

123: Drink Up

Don't drink too much wine. That cheapens your life. Drink the Spirit of God, huge draughts of him. Sing hymns instead of drinking songs! Sing songs from your heart to Christ.
—Ephesians 5:18, 19 (*The Message*)

• • ● ● ● • •

What do you think about underage drinking? I know, you've heard your parents say, "Don't drink; it's illegal—you're under twenty-one." There is something strange about us humans. As soon as we hear "don't," we want to do it all the more.

Well, I think underage drinking is great. *Any* age is a good age to begin drinking from God's Spirit. Today's passage encourages us to be filled with his Spirit, which leads to fullness in our lives—giving us joy.

When people drink alcohol, they do it to belong, to have fun, to do what everyone else is doing. Jesus says the drink that he gives does all that and more. **His drink is living water**; it's the Holy Spirit living in you!

God has given our bodies triggers that tell us when we're thirsty. Our throats feel dry, our heads ache, and our tummies growl.

START THE REVOLUTION

Pay attention to your thirst indicators. What are you drinking?

In the same way, our hearts have triggers—loneliness, anxiety, stress, depression. These are all symptoms of being thirsty—indicators that we need a drink of living water.

Look at the indicators in your life today. Are you stressed or anxious or lonely or sad? Maybe what you need today is some time in God's presence through prayer, worship, and his Word. Drink up, radical girl!

Jesus, it's easy for me to run dry, especially when I don't spend time with you. Help me to drink your living water today! Amen.

I Need Him

From the ends of the earth I call to you, I call as my heart grows faint; lead me to the rock that is higher than I.

—Psalm 61:2

••●●●••

Swimming, skiing, snorkeling; it had been a great day! Hanging out at the lake was definitely Kim's favorite way to spend a summer day. As the sun set, the group of teens headed down to the dock to enjoy the beauty. She hadn't really thought of it before, but now, with the peachy glow on the horizon creating a romantic setting, Kim started feeling left out. There with her older sister and her boyfriend, her sister's friend and her boyfriend, she was definitely the odd one.

As her eyes gazed at the stunning sunset, **her heart began to burn with the stinging feelings of being alone**. That is when Kim captured her thoughts—she remembered she wasn't alone! She reminded herself that God was there, pursuing her. Having her Love so near brought a smile to Kim's heart. She felt comforted, knowing that God had her right where he wanted her! She didn't have to fit into the mold of those around her. She had a date of a different kind—a perfect love!

Not fitting in with those around us can get really old sometimes—lots of times in fact. This is when the revolutionary girl really shines! When the truth that you are loved by the perfect one fills your emptiness, you stand out, and others see.

You can show the girl who feels she needs a boy's love that there is a perfect love for her too! There is one who wants her and is there for her in every situation.

START THE REVOLUTION

Choose a symbol—a ring, a favorite pair of shoes, sunshine—to remind you of God's love at times when you feel especially lonely.

Jesus, thank you that you are there for me every time and everywhere. Amen.

125: Be Comforted

Blessed are those who mourn, for they will be comforted.
—Matthew 5:4

••••••

Unfortunately, Joan's story is one that is way too common: "When my journey started, it began in a family filled with alcohol abuse. The sexual abuse which stole my innocence came later by a non-family member . . . someone a child should be able to trust. Because of their threats of violence, I kept this abuse a secret.

"One autumn night, feeling pushed in all directions, I took my first drink alone. I felt I would be alone forever; drinking pushed down my fear. . . . Drinking detached me from anyone or anything that might make me feel. It enabled me to ignore my mind, body, and soul. The abuse had marked me; it was a tattoo that wouldn't rub off. Though I laughed and smiled while I drank, I cried inside.

"I finally came to the darkest place, leading me to attempt suicide. **Just as he has always been, God was there.** He helped me to let go of the fearful little girl and become a more confident woman."

You may have had experiences like Joan's or know someone like her. Three million reports of child abuse are made every year in the United States (from www.childhelp .org). Maybe like Joan, you have been too afraid to tell another. Jesus tells us in today's verse that those who mourn will be comforted. That comfort may begin as you choose to reach out to your family, and to tell the police, a teacher, or a close friend. When you allow light to come into the dark situation, you open the door for healing and comfort to begin.

Don't walk alone in fear. There are others, like Joan, who have been where you are and want to come alongside you. Allow the Healer to begin healing you.

START THE REVOLUTION
If you or someone you know has experienced abuse, I urge you to tell someone you trust today, or call 1-800-4-A-CHILD.

Jesus, I know I need healing, but I am scared.
Please empower me with your courage. Amen.

I Need Him

126: Meek Is the New Bold

Blessed are the meek, for they will inherit the earth.
—Matthew 5:5

•••••••

I didn't smoke, drink, or do stuff with guys. I did do one thing . . . judge people. Jesus says in this verse that the blessed ones are the meek. I was the opposite. I was bold to the point of being abrasive at times. Not a good way to win people over. I failed to see reality: my sin of pride was just as ugly, no, probably more offensive to God than any sin of my friends. My assessment of myself was veiled in superiority, and to God, my attitude stunk.

Do you sometimes think that you are all that because of what you do or do not do? Definitely, this is no way to draw people closer to Christ. You will either give them the impression that you have to be some kind of perfect person to follow Jesus, or you will simply make them want to run away. In other words, you won't inherit the earth, you'll make it pack up and leave.

I needed to get a grip and recognize that my sin, no matter what it is, stinks just as much as the next person's. When we see our sin for what it really is—offensive to God—reality can drive us to him. We can use this desperation to our advantage to pursue Jesus, just as he is pursuing us.

Remember, in God's kingdom there are no big sins or little sins. **Sin is sin, no matter what it is.** It all leads to the same conclusion—separation from God. Whatever our condition, his desire for us is the same: to be filled each and every day with the truth of who he is, so we can pour this out to those who need him as well.

START THE REVOLUTION

Ask a friend to be honest with you and tell you how others see you, especially as a Christian. Are you too in-your-face or not enough?

God, I need to see my sin the way you do and hate it. Please forgive me and set me free. Amen.

127: Sharing in Suffering

I want to know Christ—yes, to know the power of his resurrection and participation in his sufferings, becoming like him in his death, and so, somehow, attaining to the resurrection from the dead.
—Philippians 3:10, 11

••●●●••

Daily coming to know Christ deeper and knowing the power behind his death and resurrection; that is what a revolutionary girl focuses on. The first part of this verse is so very appealing: "I want to know Christ—yes, to know the power of his resurrection."

I want to reflect Christ. I want to be free, victorious, and holy. There's a price for these.

Paul tells me the price—suffering. The price I have to pay to know him and his power is participation in his sufferings; becoming like him in death.

"Participation in his sufferings." What does that mean? I share his hurt over those who are poor, broken, and without direction, allowing that pain to impact me to the point where I *act*.

I have to become like him in death. I allow the death of me—my wants, my desires, my foolishness. Death to my attitudes, my mouth, my comfort and ease.

Here, in my own death and suffering of my flesh, I will experience knowing Christ and the power he offers. At the end of me, I find him.

START THE REVOLUTION
Make a list of the things in you that need to "die." Ask Jesus to help you give these up.

Lord, only you can take me to this place where I would never willingly go alone. Please do in me what you need to so I can know you. Amen.

I Need Him

128: Be Needy

But God will never forget the needy;
the hope of the afflicted will never perish.
—Psalm 9:18

• • ● • •

*I*t's OK to be needy.

Really, it's OK to be needy.

In our culture it's not, I know. Being needy is a bad thing; worse than bad if you're a woman! Many women don't want to be seen as dependent on anyone. A lot of women fought very hard for our rights: the right to vote, the right to work the same job for the same pay as a man, and many more.

The sad thing is in all that fighting, we lost something. We lost our need to be dependent.

Needy, when it comes to God, is good.

All of us are needy; we come into the world that way. We were completely dependent on our parents for food, shelter, and affection. As we become adults, our dependence lessens. We grow more able to be independent.

God calls us children of God for a reason. We need to be always dependent on him. He's the only one who can fill all our needs with a pure motive and unconditional love.

It is imperative that we learn to run to Jesus to have all of our needs met. When our neediness is not filled by Jesus, it becomes a force of destruction in our lives. This force is so powerful and deceptive, we can get pulled into its wake and not realize it until the damage is done.

As radically changed, revolutionized-by-love girls, Jesus' love fills us, giving us the strength, courage, and foundation we need. And it shows!

> **START THE REVOLUTION**
> Find out the needs of a shelter in your area. Work with your church to supply some of those needs.

Jesus, I'm needy. Teach me to run to
you to have those needs filled! Amen.

129: Beautiful Confidence

I am weathered but still elegant. . . . They made me care for the face
of the earth, but I had no time to care for my own face.
—Song of Solomon 1:5, 6 (*The Message*)

• • ● ● • •

*E*very girl needs to feel beautiful. Not only on the inside, but on the outside too! Our self-worth, in part, hinges on whether or not we feel beautiful.

Ever notice how, on a day when your hair flops or your jeans are too tight, that you have to fight not to be cranky or sad? Maybe it has something to do with Eve and the whole sin/fall thing. To be honest, I'm not sure. We just need to find a way not to allow these externals to drive our internals!

In today's verse, the bride says, "I am weathered but still elegant." Her darkened skin came from spending her days in the fields working, instead of having enough money to be able to be indoors. Today she'd say, "I am sunburned, but I'm still gorgeous!"

Where does a girl get that type of confidence? (Because I want it!) From her Love. Read Song of Solomon 1:1-4. Love allows her to feel beautiful, no matter what is happening on the outside.

START THE REVOLUTION
Don't let bad hair steal your confidence! Know you are loved, and lovely.

God's luxuriant love can empower you with true confidence that goes way beyond what our human eyes can see. On good days and horrible ones as well, let's look in the mirror and say to ourselves, "I may not be perfect, but I am lovely!"

Jesus, you see me as beautiful.
I need to know it. Amen.

130: Strong Words

Have I not commanded you? Be strong and courageous.
Do not be afraid; do not be discouraged,
for the LORD your God will be with you wherever you go.

—Joshua 1:9

• • ● • •

Nothing terrified me more than street witnessing. Kids in my youth group stood at the college campus, right in front of the bars on Friday night, talking to strangers about Jesus. Frozen with fright, I prayed for enough courage to get out of my yellow Volkswagen and at least stand by.

I'm not sure talking to drunken college students was the best way for *me* to share Jesus, but I do know he helped when I was so scared. Jesus knew my chicken heart. **He gave me courage to do what I believed was the right thing.**

Your terrifying experience may be way scarier than mine. Maybe you started a new school and can't find any girls who love Jesus. You feel completely alone. Whatever your fear, Jesus promises he is with you.

God doesn't make a simple suggestion in our verse today about our fear. No, instead he *commands* us: be strong. He commands us because he is with us wherever we go. His perfect love empowers us with the strength we need for whatever we face.

START THE REVOLUTION
Plan to tackle your current fears with a strategy of intentional time with God.

Jesus waits to pour into you as you step up and start to do the thing that scares you. As you take that first step—sharing your faith with the girl on your softball team, turning down the party invitation or saying yes to that mission trip—he can give you everything you need. He empowers you with courage out of his love and for his glory. Fill yourself up with the truth of his Word and do it! Jesus won't step out for you, but he will step out with you.

Jesus, pour in the courage. I need it. Amen.

131: One Word

*At the name of Jesus every knee should bow, in heaven and on earth
and under the earth, and every tongue acknowledge that
Jesus Christ is Lord, to the glory of God the Father.*
—Philippians 2:10, 11

Alex had to pass this test. If she didn't, her grade would slide to a place where there was no recovery. The pressure was pounding in her head as the numbers swirled on the page. *Maybe I'm going to black out. At least if that happened, I'd get out of taking the test for a day or so.* Finally, she laid her head on her paper and whispered the only thing she could: "Jesus."

One word. **One powerful, earth-quaking word—*Jesus.***

At some point we find that it's the only word for the dire situation we're in.

The only word that can help.

The only word that matters.

The only word we need.

Jesus.

Why is his name so powerful?

The name of Jesus carries the full force that created the universe with just his words: "Let there be light." The name invokes the one who spoke and made blind men see and crippled men run. I need his name when I'm blind to my next turn in life, or when crippling thoughts threaten to take me out. It's OK—I let them take me down. Down to my knees where I can cry out once again to that powerful name—Jesus. In my one-word prayer, I plead with him to come and help me. And he is there.

START THE REVOLUTION

What are some other words that give you comfort? Do any compare to *Jesus*?

Jesus. Amen.

132: Powers

For our struggle is not against flesh and blood, but against the rulers,
against the authorities, against the powers of this dark world
and against the spiritual forces of evil in the heavenly realms.

—Ephesians 6:12

•••●••

*J*osie's mind wouldn't stop. Was something wrong with her? At the oddest times she would have an onslaught of anxious thoughts, *Why are they staring at me? Are they laughing at me? Did anyone else have these thoughts?* She was too afraid to ask.

What Josie doesn't know is **her mind is a battlefield**; a spiritual war zone. The enemy of her heart pulls out every weapon to try to cause her to break down and run away from her love. Satan hates the relationship we have with Jesus, because he hates Jesus.

Jesus has promised us nothing can separate us from the love of God (Romans 8:38, 39).

So what's a girl to do when anxious thoughts continually fill her mind? Only one weapon can fight a battle of this intensity: God's Word. In today's verse we're told this battle is not against flesh and blood—it's not you! It is against spiritual forces of evil, and the only thing they listen to is someone more powerful than them: *Jesus*.

START THE REVOLUTION

What are your go-to Scriptures to combat anxiety?

You need to know God's Word to use this weapon. "You will keep in perfect peace all who trust in you, all whose thoughts are fixed on you!" (Isaiah 26:3, *NLT*). Write it down in your planner. Send a text to yourself. Perfect peace is ours, as we trust him. Fix your thoughts not on you, not on others, but on Jesus!

Jesus, when I become anxious, I will speak your Word to my heart. Amen.

133: No Turning Back

The arrogant mock me unmercifully,
but I do not turn from your law.
—Psalm 119:51

⋯•••⋯

Summertime, summertime, sum-sum-summertime! Carly loved summertime—especially this summer. Never before had she felt so comfortable being herself. You know what she found? She really liked herself! The girl with no makeup, running shorts, and flip-flops was the girl she now liked best. No pretenses. Just Carly.

Best of all, her faith had grown. She had taken advantage of the extra morning hours and the late nights, spending quality time digging into God's Word and letting him get into her. Jesus had truly become her best friend and love.

START THE REVOLUTION
What are the top three biblical commands that keep you out of trouble?

Now school was ramping up, and judging from Facebook, kids were too. Pictures of parties made it clear who was making dumb decisions. Carly could already feel the heat that would come from the ridicule: "Carly, you are such a goody-goody. You shouldn't take this Christian stuff so seriously. I mean, really!" Yet, these same girls were the ones who would call Carly when they were messed up and in trouble.

Carly has learned something very cool: **she has learned from other's experiences**.

The unwise person says, "I have to figure things out myself; grow up on my own." Carly doesn't see it that way. She watches the mistakes that others make and goes the opposite direction. She has decided there is no reason she needs to experience the same pain that others have. She's decided she *has* to learn from other's experience; it's the only way to escape regret.

Go ahead, let the mockers mock. I'm sticking with Carly and Jesus; I'm not turning from his law, his Word.

Jesus, I want to learn from other's experiences too. Help me see clearly what's wise and unwise. Amen.

I Need Him

134: Ever-Present

God is our refuge and strength, an ever-present help in trouble.
—Psalm 46:1

••●●●••

*E*ver fear you may find yourself in a situation way over your head? Do you have an underlying fear that, when trouble comes, you won't have what it takes to deal with it?

I had all kinds of different fears. Fear that I wouldn't pass temptation up. Fear that I wouldn't say the right thing at the right time.

The more we get to know him, the more we discover and uncover Jesus as our constant help—our perpetual strength. There is no need to fear that we'll run out of strength; he has more and more strength for us to uncover. It never runs out. **His help and strength is always more than enough.**

Psalm 46 goes on to express that even if things get really dire—if the earth gives way and mountains fall and waters roar—God is our refuge. He is our fortress. He is the place where we can always be sure to be protected and where we can stand on firm ground, even when everything around us seems pretty shaky.

This just gives us one more reason to love him. David wrote in Psalm 18:1, "I love you, LORD, my strength." What's there not to love?

START THE REVOLUTION
Ever-present. Think about all the times God has been with you, even though you may not have known it.

Jesus . . . one more reason for me to love you more. Amen.

I have told you all this so that you may have peace in me.
Here on earth you will have many trials and sorrows.
But take heart, because I have overcome the world.
—John 16:33 (*NLT*)

••●●••

*I*n this life, we are continually entering into a trial, enduring a trial, or emerging from a trial. It's a fact—one Jesus wasn't afraid to point out to us.

The question is: **how much time do we waste each day** trying to prevent coming trouble, trying to get out of present trouble, or recovering from past trouble?

The revolutionary girl knows that the first part of this verse is the answer to all our trial troubles: "I have told you all this so that you may have peace in me."

In me. Jesus.

Peace isn't guaranteed when my problem is resolved. Peace isn't promised when my life is trouble free. Jesus says it's "in me." In him. And the really great thing about it being in Jesus is that it is in him always. When we are in him, we can find that peace. It's his promise. We can choose to be in him anytime—before, during, and after a dilemma. I don't know about you, but I want to be in him all the time! I want that peace.

START THE REVOLUTION

Write down your life dilemmas. Now tear them up in tiny pieces; ask Jesus to give you his peace.

Jesus, I wish it were as easy to get rid of my troubles as it is to tear up pieces of paper. Teach me how to give you my troubles. Amen.

136: Radiant

Those who look to him are radiant;
their faces are never covered with shame.
—Psalm 34:5

••●●●••

She didn't call or text. She waited—waited to tell me her devastating news. She wanted to be in a safe place in case the tears began to flow.

"I didn't make it . . . again." Mariah has auditioned for multiple honor choirs over the past two years; this marked her fourth rejection. "Maybe God is trying to tell me I'm really not good; I'm not supposed to major in music." I hugged her, looking for the right thing to say. I hate it when those words don't come.

START THE REVOLUTION

What's your go-to song for tough times?

She downloaded a new album from a band called Gungor. Moments later, she was out the door. I hoped her voice instructor would find the words I didn't have. Surely Mariah would receive wise words from a professional. She did—just not the professional I had expected.

Later on, she explained to me the strange mix of emotions she experienced in her car as the words poured out her speakers. **Her heart hurt over the rejection**, yet as she listened to the words of Gungor, Jesus' presence filled her car. Her spirit turned to his Spirit and she began to experience his joy.

Psalm 34:5 says, "Those who look to him are radiant; their faces are never covered with shame." *Radiant* is a beautiful word meaning "emitting rays of light, shining; bright with hope and joy; the emotion of great delight or happiness caused by something exceptionally good or satisfying" (Dictionary.com).

That is who Jesus is: exceptionally good and satisfying.

When we make a choice to turn to Jesus, no matter what is going on around us, we can turn from disappointment to the one who makes us radiant and joyful. Now, we just have to make that turn.

Answer the "Start the Revolution" question.
Make that song your prayer to Jesus today.

137: Details

It was made of hammered gold—from its base to its blossoms.
The lampstand was made exactly like the pattern
the LORD had shown Moses.
—Numbers 8:4

●●●●●●

During the thirty-minute drive downtown, I felt nothing but irritation. Who has time for driving school? Yes, I'd gotten two tickets, but I was going to change!

As soon as I found a seat, my computer-like brain turned on, allowing me to multitask while sitting in the tiny classroom. Honestly, that class could not end fast enough. Finally, when I was free to leave, I rushed out of the building. Looking down at my watch, I realized I had one hour. I *definitely* had time to do one more thing.

I slipped in and out of the store in no time and was ready to fly home. I threw the car into reverse and—BOOM! Looking in my rearview mirror, I discovered my bumper curved around a fifteen-foot cement store sign. All I could do was lay my head on my steering wheel and cry.

Exhausted from the mental and physical pace I'd set for myself, God had been whispering to me for a while that I was too busy. Around that same time I was reading in Numbers, and was amazed at how God took time to attend to the details of a simple lampstand. God wasn't just concerned about the function of the lampstand but also its beauty.

START THE REVOLUTION
Commit to saying the prayer below every day this week.

I knew then that if God cared about these types of details, **he cared about the details of my life too**. I also realized I needed to slow down enough to seek his plans, instead of cramming my days with everything I wanted.

Are you too caught in the frenzy of trying to get everything done? Do you ever lie awake at night wondering how you'll do it all? I want to encourage you to try something that's helped me. Tomorrow, before your feet hit the ground, tell God: "This is your day, not mine. Whatever you want me to do, I will do. Whatever you don't want me to do, I won't." Make this your daily prayer; peace will become your new norm!

Jesus, this is your day, not mine. I'll do
whatever you want me to do. Amen.

I Need Him

138: Sunrise

Your love, LORD, reaches to the heavens, your faithfulness to the skies.
—Psalm 36:5

•••●••

In August, the brutal sun bakes me, darkening the melanin, making my skin crispy in its rays. It's a powerful thing—smothering my skin in sweat. I don't have to wonder if the sun is there, its effects are intense.

The chill in the winter air causes goose bumps to form on my skin. Though the sun is shining in the Carolina blue sky, I don't *feel* its warmth. Yet I need its light. I need the vitamins it brings to cheer my heart.

Though there are days I feel the sun intensely, and there are days when I feel it is nowhere to be found, neither one of these changes the fact that the sun is there. Every day, we can count on it rising.

The sun's consistency is just a glimpse of God's faithfulness to us.

Just as we know each and **every day the sun is going to be there**, so God's faithfulness will be. We don't have to worry about whether or not he is going to take care of our problems on time. He will. He's God. When your heart whirls with fears about your schedule next semester, choose to trust in his faithfulness. If your mind keeps replaying your parents' fight over and over again, picture Jesus, entering the room, bringing his peace.

Keep believing; don't give up. You'll see him.

START THE REVOLUTION
Every time you put your sunglasses on or squint in the sun, thank God for his faithfulness.

Jesus, thank you for your faithfulness. Amen.

139: The Fog

*I have swept away your offenses like a cloud, your sins like
the morning mist. Return to me, for I have redeemed you.*

—Isaiah 44:22

•••••••

My favorite place to be is early morning in the mountains. I like to wake up
before anyone else, grab my journal and Bible, and head for the nearest
porch. Often, there will be a heavy haze; so thick you can barely see past the rails.
As I sit there and spend time with Jesus, I watch as the air heats up, burning away
the fog. As it slowly lifts, the majesty of the mountains is
revealed. It is so beautiful; it often brings tears to my eyes.
Even though I have seen this transformation many times, I
am still astounded that something so incredibly breathtak-
ing is just behind that curtain of gray. **The gray hides
the beauty.**

Sin in our lives can be like the fog, holding us from
Jesus and his beauty. Consumed with only what is directly in front of us—friends, school, sports, Facebook,
cell phones—we miss the best. For a while, we may think
that this is it; this is all there is, so it seems pretty good.
But, if we will hear the voice of the one who wants us and
draw close to him, he will lift the fog of our sin, revealing
our purpose in his love.

**START THE
REVOLUTION**
Think about it.
What or who
helps you see
more clearly
when your
vision is
clouded?

The fog of sin is just a front from the enemy to stop you from seeing Jesus' beautiful love. Ask Jesus to burn it off to reveal his best for you.

*It's so hard not to become consumed with everything
around me and forget about you, Lord. Forgive me and
cause me to put you above all. Amen.*

140: Unbreakable

I am with you and will watch over you wherever you go,
and I will bring you back to this land. I will not leave you
until I have done what I have promised you.

—Genesis 28:15

•••●•••

roken promises. Nothing breaks a girl's heart like broken promises. A dad who never shows. A boyfriend that breaks up. Friends who get better plans. He knows how these pain you.

God cannot break promises; it's not in his DNA. It's impossible, because he is perfect! He always shows and never breaks up. He has better plans, and those plans include you!

When you give him your life, he makes you a promise. He has begun a great work in your life and he will complete what he has started (Philippians 1:6)! That message is echoed in today's verse, "I will not leave you until I have done what I have promised you." That completion will not take place until we are in Heaven with him, so we can know he will be with us always!

START THE REVOLUTION

Have you ever broken a promise? Why? If possible, ask forgiveness today from the person you made the promise to.

It is so good to know that even if nothing else is stable in my life, Jesus, you are. Amen.

141: Conviction

So the LORD said to Solomon, "Since this is your attitude and you have not kept my covenant and my decrees, which I commanded you, I will most certainly tear the kingdom away from you and give it to one of your subordinates."

—1 Kings 11:11

•••●••●•••

There are times when Jesus speaks to us, and it isn't fun or fuzzy. In fact, sometimes it's a downright bummer.

Ever have that feeling, the one where you feel icky in your heart, or **like someone punched you in the stomach**, and you know it's God? My friend Kim and I used to say, "Jesus just slapped up me!" Christians call it *conviction*. Conviction is when your heart and mind realize you're guilty; you've offended God in some way.

There are times when what God has to say to us is for our correction. In today's verse, God was not just delivering correction, but he was also giving the consequences for Solomon's bad attitude. God wasn't messing around. He had told Solomon to obey, but Solomon hadn't taken God seriously. Now Solomon was going to lose the one thing most important to him.

START THE REVOLUTION

What are you feeling icky about? What can you do to fix it?

When we have our hearts and ears open to hear from God, we need to be sure that we are not using selective listening. Yes, God wants to tell us that he is crazy about us. Of course, he wants us to know that he is always there for us and will give us everything we need. But he will also deliver the news when we need adjustments in our attitudes and actions.

❦

Jesus, I don't want to have sin in my life. I'm trying hard not to, but when I do, help me to have a heart that says "Forgive and fix me!" Amen.

142: Who, Me?

*But Moses said to God, "Who am I that I should go
to Pharaoh and bring the Israelites out of Egypt?"*
—Exodus 3:11

•••●●•••

"Don't pick me; I'm nobody!" was Moses' response. God had said, "I've got a mission for you; rescuing my people from slavery." Moses was terrified! How was he going to go before a king when he had a speech impediment! "Please, I don't talk well. I've never been good with words, neither before nor after you spoke to me. I stutter and stammer" (Exodus 4:10, *The Message*). God told Moses to keep going; he'd give him the words.

Moses tried again, **"Please! Send somebody else!"** (v. 13). God's response? Nope. Moses, the guy who couldn't talk well, was just who God was looking for.

Was he out to embarrass Moses? Not at all! God was all about his glory. He was about to do a miracle and he purposely chose someone who couldn't say, "See what *I* did for God!"

> **START THE REVOLUTION**
>
> Think about it. What's God calling you to do?

What does your school need? Someone on the student council? A captain for the volleyball team? A new debater? What does your church need? Someone to lead worship? A girl to mentor other girls?

What is God calling you to do?

Don't be afraid that you can't do it; you probably can't! That makes you the perfect fit! God specializes in using the unqualified. He can shine best through those who don't think they're all that. If you step out, he'll supply what you need. When Moses asked God, "Who am I?" God answered with who *he* was: "I AM WHO I AM."

Be brave! God doesn't want someone else; he's chosen you. And he will be with you.

Jesus, I'm scared. I guess that is a good place to be, because then I need you. Help! Amen.

143: Hazards

When you pass through the waters, I will be with you;
and when you pass through the rivers, they will not sweep over you.
When you walk through the fire, you will not be burned;
the flames will not set you ablaze.

—Isaiah 43:2

How could this have happened? Samantha's dad had accepted a new job at the worst possible time, the beginning of her eighth-grade year. She would have to move over a thousand miles away to a tiny town where people didn't even talk the same!

Has there been a time when **you just wanted to crawl under your covers and stay there**? If you're a girl, the answer is probably yes! I've had days when I just didn't think I had what it took to get out of bed; the world was too hard from where I was looking.

It's times like these when it's so comforting to know Jesus is with us. Today's verse was written to God's people when they were getting ready to go into the land he had just provided for them. The problem was, they had to go through some tough stuff to get it—crossing the Jordan River at flood stage!

If you've ever seen a flood on TV or have actually lived through one, you know that water can be life-threatening. Jesus promises us that even when our troubles seem like they will take us out, he is with us. He won't allow us to be swept away.

START THE REVOLUTION

Take today's verse and fill in your own trouble: "When you are failing algebra because you just don't get it, I will be with you."

Lord, I know hard times are just part of life. I need you; thank you for this comfort. Amen.

144: Them

The LORD is with us. Do not be afraid of them.
—Numbers 14:9

•••●●•••

"Do not be afraid of them." Who are "them" in your life? Who have you been afraid of? Sometimes my "them" was my piano teacher; I hadn't practiced. Other times my "them" was my boss at work; I was late. I should have been afraid of them; I did something that was my fault.

But what about when we haven't done anything wrong?

What about the "them" that makes fun of you for remaining pure when it comes to guys? You are different. They don't get why, so the easy thing to do is rip you to shreds.

How about the "them" who are the upperclassmen on the basketball team? The ones who pick on you as if they weren't freshmen just four months ago?

The Lord gives a command here—don't be afraid of them. We have a choice: to be fearful or not. If we give in to the fearful thoughts in our minds and allow them to play out in our actions, we could be disobeying God.

Fear cripples. **Fear imprisons**, making us incapable of revolutionizing our world around us with the truth of Jesus' radical love. How can you display the power of Jesus' love to people if you are too afraid to speak to them? It's impossible.

Instead of being a slave to fear, make fear your slave. Recognize when it is attempting to invade your heart through your mind. Fight back with the truth of God's Word: he is with you. If God is for you, who can be against you?

START THE REVOLUTION
Really think about this one. If God is with you, who are you afraid of?

Jesus, when I am scared, you aren't always the first thing that comes to mind. I want to remember you are with me, so I won't be afraid. Amen.

145: A Winning Pass

Therefore he is able to save completely those who come to God through him, because he always lives to intercede for them.

—Hebrews 7:25

•• ● ●••

When I met Greg, my future mother-in-law gave me some terrific advice: "You can either hate football or learn to love it." I chose loving it. I've learned there's this move in football called the interception. An interception is when a team intercepts (or prevents) the opponent's pass. It stops the game from moving in one direction and reverses it.

An interception stops a connection from happening. It prevents the team's progress. In contrast, an *intercession* makes a connection possible.

Satan wants to intercept the messages God sends us. He wants to stop progress from happening. He wants our game to be over, or to completely reverse anything God has accomplished.

Jesus, on the other hand, lives to intercede for us. He acts on our behalf, pleading for our case before God. Restoring our connection with our Father, so God can continue to make progress in our lives.

Feel like your game of life is moving in the wrong direction?

You made a really unwise decision, and now the consequences are looming. Or are someone else's choices causing heartache and pain in your life?

You are not alone in these troubles. Jesus is constantly before our Father God, making a case for you. He is acting on your behalf, praying for you, and making reconciliation possible. He can make the winning pass complete. All you have to do is accept his work on your behalf, and don't let Satan get you off your game.

START THE REVOLUTION

Fill in the blank. Jesus, restore the connection to God for me in the area of

_____.

Jesus, thank you for taking these troubles to God. I need you! Amen.

I Need Him

153

146: Guardian Wanted

And the peace of God, which transcends all understanding,
will guard your hearts and your minds in Christ Jesus.
—Philippians 4:7

••●●●••

Take a stab at how many advertisements you see a day. I've heard it's three thousand. Three thousand. Three thousand times a day someone tells you:

- what you lack
- what's wrong with you
- what you need
- why you aren't good enough
- why what you have isn't good enough

And we wonder why we feel so bad about ourselves some days!

You know what we need? **We need a bodyguard**; a guard that will protect us from the three thousand lies a day that pound into our hearts and minds.

We have one. We have a personal bodyguard, Jesus. And his defense weapon of choice is his peace. His peace can cut through three thousand lies, bringing us the truth of his contentment and everything we need.

START THE REVOLUTION

Think about it. How can you avoid being influenced by advertising messages?

Jesus, thank you for guarding my heart and mind today.
Help me to guard it with you. Amen.

147: Radical Message

I told you that you would die in your sins; if you do not believe that I am he, you will indeed die in your sins.
—John 8:24

••●●●••

Death is a scary thing. There is so much we don't know about it. How will it feel? How will I die? What happens next?

One thing we can be certain of: we need Jesus. We need to believe that he is who he said he is: the Son of God. Believe that he is the only way to Heaven; his is the only truth and in him is true life (John 14:6). We need to believe that without Jesus we will spend eternity separated from love. Separated forever from his love and any love we have ever known—completely alone. Serious stuff.

Don't ever let anyone tell you that they're going to Hell with their buddies. Hell was not created for buddies. It was created for the devil and his demons; not for people. Yet, because people refuse to admit their need for Jesus, that is where they are heading. When they choose not to follow him, they choose an eternity of aloneness.

That is why we have to be bold about the truth. We need to be radical when it comes to telling others that what they are buying into is a lie: sin has a price, and that price is eternal death.

No matter how we struggle, let's decide. Let's make up our minds that from now until eternity we will believe Jesus is the one—the one who can keep me from dying in my sins and give me eternal life.

START THE REVOLUTION

Do your friends and family know about Jesus? If not, tell them today!

Jesus, I believe you are the Son of God and the only hope I have of eternal life. Amen.

148: Doubt

But he said to them, "Unless I see the nail marks in his hands
and put my finger where the nails were,
and put my hand into his side, I will not believe."
—John 20:25

•••●●•••

There are days when you might struggle with doubt. Is Jesus really who he said he is? Is this Christianity thing real? You are not alone. Mariah and Mary are both believers, and they are both struggling. They made a decision to read *Mere Christianity* together this summer to strengthen their faith before they head off to college.

Even one of Jesus' own disciples struggled. Take a minute and read his story in John 20:19-31. Thomas had just spent the last three years with Jesus. Yet when the other disciples said, "He's risen from the dead," Thomas said he wouldn't believe it until he could see it. Thomas lacked faith.

Faith is confidence in what we hope for and assurance of what we do not see (Hebrews 11:1). It means that, even though we can't see the thing we believe in, we still believe.

Some people call it something different. They say it is being naive, or blind or dumb. They may argue with scientific or historic facts (even though there is so much evidence that Jesus was here on earth and was divine). But here's the deal: **they can't argue with my story**. My story of how he has changed me and of his presence in my daily life is proof.

Unlike Thomas, I don't have the luxury of being able to wait for a few hours for Jesus to return. I can't see the nails marks in his hands and put my hand into his side. I can, however, see his work through my hands and see his presence in my life.

Build your history with God, evidence in your life of his work. Evidence dispels doubt when it creeps in.

START THE REVOLUTION

Assess your doubt level. Are you looking for signs, or are you secure in your faith?

Jesus, I have struggled with doubt. I am going to keep trusting you, seeing you work in my life, and building a history with you. Amen.

149: Good Morning!

Satisfy us in the morning with your unfailing love,
that we may sing for joy and be glad all our days.
—Psalm 90:14

••••••

Morning time is a hard time. If you're not a morning person, just getting out of bed is a challenge, let alone getting the day off to a good start. You've probably heard someone say this before: "Looks like she got up on the wrong side of the bed." Often the way we begin a day is the way that entire day goes.

Could that be why David says in today's psalm, "Satisfy us *in the morning* with your unfailing love?" He might be on to something!

If we make a decision to have our needs for affirmation, attention, and approval met by Jesus first thing in the morning, we will go about our day *filled*. When our hearts are full of his love, we're not so needy and not so apt to turn to people and things to make us happy (things that often disappoint).

> **START THE REVOLUTION**
> Start the day off right. Have some Bible verses with your breakfast.

If your heart is already satisfied with the unfailing love of Jesus, when you see that guy you are crushing on, you won't feel desperate for his attention. You're full already. You don't *need* to make that play, get that grade, or have that friend. All those things are icing on the cake; they make life better, but your happiness is not dependent on them.

It doesn't take long to get filled. A Bible verse or two, that you can think on all day, might satisfy you. Type it in your phone. Write it on a card. Just make the time to fill up.

Jesus, morning and I aren't friends. Help me to be disciplined enough to read even just a verse or two, so that I will be satisfied in the morning with your unfailing love. Amen.

I Need Him

150: Be Perfect?

Be perfect, therefore, as your heavenly Father is perfect.
—Matthew 5:48

••●●●••

*J*esus sounds pretty harsh in this verse. Be perfect! When it comes to our hair, bodies, and all that outside stuff, it is exhausting trying to get everything just right. You mean Jesus wants us to be that way on the inside too? It just about makes me want to give up!

But wait—what does he mean by *perfect*? I checked it out in my Greek dictionary. This word for perfect is *teleios,* meaning "perfect, mature, complete, finished."

Let's plug that word in: "Be complete and mature just as your heavenly Father is complete and mature." Sounds like something we want!

We want to be complete, not lacking anything. **We want to be whole—not broken.** Jesus wants that for us too!

My friend Lisa Whittle poses this question: whole or hole? When you look at your heart, do you see one that has been made whole, despite what you might have already been through in your short life? Or do you see a hole, one created by your situations or choices, that desperately needs to be filled?

If you see a hole, you need him. You need him to come and heal you; make you perfect and complete. He can and will; just take his hand and let him take you there.

START THE REVOLUTION

What parts of you need to mature and be made complete?

Look up the chorus to the song, "Healer," by Kari Jobe, and make those lyrics your prayer today:
"I believe you're my healer. . . .
Jesus, you're all I need." Amen.

151: Forgiveness Heals

Praise the LORD, my soul, and forget not all his benefits—who forgives all your sins and heals all your diseases.

—Psalm 103:2, 3

•••●••

*I*t was a constant reminder. Every time she saw the scar on her arm it was a reminder to Josie of the painful time she had cut herself. Fortunately, the reminder itself was not painful; in fact, the reminder caused her to be grateful. She has been healed.

In Jesus, there is healing. In him, we can reach a place where, though we still remember painful things, we no longer feel pained by them. The memories no longer have the power to hurt us.

It begins with our need for forgiveness—forgiveness for us or forgiveness towards others. Without first going through forgiveness, there will never be healing. **Forgiveness is a step that can't be skipped.**

Then, after forgiveness, Jesus can heal all of your diseases. Diseases of betrayal, rejection, self-hatred, eating disorders, addictions, abuse—Jesus has the desire and power to heal them all.

You need to take the first step. He'll help.

START THE REVOLUTION

Do you have scars—inside or outside—that remind you of pain? Have you forgiven the person who caused your wound (even if that person is you)?

Thank you that you want to and will heal me, Jesus. Empower me to take the first step of forgiveness. Amen.

152: Rescue Mission

*Who redeems your life from the pit and crowns you with love
and compassion, who satisfies your desires with good things
so that your youth is renewed like the eagle's.*

—Psalm 103:4, 5

••••••••

$\mathcal{E}$ver feel like you are so low the only way to look is up? **Your life is a pit.**

David knew what it was like to be in a pit. Spending many years of his life running from someone trying to kill him, he learned to depend on God to pull him out of the hole in the ground—literally.

When we find ourselves at the lowest of lows, it's the perfect place for a God rescue. He specializes in rescue missions, pulling us from the hardest of times to a place where we are filled with love. And you know what? Our situation doesn't even have to change! That's one of the coolest things about God. When we in need reach out for his help, he has the power to lift our hearts out of our absolute worst condition, even while nothing around us changes. What changes is us! When we fill our minds and hearts with the truth of his love for us, he brightens our hearts, meets our needs, and gives us strength to keep going.

START THE REVOLUTION

Is there anyone down in a pit with you? Have you told them the way to get rescued?

*Jesus, thank you that my need isn't a turnoff for you.
I need a rescue mission in my life.
Brighten my heart, O Lord. Amen.*

153: Full Life

The thief comes only to steal and kill and destroy;
I have come that they may have life, and have it to the full.
—John 10:10

•••◦●◦•••

Do you believe in fate? I believe in lots of things, but fate isn't one of them. The beliefs I hang onto the most come from God's Word:

- I believe Jesus loves you and is for you (Romans 8:31).
- I believe Jesus is crazy about you (Psalm 45:11).
- I believe Jesus says you are beautiful (Song of Solomon 4:7).
- I believe Jesus has a plan for good for your life (Jeremiah 29:11).
- I believe that Satan hates your guts (John 10:10).

Yep, hates your guts.

Jesus said that Satan, the thief, has one script—to kill, steal, and destroy. Me. You. Your friend.

Fate isn't fate at all. Jesus and the enemy are both at work in your life.

That's just another reason why we need Jesus. We have a target on our backs, and **the enemy is aiming right at us**. Before we freak out and give up, we've got to finish the verse: "I have come that they may have life, and have it to the full." That's Jesus talking. He came to earth and died so that we could experience a life that is full—full of life, goodness, and purpose.

It's important for you to know that the enemy hates you and to recognize what some of his tactics are for killing, stealing, and destroying those God loves. They're not super tricky. One of Satan's best weapons against me is me. Lots of times he uses us to pull ourselves down!

Most of all, know that you need and have Jesus. He's got your back.

START THE REVOLUTION
What do you believe in? Make your own list.

Jesus, I have all the power I need in you to experience the full life you came to give me. Help me to see that. Amen.

154: Wisdom

If any of you lacks wisdom, you should ask God, who gives generously to all without finding fault, and it will be given to you.

—James 1:5

•••●•••

I f you want to know what God thinks about dating someone who doesn't know him, that's easy. "Don't become partners with those who reject God. How can you make a partnership out of right and wrong? That's not partnership; that's war. Is light best friends with dark?" (2 Corinthians 6:14, *The Message*).

How does he feel about partying? He's clear: "Don't be drunk with wine, because that will ruin your life. Instead, be filled with the Holy Spirit" (Ephesians 5:18, *NLT*).

How does he feel, though, about things that are not so clear? Where should I go to school? What classes should I take? Should I buy a car? If so, what kind? **What about questions that don't have clear biblical answers?** Today's verse gives us a clear answer: "If you don't know what you're doing, pray to the Father. He loves to help. You'll get his help, and won't be condescended to when you ask for it. Ask boldly, believingly, without a second thought" (James 1:5, *The Message*).

When you need an answer:

• Ask God; he wants to give you the answer.
• Trust God; he doesn't think you are dumb for needing his help.
• Believe God; he will give you the wisdom you need.

Now don't doubt that he will come through: "But when you ask, you must believe and not doubt, because the one who doubts is like a wave of the sea, blown and tossed by the wind. That person should not expect to receive anything from the Lord" (James 1:6, 7). Trust him; he'll give you the wisdom you need when you need it!

START THE REVOLUTION

Got a question today? Ask God. Trust God. Believe God.

Jesus, life has so many questions and I need so many answers. Teach me to trust you one issue at a time, and with your help, I'll make wise decisions. Amen.

155: Fixed

But my eyes are fixed on you, Sovereign LORD; in you
I take refuge—do not give me over to death.
—Psalm 141:8

•••••••

*E*ver notice the more you think about a problem the more it grows?

Heading to your closet to wear your favorite shirt, you discover it's gone. Immediately you think, *She's taken it again!* Infuriated with your sister, you yell, "Why does she always take *my* stuff?"

You begin a list of all the things she's "borrowed." As the list grows, your anger heats up. You erupt! Like a river of destructive molten lava, you pour out of your room, burning anyone in your path. Enraged words overtake your victim.

Beginning to cool off, you feel so much better. The pent-up anger is gone; now it covers your deserving sister. With relief, you walk away, having scorched her to death.

Radical girl—this is not God's way. When anger is erupting in our hearts, **self-control is beyond hard**. That's why we need him so! We need God to help us keep from making anger our focus.

When something sets you off, a tiny hot spot gets sparked in your heart: "She makes me so mad." That's the spark—let it become your warning. Quickly turn your thoughts to Jesus. He commands you to focus on him.

> **START THE REVOLUTION**
> Rest. Be still and quiet until the anger has burned out, and then remedy the problem.

Program your mind to immediately fix your eyes on Jesus. Turn your eyes to his love for you, and on his love for *her*. Fix your eyes on his forgiveness for you and his forgiveness for her. Remember his patience for you and choose patience for her.

Jesus, my anger feels justified. I need to fix
my eyes on you so I can choose right. Amen.

156: He Can Take It

Cast all your anxiety on him because he cares for you.
—1 Peter 5:7

••●●●••

Tammy never knows which mom she'll get each day after school. Happy mom—snack on the table, smile on her face, and ready to hear about her day. Or stressed, overwhelmed mom—short-tempered, easily angered, and unavailable.

Not knowing which mom she'll find creates anxiety in Tammy's heart. She loves going home to happy mom. When her mom is in a good mood, there is no one she would rather be around. But when she isn't . . . Tammy would rather be anywhere but home. Not knowing which mom she would have to deal with made Tammy's stomach ache.

Relationships are just plain hard; these combinations of personalities and emotions can be confusing and difficult. Sometimes they are too much. We need the comfort and strength of Jesus. He tells us we can take the things in our lives that produce stress and give them to him. Actually he tells us to cast, or throw, all our anxiety on him.

Why him? It's not his problem!

We can give our stress to him because he cares for us and his perfect strength can handle what we can't.

When you sense trouble building in your heart—worried thoughts, racing pulse, swirling emotions—stop. No matter where you are or what you're doing, tell yourself to give the problem to Jesus. Do it the first time, the second time, the hundredth time. He has what it takes, especially when you don't.

START THE REVOLUTION

When you feel the pressure rising and your emotions swirling, stop. Take a minute and imagine handing over your bundle of troubles to Jesus.

Jesus, things seem so heavy sometimes. Help me to give them to you. Help me feel lighter. Amen.

157: Rejection as Freedom?

Then you will know the truth, and the truth will set you free.
—John 8:32

•••●•••

Cut again! Looking at the board in the locker room, Karry was unable to believe she had failed to make the track team for the second year in a row! She had tried so hard and she was the only one of her friends to not make it. "God, why? I tried my hardest, prayed, asked my mom and some friends to pray. I even posted a verse about courage on my FB page! Why did you let this happen *again*?"

There is nothing harder than rejection, nothing worse than feeling like we've failed. So if it hurts so bad, why does God let it happen?

Mariah asked this same question when she didn't make the basketball team in middle school. At 5'11", she was sure she'd make the team—everyone said so! So after three grueling days of tryouts, when the coach took her aside and told her the devastating news, she was completely shocked. "Everybody, including myself, expected me to make the team," says Mariah, now eighteen. "The worst thing is when people say things like 'This is for the best.' But it really was true."

Not making the basketball team caused Mariah to ask herself some tough questions. *Was basketball her passion?* Mariah had to face it: basketball was not her passion, nor was it her gift. What she loved was music.

START THE REVOLUTION

Have you ever been rejected? Can you see how God used this in your life?

Mariah took the rejection and turned it around. She joined a prestigious choir that practiced at a higher level than most and traveled. She began voice lessons and piano too. She began to invest her time and efforts into what she *was* gifted in.

So how has this new motivation turned out? Mariah traveled to Italy and even sang in the Vatican with her choir. She tried out for her school's exclusive chamber choir, normally reserved for juniors and seniors, becoming the only sophomore to make the group. She followed her passion which led her to find her niche.

Lord, the next time rejection comes my way, help me see it for what it is: something you can use! Amen.

I Need Him

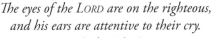

158: Peace in the Dark

The eyes of the LORD are on the righteous,
and his ears are attentive to their cry.
—Psalm 34:15

•••●•••

*F*lying straight up, Sarah squinted, her eyes not adjusting fast enough to the pitch-black room. Exhausted, she had gone to bed early, knowing her parents would be home soon. But now, she thought she heard someone knocking at the door. Who would be knocking at the door at this time of night? What if, when she didn't answer, they tried to break in? All she knew to do was whisper, "Jesus."

Have you ever experienced fear in the dark like Sarah? A time when you feared the unknown?

I have. Even though my heart was pounding and my mind tried to create the worst possible scenes, I made myself pray. I knew that Jesus could bring his peace even in the most fearful situation. It didn't come immediately, but as I forced my mind to turn from my fear and toward faith, peace came.

It is so comforting to know that no matter where we are or what is happening, **the Lord's eyes are on us; his ears are just waiting for our prayers**. Knowing the powerful, majestic God is looking and listening to you can quiet your screaming heart.

START THE REVOLUTION

Draw a picture of what you think Jesus' eyes and ears look like. Remember he sees and hears you.

Jesus, I needed to know today that you are looking and listening to me no matter what is happening in my dark. I love you so! Amen.

159: When You're Stuck

It is for freedom that Christ has set us free. Stand firm, then, and do not let yourselves be burdened again by a yoke of slavery.
—Galatians 5:1

••●●••

o you ever feel stuck? Stuck with the same group of friends? Stuck doing the same bad things over and over again? Stuck in a relationship you need to get out of?

Stuck.

Christ died to make us unstuck but he's not going to do the "unsticking" for us. He will help. His Word promises he is an ever-present help in time of need (Psalm 46:1). *We* have to take that first step to get unstuck.

What is your first step? Asking a new friend to hang out? Getting a filter on your computer? Becoming "friends" with your mom on Facebook? Sharing with your youth director your secret sin? Breaking up with that guy once and for all?

> **START THE REVOLUTION**
> Change your thoughts and you'll change your walk.

Jesus died to set you free from what's dragging you down, but before he can do that, you have to hate being dragged down. Get to the point where you're over being a slave to this thing in your life. Call it what it is—sin. Ask Jesus to forgive you for it and then do something. Change the way you think. If you change your thoughts, you'll change your walk. Stop dwelling on the guy; think on Jesus. Stop texting old friends; call out to your new friend. Walk away from the computer. Take action to be free—let that first action begin with your thoughts.

Today's verse tells us that Jesus did not set us free for us to get stuck again. He set us free so we can *be* free; completely and permanently.

Jesus, I am over being stuck in my sin. Please "unstick" me. Empower me, one thought at a time, to change my thinking so I can keep being free. I need you, Jesus. Amen.

I Need Him

160: Be Prepared

Wait for the LORD; be strong and take heart and wait for the LORD.
—Psalm 27:14

•••●••

"I'm tired of waiting." Ever said this? Thought this? Tired of waiting for a boyfriend. Tired of waiting to succeed in your sport or music. Tired of waiting for your parents to give you more freedom. Tired of waiting to do stuff with guys. Tired of waiting.

It takes courage to wait, to not fix or manipulate. To not force or rush into something.

Waiting takes maturity. **Waiting is true power.** Look at the winner in a race; the winner knows just the right time to pour it on. She doesn't sprint at the beginning. A girl who can wait is a girl who is truly free! Free from the pressure of deciding "when." She's made up her mind that the "when" is when God says so.

Waiting is not a matter of just sitting around until something happens. *Wait* is a verb—it means "to be available or in readiness" (Dictionary.com).

When you are waiting you are preparing for the thing you are waiting for. Preparing for the right guy that God brings in his right timing. Practicing to improve in your sport or music. Becoming the girl who can be responsible with more freedom when it is given. Remaining pure until your wedding night when you won't have the boundaries you have today.

Be radical and see waiting as the privilege to receive God's best at the right time in the right way.

> **START THE REVOLUTION**
>
> What are you tired of waiting for? Stop being tired and get up and get prepared instead.

Jesus, I need you to empower me to wait. Make me strong in my mind and in my heart so that I will one day receive your best. Amen.

161: Grow the Seed

No one who is born of God will continue to sin, because God's seed remains in them; they cannot go on sinning, because they have been born of God.
—1 John 3:9

• • ◦ ● ◦ • •

Jane said she was a Christian. She went to youth group; she was even on the leadership team. Yet, the rest of her life didn't reflect that. Not the way she talked, not the things she did.

Confusing, isn't it?

A child of God should look like a child of God. She should reflect his character: kind, patient, and loving. She should treat her body like the temple of God, using it only for what pleases him. The revolutionary girl doesn't allow known sin in her life; her heart wants only to please her king.

Sound difficult? It is. It is almost impossible except for one thing: God himself is living inside of you. Today's verse tells us that when God's seed remains in us, we cannot go on sinning; we've been born of God.

I planted a salsa garden: jalapeños, peppers, and tomatoes. When I went to harvest my vegetables, I got exactly what I planted. I didn't get lettuce, carrots, and radishes.

Friend, if you haven't seen God's produce in the garden of your heart, **what have you been planting?** Selfishness, unkindness, gossip? Don't allow space in your heart garden for sin to grow. Ask Jesus to bring the tiller of repentance and start planting God's seed. You'll find the person that you say you are and the person that you are is the same.

START THE REVOLUTION

If someone asked the people you see every day if you were a Christian, what would their answers be?

Jesus, I don't want to be a hypocrite. That's embarrassing to you and to me. Today, I will pray, read your Word, and obey what it says. I'm making room in my heart for your seed. Amen.

I Need Him

162: Family

Though my father and mother forsake me, the LORD will receive me.
—Psalm 27:10

•••●••••

ily's family was falling apart. It started when they found out her sister was on drugs. Her parents started arguing, then not speaking to each other. Now, they weren't speaking to her either.

Why me? She thought. *We always had the perfect family, the one others said they wished they had. Why is all this happening?*

Nothing hurts like family problems. Your home is supposed to be the one place where you are safe; where you can be yourself. When that one place is crumbling, it's hard not to feel helpless.

We may feel helpless, but we are never alone. God promises us that no matter what happens, even if my mom and dad desert me, he will always be there for me. Whenever I need him, he can be counted on. He'll never let me down.

Our families are made up of humans—humans who mess up. But God doesn't mess up. He cannot be unfaithful, unkind, or unloving. He is perfect . . . always.

START THE REVOLUTION

If you have family members who support you and love you, hug them today!

Jesus, thank you that you will never leave me or forsake me. I need that. Thank you that I can always depend on you. Amen.

CHAPTER FIVE

I Go After Him

163: One Thing

One thing I ask from the LORD, this only do I seek:
that I may dwell in the house of the LORD all the days of my life,
to gaze on the beauty of the LORD and to seek him in his temple.
—Psalm 27:4

········

*H*ow do I get his attention? How can I lose weight? How do I get my hair to do what hers does? Our energy and minds are consumed with things that are *huge*! Or are they?

What would happen if we funneled our energy toward something truly valuable—eternal even? What if we put all the time we spent thinking of the guy in Spanish class toward thinking about the one who is already in love with us? What would happen?

We would become girls who are confident, secure, filled with true joy. Whatever we stare at, we become. **Our focus becomes our future.**

David knew this secret. In Psalm 27, he says he wants to steadily focus on one thing—just one. The beauty of the Lord. Gazing at the beauty of the Lord would cause him to become beautiful. We become what we focus on.

Don't we want to be beautiful? To become so like Jesus, we look like him?

Be deliberate today. When your mind turns to that guy you're crushing on, turn your mind toward Jesus. When your focus becomes the zit on your forehead, turn your focus to him. It won't happen by itself and it won't be easy, but it will be a huge step toward becoming the girl you want to be.

START THE REVOLUTION

If you have a microscope or a camera with a zoom lens, practice focusing. You need to practice your focus on God too!

Jesus, today I'll stare at you and become beautiful as you are beautiful. Amen.

104: Get Bossy

My heart says of you, "Seek his face!" Your face, LORD, I will seek.
—Psalm 27:8

•••●•••

Hearts are liars. I know because my heart lies to me. It lied to me when I was trying to find a publisher for my first book. Nineteen times I heard, "No one is going to publish you. You're not good enough." At first, I cried and agreed, "It's true!" After a while, I got smarter. As my friend Renee Swope says, I started bossing my heart around. I ran to Jesus with these disappointments. Some days, it was easy. I felt strong and said confidently, "I'm trusting Jesus." Other days, it was a constant battle not to listen to the cruel voices. I had to get bossier on those days.

START THE REVOLUTION
Write your own psalm from your heart. What does your heart say?

I bet you have a lying heart too, telling you things that aren't true:
- "Your parents are disappointed in you; you can't *ever* please them."
- "You could never get into a college like that; it's only for smart kids."
- "Your artwork isn't that beautiful."

Our hearts see things as they *aren't*. They lie, telling us how to feel when we shouldn't feel that way at all.

In today's verse, David appears to be having issues with a split personality; he's talking to himself: "My heart says of you, 'Seek his face!'" Then David turns around and answers himself! "Your face, Lord, I will seek." This is a psalm of complaint. David doesn't like what is going on, yet he's trying to get past it to pursue God.

To become a radical girl, you've got to take control of your heart. This isn't for the weak. This isn't for the girl who is just living for today and doesn't care about tomorrow. But you're not that girl anyway, right?

Today, I'm bossing my heart around, Lord. I'm going to seek you no matter what. Amen.

I Go After Him

165: Heart Exercise

Do you not know that in a race all the runners run, but only one gets the prize? Run in such a way as to get the prize.

—1 Corinthians 9:24

••●●●••

o you like to work out? Often I don't. I hate sweating, forcing my muscles to hurt, and taking time away from more fun things. There are so many things I would rather be doing. Does that mean I don't work out? No, I know my body needs exercise, so I make myself do what I don't want to do because it's best for me.

There will be days, many days, when you won't feel like seeking God. You won't feel like being a Christian. You won't feel like reading your Bible, praying, or spending time at church. You *will* feel like doing what everyone else is doing—fitting in. You'll have a choice: doing what is best anyway or doing what feels good.

Making the choice to go after him will keep you on the way that will lead to what you ultimately want: God's best. A runner in a race, when you choose to keep going after God, even when you feel exhausted from going against the crowd, in the end you win! The question is, will you keep running?

There are prizes for the girl who goes after him: peace, joy, blessings. There is life, without regrets for poor choices made. The cost of the workout is worth the prize.

START THE REVOLUTION

Figure out an exercise routine for your heart. What parts do you need to strengthen?

Teach me to exercise my heart, Jesus, so that my faith is fit in you. Amen.

166: Attention Deficit

No one serving as a soldier gets entangled in civilian affairs,
but rather tries to please his commanding officer.
—2 Timothy 2:4

Being good is getting old. That's how I started to feel my senior year. Angelica did too. Up until then, her life had gone pretty smoothly. But during her senior year, things began to change. She had really blossomed and become more aware of her appearance. Her fashion taste ramped up and so did her interest in boys. One thing led to another, right up to dating a bad boy. Fortunately, she got wise and broke up with him, as she headed off to college.

Her freshman year in college was a rerun of her senior year in high school. College was filled with all kinds of interesting guys. She again found one who caught her eye, leading to another bad decision. All her Facebook statuses were love songs. The worst part of this journey was her suffering relationship with the Lord. **The closer she got to the guy, the further she got from Jesus.**

Sometimes what's best for us is to back up and get a fresh perspective on our lives. Taking a break from our surroundings is needed. When Angelica returned home for summer break, she got the right perspective back. Investing in her relationship with Jesus again became a priority. A total transformation began in Angelica's heart; she became the person she used to be. Now, her statuses showed her focus and heart were back on the Lord.

Split attention is not 100 percent attention—you can't focus on investing in Jesus with all of your heart and a guy at the same time. If you find yourself thinking about a new crush more than you are thinking about Jesus, don't delude yourself. Admit that the guy has become more important than your God and turn your heart around.

START THE REVOLUTION
Check yourself out. Compare the time you spend with God to the time you spend dreaming about, talking with, or worrying over that guy.

Jesus, crushes are powerful. Help me not to give my heart to a guy right now and to keep my heart focused on you. Amen.

167: Perfect in Weakness

But he said to me, "My grace is sufficient for you, for my power is made
perfect in weakness." Therefore I will boast all the more gladly
about my weaknesses, so that Christ's power may rest on me.
—2 Corinthians 12:9

* * * * *

*W*hat do I have that God could use? I've struggled with my answer to that question a time or two. There's really nothing extraordinary about my life—nothing I've *excelled* at. I'm really quite ordinary.

I loved to sing and took piano lessons, but I wasn't great. I ran cross-country and track, but I wasn't fast. I got decent grades, but I wasn't a scholar.

I guess that's why God *could* use me; there's no way I can take credit. I can't say I write because of my writing degree; I never went to college. I can't say specialized training opened speaking doors for me; I had none. When God began to use me, it had to be him. Unqualified was exactly what God found in me.

When we take our focus off how unqualified we are and put our focus on him, he can really begin to show off.

Our verse today is from Paul's letter to the Corinthians. Here he is talking about a specific problem he had, "a thorn in [his] flesh," but he repeats this same kind of thinking elsewhere in his letters—that he is nothing without God. God's power is shown off through what he accomplishes in our weakness.

Jesus can show others the power of his love to transform a life; power to take the ordinary and make her extraordinary. To make the weak, strong. This power from God is released in our lives when we gain a right view of who we are: not good enough to gain his love, but **loved enough to gain his good**.

> **START THE REVOLUTION**
> Are you giving God the glory for the things you have done? How?

Jesus, I guess I have all the right qualifications to be used by you: nothing but you! I'm ready. Take my weakness and show your strength. Amen.

168: Take Charge

*When his master saw that the LORD was with him and that the LORD
gave him success in everything he did, Joseph found favor in his eyes
and became his attendant. Potiphar put him in charge of his household,
and entrusted to his care everything he owned.*

—Genesis 39:3, 4

••●••

Dragged to a country unlike his own, this teen boy was sold into slavery to a government guy named Potiphar. But then things started to look up! Potiphar saw something special in Joseph. Even though Joseph thought he was in the wrong place, he worked hard to do the right thing. God's favor carried him the rest of the way. He saved an entire nation from starvation!

In a sermon once, pastor Steven Furtick described God's favor as the guarantee of God's presence and the provision of his power to accomplish his special purpose in and through my life.

START THE REVOLUTION
The choice is yours. Press in or push away? Which is it going to be?

Like Joseph, there will be times when you will feel you are in the wrong place at the wrong time, and you had nothing to do with it. Your family moved. Your school district redrew the lines. Money ran out and changes were made in your family. Whatever your situation, radical girl, you can go after God right where you are and find his favor.

In these difficult times, make this decision: **define your situation, don't let it define you**. Take the opportunity and press into God; don't allow the opposition to push you away from God.

God has big plans for you—plans for you to spread his love so that others' lives are also revolutionized. That was his purpose for Joseph; it's his purpose for you.

*God, hard times make me want to run.
Help me to run to you! Amen.*

I Go After Him

169: Filling Up

Blessed are the pure in heart, for they will see God.
—Matthew 5:8

••••••

It is so refreshing being around P. J. She is really discovering a relationship with Jesus for the first time, and her heart to dig in and know him better inspires me.

P. J. shared her story with me—her early days of high school partying. That was before she became a camp counselor last summer. Hearing stories of Jesus each day and then attending Bible study for the staff sparked her attention.

It was worship, though, that really grabbed her heart. Having never experienced God's presence like that before, she got hooked. Studying God's Word, being in church, and participating in worship are now what gets her pumped. P. J.'s heart has a new focus: she wants to know God and is doing whatever it takes to learn about him.

Jesus promised those who were pure in heart would see God. I see this purity when I look at P. J. Does she have it all together? I doubt it. What she does have is a heart that wants Jesus more than other things.

START THE REVOLUTION

Is your heart empty or full, or somewhere in the middle?

I asked P. J. if she missed partying. This was her reply: "When I first quit partying, I quit because I knew it wasn't good. I missed being around those people who had been my friends for a really long time. Now, I don't party because **Jesus fills that spot.**"

When we quit doing wrong stuff just because it's wrong, for some of us, that isn't enough. We need a deeper reason, a bigger why. Knowing God is that "why."

Knowing God—experiencing a life that is filled with him—fills our hearts. He fills the lonely heart. He fills the broken heart. He fills the bored heart. When we truly see God, we see for the first time what real life is. That's when we are ruined—ruined for anything short of everything he has to give!

Jesus, ruin me for any life outside of being filled by you! Amen.

170: The Life I Now Live

I have been crucified with Christ and I no longer live,
but Christ lives in me. The life I now live in the body, I live by faith
in the Son of God, who loved me and gave himself for me.
—Galatians 2:20

Rights are a big deal to Americans. I have the right to privacy. I have the right to my opinion. Does Jesus believe in rights? Is this his idea?

In today's verse, Paul says "I have been crucified with Christ."

What happens when I'm crucified? I'm dead. I no longer exist. Christ is living in me. So this life that I'm currently living is his life in me.

Wow! If I look at my life, it doesn't always reflect that. Thoughts I think aren't always his thoughts. Words I say aren't always his words. That's why I have to die *every* day. I have to say no to my screaming wants and live by faith, with the purpose to live for him.

This **love is what compels me** and drives me each and every day to do the things that I do. I want this love to be the motivation behind the choices I make, the words I say, and the things I do.

Is this your heartbeat? Your motivation? If not, ask Jesus today to give you the heart to *want* to run after him!

START THE REVOLUTION
See what the Bible has to say about your rights. Do Christians have any?

I can't imagine dying to all of my selfish ways, Jesus, but I want your life to pour out through me! Amen.

171: Joy

Though you have not seen him, you love him; and even though you do not see him now, you believe in him and are filled with an inexpressible and glorious joy, for you are receiving the end result of your faith, the salvation of your souls.

—1 Peter 1: 8, 9

"**You have to be a fool to believe that!**" When I first heard this, it would startle me. *Maybe I was a fool. What if all this was just a hoax and I was spending my whole life believing and investing in something that was not even real?*

As I grappled with these thoughts, I watched the lives of those around me who didn't believe. Girls who didn't fill up their hearts with the truth that Jesus was crazy about them, and instead filled up their hearts with "Joe's" love for them. That is until "Joe" dumped them. Guys who based their happiness on how great they did in the football game on Friday night until they tore their ACL and were told they wouldn't ever play the game again. Kids who got stoned each weekend to escape the pressure and sadness of their weekday lives.

I looked at these kids and asked myself, "That's what I would trade Jesus' love for?" I decided that even if everything I believed in was not true (which I know it is!), my life was still better than the lives of those around me. The hope that empowered the decisions I made created a life that was worth living.

As today's verse says, though I have not seen him, I love him; and even though I do not see him now, I believe in him. Because of this love and belief, I am filled with an inexpressible and glorious joy. That alone is worth me going after him each and every day!

START THE REVOLUTION

Make a list today of all the reasons that believing in Jesus is good for you. A grateful heart is a joyful heart!

Jesus, thank you for the peace, joy, and security you bring to my heart each day when your love fills my heart. Amen.

172: Leaving Behind

*Then, leaving her water jar, the woman went back to the town and
said to the people, "Come, see a man who told me everything I ever did.
Could this be the Messiah?"*

—John 4:28, 29

••••••••

What will you get when you lose? In order to go after Jesus, in order to tell others about the truth of his revolutionary love, what do you need to leave behind?

Coming to the well like she did every day, the Samaritan woman had no idea her life was about to be radically changed. Looking for someone to love her for her, she had tried five husbands and the guy she was currently living with. Who would have guessed that the one she would meet that day would be the one she'd always looked for?

Her life was changed, never the same. Like the jar filled with water, her heart was filled with acceptance and love from Jesus. She had to share it—and fast! But she had that huge water jar that was now so heavy. There was no getting anywhere fast with that huge thing! If she was going to tell everyone she knew while Jesus was still in town, she would have to go now! The water jar was going to have to be sacrificed and left behind.

In order to go after Jesus, what do you need to leave behind? The woman had to leave behind something very important, but it wasn't more important than him.

What will you give up to go after Jesus? Your fear of speaking about Jesus so your friends come to Christ? Your "me first" attitude to become more of a servant? Your worries about what people think of you in order to gain confidence in Christ?

There's a lot to gain when you decide to lose.

START THE REVOLUTION

Make a list of what you will gain when you leave behind whatever you need to get rid of. Keep the list safe and look at it a year from now.

---

*Jesus, it's time for me to lose. Give me
the confidence I need to let go. Amen.*

173: The Important Things

Take me away with you—let us hurry!
—Song of Solomon 1:4

*E*xcitement brings one speed—fast. When you're pumped to go somewhere cool, you can't get there quick enough. Other things are thrown aside; they no longer seem important. You don't stop to get on the Internet, make a snack, or watch a show. You are out of there!

That's the type of excitement I hear in the girl's voice in today's verse from the book of the Song of Solomon. "Take me away with you—let us hurry!" My Bible calls her the Beloved. **Nothing is distracting her**; nothing is as important as spending time with the one she's crazy about.

Radical girl, does this describe you? Are you so taken with Jesus that you set other things aside in order to get away with him? If not, what are you waiting for? Is what everyone's doing online as important as the one you are going to spend eternity with? Will that show you're watching benefit the most important thing in your life?

START THE REVOLUTION
School, sleep, food, friends. What other things take up your time? Which ones need to go?

"It's not just fun stuff! I'm busy doing really important things," I hear you say. I'm sure you are. But think on this: when you stand before Jesus one day, will that softball game, bio quiz, or music lesson be the thing you wished you had spent more time on? I doubt it. My guess is all of us will finally see clearly what life was really about—and many of us will have missed it.

Be like the Beloved! Say "Jesus, take me away with you—let us hurry!" Do whatever you have to do in order to spend more time with the one who is crazy about you!

Jesus, I know you can't wait to talk to me!
I want to be the same with you. Amen.

Come near to God and he will come near to you.
—James 4:8

•••◉••••

*P*ick out an object on the other side of the room. Your dresser? Your closet? Now, if you wanted to get to that object, how would you do it? You would take a step, one after another until you arrived. Simple, right?

Getting close to God is really that simple too! You take one step at a time toward him. James said, "Come near to God and he will come near to you." Shortly before this verse he said, "Submit yourselves, then, to God. Resist the devil, and he will flee from you." So those actions are part of the steps you have to take. You submit to God—you give yourself, your time, your mind, and your heart over to him. You spend time reading his Word, praying, and listening for him to speak. You listen to other speakers share what his Word means.

And through doing this, you get strength and wisdom to take the other step—resisting the devil. Saying no to deception and temptation and destruction. When you resist the devil, he runs away from you, leaving your path free to take more steps to come near to God. Each step you take draws you closer to his heart.

You know the really cool thing? Today's verse tells us that as we are walking closer to him, he's walking closer to us! It's not all up to us; it's not all up to him. It is us together!

START THE REVOLUTION

Besides the Bible, what books or speakers help you learn about God? If you don't know, ask a pastor or someone else you trust to give you a reading list.

Jesus, even though getting close to you is simple, it still takes discipline and effort. Today, remind me to be diligent to take deliberate steps closer to you. Amen.

I Go After Him

175: High Honors

Whoever serves me must follow me; and where I am,
my servant also will be. My Father will honor the one who serves me.
—John 12:26

•••●●•••

Do you ever find yourself experiencing spiritual envy? Sitting in church, looking at the girl leading worship, thinking, *I wish I was doing that.* Watching a girl leading Bible study, so confident—*I wish I could be like that.*

Those people being used by God didn't just get there by accident. The blessings they are experiencing have come out of sacrifices they made. **Positive consequences come from positive choices.**

In order to experience God's blessings, you and I have to make sacrifices and positive choices:

- Not getting too wrapped up in the newest TV series.
- Having core friendships with those who are passionate about following Jesus.
- Not giving in to what we want, but giving in to what God wants.

Jesus says "Whoever serves me *must* follow me." In order to follow him, we have to know his ways—what he is doing. We have to recognize him. We learn to recognize him by reading his Word and learning the things that are important to his heart. The poor, the unheard, the weak, the broken—these people are important to God.

When we follow him in what's important to his heart, our Father God will honor us!

I can think of many ways this world honors people. Trophies, affirmation, attention, and money are just a few of the ways. They all have something in common; they're short-lived. Trophies end up in attics. Affirmation and attention feel good, but are quickly forgotten. Money gets blown through quickly, and purchases end up at the dump! But God's honor never fades. His blessings last forever!

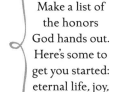

START THE REVOLUTION
Make a list of the honors God hands out. Here's some to get you started: eternal life, joy, peace . . .

Jesus, help me to see the difference between the world's choices and your commands. Empower me to follow you. Amen.

Devotions for a Revolutionary Year

176: Turn to Him

Turn to me and be saved, all you ends of the earth;
for I am God, and there is no other.
—Isaiah 45:22

•• • ● ●••

When trouble comes, what is your first reaction? Text your best friend. Call your boyfriend. Express your problem in 140 characters or less. Update your status online.

START THE REVOLUTION

Next time trouble or worry hits, put that phone or computer away. Open your Bible instead.

Whatever your reaction, what does that say about you? Are you hoping your friends will feel miserable with you? Are you counting on your boyfriend for comfort? Or are you just looking for a few sympathetic tweets or encouraging comments from your virtual world?

On the one hand, there's nothing horribly wrong with any of these actions, but on the other hand . . . *you* are becoming a radical girl—a girl revolutionized by *God's* love. So what's a radical girl to do when trouble comes her way?

Turning to Jesus should be your first action. It doesn't matter if you've just been handed an F on your Spanish test, failed to make the swim team, or been blasted with rude comments by your best friend. The radical girl turns to Jesus for words of comfort, encouragement, and strength—whenever and wherever trouble comes. There is no other who can give you exactly what you need to make it through.

This reaction isn't natural, not for most of us. Responding to trouble by turning first to Jesus takes a lot of discipline. You have to train your mind not to go to the first available person. **How often should you turn to Jesus?** Not pretty often. Not almost always. *Always*. As you always turn to him, you'll always find him faithful, available whenever you need strength. When you seek his face, you can face your need.

Is something looming over you today? Make today's verse your prayer: "Jesus, you are God, and there is no other. Help me turn to you." Amen.

*Those who know your name trust in you, for you, LORD,
have never forsaken those who seek you.*
—Psalm 9:10

·····•····

bby just didn't get it. Connie had asked her to go to the football game, but once they got there, Connie was nowhere to be found. Abby found herself sitting in the stands, surrounded by people she barely knew. She thought Connie had wanted to go *together*. If they were there together, then where was Connie? Even in a sea of people, Abby felt completely alone. *What's wrong with me? Why did Connie ditch me?*

Situations like these can make us feel unimportant; invisible. In today's verse God promises those who know and seek him that he will never forsake them—never turn his back. Security comes when we truly understand we are never alone. **Never alone.**

In fact, the more you seek Jesus, the more you'll sense you're never alone. You'll begin to recognize his faithfulness in your life every day. Sometimes our eyes need a little nudging to see him. You may turn to him for help with a bad grade or words to say during a fight. You trust him in that situation and discover he is there with you; giving you direction and wisdom.

START THE REVOLUTION
Next time you feel alone, open your Bible and read all the Psalms you can.

As you find him faithful in small things, you begin to trust him for the bigger things. And as you trust, you'll experience his peace and his assurance that you're not alone.

It is so important to seek him each and every day; to not let a single day go by where you are not connecting with him through his Word and in prayer. I know I keep saying this over and over again. That's because it is so important and so few of us do it!

*Jesus, thank you that you never leave
me alone. I love you. Amen.*

178: Strength

He gives strength to the weary and increases the power of the weak.
Even youths grow tired and weary, and young men stumble and fall;
but those who hope in the LORD will renew their strength.
—Isaiah 40:29-31

••●●●••

*B*ryce Canyon National Park is beauty like I've never seen before—definitely some of God's best work. Look up some pictures online; it is amazing!

When we visited I figured, "What better way to see the canyon than a seven-mile hike through the middle!" I had to get *in* it! After a few miles, the fun wore off; my family was over it.

To encourage them, I got out front, turned around backwards and inspired them, "Don't give up; you can do it!" The only problem was, I wasn't watching where I was going. My foot slipped, sending me off the edge. I have no idea how deep that drop-off was, but some cliffs in the canyon are eight thousand feet off the ground! I dangled off the precipice by only my forearms. Within seconds, Greg pulled me up from what might have been my sudden death!

Sometimes in life, we're on the right path when we make an unwise decision. We just don't think through the ramifications of our choices. And sometimes we just get tired. We let down our guard and temptation comes in. Even then, **Jesus is right there**. He stoops down, grasping us, pulling us to safety. He gives us the wisdom we need to make our wrong right, and he renews our strength, giving us hope to endure the consequences that follow.

When you stumble, call out to Jesus. Ask for forgiveness. He is very near; he'll give you his arm of strength.

START THE REVOLUTION
Think of a time you took a wrong step on a right path. How did you get back on track?

Jesus, I'm slipping. Please rescue me from
_____ today. Thank you for saving
me from myself! Amen.

179: Hunger and Thirst

Blessed are those who hunger and thirst for righteousness, for they will be filled.
—Matthew 5:6

•••●•••

Reese's Cups, broken-in sweatshirts, boots—these are just a few of the things I can't get enough of. They all make me happy, but never last long enough. Reese's Cups are just four quick bites and they're gone. You can't wear sweatshirts in the hot summer; and winter's just too short in the Carolinas to enjoy boots!

I can't say I "hunger and thirst" for these things, but I will go out of my way to get them. What are the things you go after? People you want to be friends with? Grades you want to get?

START THE REVOLUTION
Do you feel filled or empty? Take a look—what's happening in you?

Here's the promise Jesus makes: those who go after righteousness—what pleases God—will be filled.

According to Dictionary.com, here are some meanings for *fill*:

• to supply what is missing
• to complete
• enough to satisfy want or desire

When Jesus is the one thing we go after, we will be fully satisfied. Loneliness, stress, or anxiety will be squeezed out. When you're filled, there is no room for them.

Jesus said, "Blessed are those who hunger and thirst." When we have this kind of need and want, we are blessed because we are in a perfect spot to be filled by the only one who can satisfy us. **Blessing is not determined by what happens to me; blessing is determined by what is happening in me.** A blessed life is not determined by circumstances; a blessed life is a by-product of Jesus' love pouring into me!

Jesus, I am tempted to feel happy or unhappy based on what is happening to me. Empower me to want what is right and then be blessed! Amen.

180: Love and Obey

If you love me, keep my commands. . . .
Whoever has my commands and keeps them is the one who loves me.
The one who loves me will be loved by my Father,
and I too will love them and show myself to them.
—John 14:15, 21

•••●•••

*I*n the first section of this book, you soaked in the truth that Jesus wants you, knows you, and speaks to you. Hopefully, your heart was filled to capacity when you put all that love inside it!

So what is a full heart supposed to do with that love? Return it! We show we're thankful by loving him right back. We do that by obeying his commands. Obedience proves our love is sincere and not just a bunch of empty words.

If your best friend said she loved you, you would expect her to show it. If she dissed you in the hall, didn't text you back ever, or ignored your phone calls, you wouldn't believe she really cared.

START THE REVOLUTION
Take inventory today. Is there evidence of obedience in your life, proving your love?

The same is true in our relationship with God. **If we love him, our actions should show it's true.** The way we spend time, the words we say, and the worship we give should all reflect our love!

When we love him there's a great promise. Jesus says we will be loved by his Father and "I too will love them and show myself to them." We get to see Jesus and begin to understand him. That's a pretty deep concept—to understand and have spiritual insight about the Son of God. Seeing Jesus means you become aware of his ways: how he thinks and how he acts. You recognize when he is at work. That's what it means to really be mature!

Jesus, even when it comes to loving you, I need your help. I want to prove to you I love you by obeying you. Give me your power to do that. Amen.

I Go After Him

189

181: Addicted

Simon Peter answered him, "Lord, to whom shall we go?
You have the words of eternal life."
—John 6:68

•••●••

I'm addicted. I'm enslaved. If I stopped, it would cause severe trauma. I'm addicted to Jesus; my son told me. What a compliment! I am. Jesus is my life. Everything I do is wrapped up in him!

Are you addicted to Jesus? Is your life so centered on him that if he was no longer in your life, you would fall apart?

Take a minute to read John 6:60-69. Many of Jesus' disciples were ditching him. He was teaching challenging lessons, and his followers were freaking out. Jesus asked the twelve disciples, "You do not want to leave too, do you?"

Simon Peter's answer is in today's verse: "There is no one for us to go to! You are it; you are everything to us." Sounds like an addiction to me!

START THE REVOLUTION

An addiction is something you cannot live without. What are your addictions?

Maybe you've hit a spot where you're pondering your faith, what it means to live as a Christian. Maybe you're thinking, *Following Jesus costs too much.* Hanging with certain friends, partying, doing stuff with guys, having bad attitudes, and hanging on to selfish rights—it all seems like too much to walk away from. **Ask yourself: "What am I turning back to? Is it worth everything—is it worth eternal life?"**

Jesus, you are what I want to be addicted to. Amen.

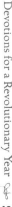

182: Be Free

He has sent me to bind up the brokenhearted, to proclaim freedom for the captives and release from darkness for the prisoners, to proclaim the year of the LORD's favor and the day of vengeance of our God.
—Isaiah 61:1, 2

•••●●•••

y first love was in sixth grade. But he didn't like me back. That crush crushed me! After high school, I went on to Bible training school. At this school, I discovered the love I was looking for: Jesus. He wanted me.

Studying his Word, my heart began to be filled up. The loneliness and the fear that I would never find the "right" one for me began to go away as I grasped hold of the truth that Jesus was the Right One. The rejection that I had allowed to dominate my heart began to go away. God bandaged up my wounded heart, and I found freedom in his truth.

Maybe you too have experienced rejection; you know the heartache of liking someone and not having your feelings returned. You've become a prisoner to your hurting feelings.

God's Word brings us freedom! As we go after him, his love for us fills the love gap in our hearts, freeing us to enjoy life. Breaking us out of the cycle of gloominess we find ourselves spinning in.

Take time today to seek God through his Word. Let him heal your heart from the pain of rejection. **Walk toward Jesus and the freedom his truth brings.** It's not going to happen on its own; your heart needs you to replace the depressing thoughts that dominate your mind with the truth of God's crazy love. As you take these steps, you'll find freedom.

> **START THE REVOLUTION**
> A lot of people see being a Christian as being imprisoned by rules. How would you tell someone that following Christ makes you free?

Jesus, I want to be free in my heart and my mind. May your Word fill my thoughts. Amen.

183: Stumbling, Not Falling

The LORD makes firm the steps of the one who delights in him;
though he may stumble, he will not fall, for the
LORD upholds him with his hand.

—Psalm 37:23, 24

•••●••

*F*lipped upside down—that was me. That summer I sensed Jesus was saying no to going to college, where I'd planned on going. Bible training school was what he had in store for me instead. The problem was, there were no openings for the fall. So, trusting Jesus, I waited. It started out good, but like David says in today's verse, I began to stumble.

START THE REVOLUTION
What are stumbling blocks for you?

I started dating a terrific Christian guy. He loved Jesus, wanted to go into ministry, had great character too—but that didn't mean he was God's best for me. I let this relationship become really important—too important.

In the middle of this whirlwind, a spot at the school opened! I had just a couple of days to get myself ready to go, but I still could have made it in time for the new semester! But I didn't. **The relationship I was in had become more important to me**—I didn't want to leave it. I stumbled.

I loved Jesus, but my priorities were misplaced. Asking for forgiveness, the next semester I headed off to Bible school. Jesus was so good to help me get back on the right track.

When you're going after Jesus, even if you mess up, quickly ask for forgiveness and turn around. Jesus will make your next steps firm as you go after him whole-heartedly once more.

Jesus, thank you for holding me up and keeping my steps firm. Open my eyes to see each step clearly and empower me to keep going after you alone! Amen.

184: Daily Bread

Jesus answered, "It is written: 'Man shall not live on bread alone,
but on every word that comes from the mouth of God.'"
—Matthew 4:4

• • • • • •

Now often in a day do you eat? For me, it's about every three to four hours. I feel that grumbling going on in my tummy and know that it is about time to put something in there! Just enough of a nibble to make myself feel satisfied.

My body was created to be fed daily. I don't go several days without eating, then pile food on a plate as high as I can and try to feed myself for an entire week all at once. I could probably survive that way, but just barely. My body was not made to endure that type of treatment. **It was designed for steady nourishment.**

God made your heart and your stomach a lot alike. Jesus said, "Man shall not live on bread alone." You were made to need more than bread; you were made to need God's Word. And it's important to get this Word on your own directly from God.

Think about it. If you came over to my house for dinner and I gave you everybody's leftovers from their plates, would you be excited about that? Yuck! How gross!

Don't be satisfied with leftovers when it comes to God's Word either. Devotional books and sermons are great, but you need to read God's Word for yourself. Some parts might be difficult to understand—seek help from more mature Christians or from solid reference books. But try to hear the message God's sending directly to you. Read it every day, and even more than once a day. You don't have to read a lot at once—there's a lot in there. A little nibble every now and then will keep you satisfied.

START THE REVOLUTION
Find a Bible reading plan that will work for you. Check out www.bible gateway.com /resources /readingplans/.

Jesus, put a hunger in my heart to desire your Word every day. Amen.

I Go After Him

193

185: Total Commitment

Take delight in the LORD, and he will give you the desires of your heart.
Commit your way to the LORD; trust in him and he will do this:
He will make your righteous reward shine like the dawn,
your vindication like the noonday sun.

—Psalm 37:4-6

• • • ● • • •

So, you're doing homework when a text comes. You stop and reply. It's just not possible to give 100 percent of our attention to two things at the same time, right?

When I was at Bible school, I committed not to date so I could focus on the True Love of my life. Guess who called me during that time? Greg! My crush of seven years! He was coming a thousand miles from home and wanted to see me. I was crazy excited!

That is, until my counselor reminded me of my commitment. I was a mess! I just knew if I passed Greg's offer up, I'd never have another chance. **I decided to trust God** and go after Jesus. Telling Greg he couldn't visit because I was committing this time in my life to Jesus was my act of obedience. I can't tell you how much it pained me, and how scared I was that I was giving up the best thing of my life.

After school was over, I went home to visit my parents. Greg was in church that night. As my heart was doing flip-flops, he asked me out. I knew it was OK this time; I had given God the desires of my heart. We were married a year later! Talk about a "righteous reward"! It just doesn't get any better than that!

Most of the peace and joy I've had in life has come from trusting God. Jesus needs to be the thing we go after more than anything else: more than the love of our friends or family, the attention of a boyfriend, success in a sport or school. Nothing comes before him and we should want nothing more than him. He is our everything!

START THE REVOLUTION

Fill in the blank:
I need to
want Jesus
more than

_____.

Jesus, I want to make you number one! Amen.

186: Called and Changed

*When the LORD saw that he had gone over to look, God called
to him from within the bush, "Moses! Moses!"*

—Exodus 3:4

•••●●•••

*M*oses probably didn't wake up on this particular day and say, "I bet God is going to completely change my life today." But he did position himself to have his life changed by God.

Read Exodus 3:1-3: "he led the flock to the far side of the wilderness and came to Horeb, the mountain of God." Moses was doing his normal job, but even in the everyday event of watching his sheep, he made his way to the mountain of God. It was there that "the angel of the LORD appeared to him in flames of fire from within a bush. Moses saw that though the bush was on fire it did not burn up. So Moses thought, 'I will go over and see this strange sight—why the bush does not burn up.'"

Moses put himself in a place, God's mountain, to hear from God. Then, when he thought he saw something that could possibly be God, he moved closer still. Sure enough, God spoke to him and changed his life.

Be like Moses. Each day, put your heart in a place where you are near to God. Look for and expect God to speak to you and do something great in your life.

When we are in a place where we are looking for something, we are in a place to find something. Go after God; seek him. You'll find what you are looking for!

START THE REVOLUTION

Today, be more aware of God's presence. Expect him to use you, speak to you, or do something for you today.

*Jesus, my eyes are open. Show me your work today!
Amen.*

I Go After Him

195

187: Three Steps

*No, O people, the LORD has told you what is good, and this
is what he requires of you: to do what is right, to love mercy,
and to walk humbly with your God.*
—Micah 6:8 *(NLT)*

M aybe this whole concept of going after God is new to you. Your whole life you've simply done whatever you wanted to do with little to no thought about what someone else wanted or what would be the right thing. **It's time to start pleasing God** and following his ways, if you haven't already.

Today's verse gives us very clear direction on three things God considers good and pleasing: doing what is right, loving mercy, and walking humbly with God.

Doing what is right simply means making right choices, deciding on good over bad.

Loving mercy means showing compassion to someone who has offended you or who doesn't deserve it. When we demonstrate kindness to those who don't deserve it, we are the most like God.

Walking humbly with God means choosing not to be proud or arrogant. This puts us in a position where we are most capable of learning and becoming more like Jesus. When we walk humbly with him, we will be in a position to be his friend and in turn be used by him.

Three simple steps—do what is right, love mercy, and walk humbly with God. Three powerful steps.

**START THE
REVOLUTION**

Which one
of these three
steps do you
struggle with the
most? Make this
struggle your
prayer today.

*Jesus, I want to go after you because I want to
become like you. I need your help most in the area of
_____. Teach me to be like you. Amen.*

188: Get Rid of Stuff

At this the man's face fell. He went away sad,
because he had great wealth.
—Mark 10:22

•••●•••

What will it cost you to go after Jesus? Yes, his salvation is free, but to daily be in a place where you are drawing close to him and becoming more like him will cost you something. That something is everything.

START THE
REVOLUTION
What stuff do
you need to
clear out?

Stop and take a few minutes to read in Mark 10:17-27 the story commonly known as the rich young ruler. Here was a young guy who wanted to know what it would take to inherit eternal life. Following God's laws had been his norm, but he needed to make sure he had done it all just right. So he asked Jesus, **"What do I have to do to inherit eternal life?"**

Jesus knew his heart; he knew what was holding him back from going all out for Jesus: stuff. He had lots of it; he was rich. He had stuff and he liked stuff. Listen to what Jesus told him: "'One thing you lack,' he said. 'Go, sell everything you have and give to the poor, and you will have treasure in heaven. Then come, follow me.'"

Jesus didn't tiptoe around the issue. He just said it boldly—sell it all. What harsh words!

We all have stuff that holds us back from following Jesus wholeheartedly.

Popularity. Looking cool. Anxiety. Certain friends. Certain plans. A boyfriend. Having fun. Fear.

Jesus says the same thing to you today: get rid of it. If you really want me, get rid of the one thing you love more than me and come after me. It's not just about getting rid of the stuff; it's also about taking the next step to follow. Then you'll really get him.

Do it. He's worth it!

This terrifies me, Jesus, yet I am miserable trying
to have all of that stuff and all of you too.
Please help me. I really want you more. Amen.

I Go After Him

189: What's He Like?

When Jesus spoke again to the people, he said, "I am the light of the world. Whoever follows me will never walk in darkness, but will have the light of life."
—John 8:12

•••••••

START THE REVOLUTION
Grab a notebook and start reading the book of John. Write down what Jesus is like—kind, compassionate, loving to all types of people …

W hen you were growing up, were you ever afraid of the dark? Sleeping with the hall light on, even in sixth grade, I just couldn't stand the thought of what might be coming up my steps when my eyes were shut. Darkness terrified me.

Darkness for many people conjures up creepy or scary feelings. That's why trick-or-treating is in the dark!

Jesus tells us that when we walk with him, we will never walk in the dark. **He is the light in our life.**

So, how do we discover how to walk with him?

If you wanted to learn what I was like, you could read what I write. My blog, my journals, my Facebook, *His Revolutionary Love*. By reading what I write, it gives insight into the person I am.

When you read God's Word, what he wrote, you learn about the person of God. When you read Matthew, Mark, Luke, and John, you hear the words Jesus said and the actions he took. And when you learn about the person of God, you will find it easier to make choices that make you a person like God.

It is comforting to know, Jesus, that following after you means I am walking in light, going the right way. Amen.

190: First

But seek first his kingdom and his righteousness,
and all these things will be given to you as well.
—Matthew 6:33

•••●••

*H*ave you ever noticed how busy-ness just seems to suck you in? From the time Jo was in elementary school, "they" said high school was so important—it would determine where she could go for college. In middle school "they" said college was so important—it would determine her career.

In her junior year—maybe the most important year of high school—focusing on her grades became her everything. Bible studies with friends and quiet time with Jesus went away. There just wasn't enough time to do everything, and getting a good GPA was the most important thing, right?

She learned too late it wasn't most important. Her health and heart suffered from her anxiety-induced schedule. She wished she had let some important things be not so important. She wished she would have made Jesus the most important.

Jesus makes this promise to us in today's verse: "But seek *first* his kingdom and his righteousness, and all these things will be given to you as well." He promises us that if we will make God number one, he will see that we get the things we need.

If we make time to read his Word before we study for that chemistry exam, he will help us study. If we spend time praying about that difficult relationship before we try to solve the problem, he'll give us the wisdom to work it out. Jobs, financial issues, decisions, relationships, grades—yes, all these things are important, but if we will make Jesus our first priority, he will take care of all the other important things. We can trust him. Put the first things first.

START THE REVOLUTION
What "important" things are on your daily schedule? What's most important?

Jesus, I'm going to trust that, as I make you first, you will help all the other things in my life come together. Amen.

I Go After Him

191: Always on Him

I will extol the LORD at all times; his praise will always be on my lips.
—Psalm 34:1

•••●•••

It had been more than a terrible day. Everything that could go wrong did. She left Chapstick in her pants pocket—the pants that just went through the washer and dryer. Now her favorite clothes were ruined—oil spots everywhere. Her face, a million shades of red, revealed her heart as her teacher announced, "You did it wrong!" Her special earrings had gotten buried in the landfill under her bed, and too little sleep left her too exhausted to dig under the rubble. Now it was time to do her homework. Jenna felt like **she just didn't have anything left to give out**.

Getting up from the dinner table, she told her mom, "I'm going to listen to a new worship song before I get started." She shut the door to the office and pulled up the new song on YouTube. Once, twice, three times she listened. As she began to sing praises to Jesus, her spirit lifted. The heaviness of the day melted away as she focused on the best thing in her life.

> **START THE REVOLUTION**
> Stop what you're doing and take time right now to focus on Jesus.

Minutes later, she emerged from the small room, not unlike a butterfly from its cocoon, ready to tackle her homework, even though nothing had changed. Really *everything* had. Going after Jesus before she went after her homework shifted her perspective and gave Jenna the hope she needed.

There are many things you cannot change in your world. Your teachers, your troubles, your time commitments. One thing you can change: your attention. Take time, even right now, to focus on your king and find the peace you need.

Jesus, you are everything and all that I need for this day and tomorrow too. I praise you because you are worthy. Amen.

192: Morning and Night

It is good to praise the LORD and make music to your name,
O Most High, proclaiming your love in the morning
and your faithfulness at night.

—Psalm 92:1, 2

••●●●••

Going after Jesus is an all-day thing. I go after him morning and night. His love is what fills me as I awake. Lying still before I greet the world, I talk to him about what is to come. I think of his love for me, taking it in, preparing me for whatever the day might bring.

If you fill up with Jesus' love and truth in the morning, **when life hits, jostling you around, *he* pours out!**

When the dog runs away, loving patience flows out. When your sister wears your favorite shirt without asking, love reacts. When that kid in biology makes fun of your purity ring again—love spills.

At night, when you finally lay your head on your pillow, thank him for his faithfulness. He was with you through it all, helping you to overcome temptation, keeping you safe, and pouring his presence in when the world tried to pour you out.

START THE REVOLUTION

Proclaim his love by morning; his faithfulness by night.

Jesus, your love is perfect for me. It completely fills the love gap in my heart. Thank you that you never leave me or forsake me. You are mine and I am yours. Amen.

193: With All Your Heart

*"You will seek me and find me when you seek me with all your heart.
I will be found by you," declares the LORD, "and will
bring you back from captivity."*
—Jeremiah 29:13, 14

• • ● ● ● • • •

Borrowing your brown boots. Helping with her homework. Hanging out at your house, because she's got a crush on your brother. She's using you—that's how you feel, because the only time your "best friend" seeks you is when it's about her.

I bet that's how God feels sometimes. **Used.**

Because the love that I often seek him with is love that mainly benefits me.

Think about it. When do we most often come to him? When we've strayed away from God, what is it that brings us back usually? Are our prayers filled more with asking for ourselves or giving praise? Consider even the worship you give—is it more about how you feel or more about loving and honoring him?

START THE REVOLUTION
What is one way today you can show Jesus you love him?

God loves us perfectly with perfect love. His love is *agape*—love that is rooted in the mind and will, expressing value and esteem; love that is for the benefit of the object of that love.

The funny thing is, the more we try to love like him, with all our hearts, the more "used" we will feel. Used by him and for him, to accomplish what he created us to do—to serve his kingdom.

Mature love is aimed at the benefit of the receiver. Let's take our love for Jesus to the next level. Let's seek Jesus as number one in our lives, seeking him with all our hearts because we love him—and that is reason enough.

Jesus, I do thank you for what you do for me, but I want you to know I love you for you. Amen.

194: One Thing I Know

He replied, "Whether he is a sinner or not, I don't know.
One thing I do know. I was blind but now I see!"
—John 9:25

•••●••••

John tells us the story of a man born blind who encountered Jesus. Jesus did not judge the man, as others did. He said that the man was blind so that "the works of God might be displayed in him" (John 9:3). Then Jesus healed the man, and it happened to be the Sabbath.

When the Pharisees heard this tale, they put the man who used to be blind through a series of questions, trying to get the man to say something against his healer. But no matter what they said, the man stuck to his story. He didn't try to make fancy arguments or elaborate on the details—he just told his personal story of what happened when he met Jesus. **He told the one thing he was sure of.**

START THE REVOLUTION
What's the one thing you know about Jesus?

If you have been a Christian for any time at all, you've probably met people who wonder why you follow Jesus. They might have even tried to argue you out of believing in him—saying Jesus was just a nice teacher, or a good man, or perhaps just a story.

What do you say when people ask you who Jesus is, or want to know why you are a Christian? I know what I do. I hold on to the one thing I am sure of—my story of what Jesus has done in my life. That is the one thing I know I'll get right, and the one thing no one can take from me.

When you go after Jesus, he will do many great things for you. And he will also probably be the reason you lose some friends, or get in some uncomfortable situations. But just hold on to the one thing you are sure about. Tell the one thing you do know—what Jesus has done for you!

Jesus, help me to stick to my story and to let my story make others want to go after you. Amen.

I Go After Him

195: Joy in the Path

You make known to me the path of life; you will fill me with joy in your presence, with eternal pleasures at your right hand.

—Psalm 16:11

•••••••

Life. Joy. Eternal pleasures. Does all that sound as amazing to you as it does to me? It sounded pretty good to David too. In Psalm 16 he tells us how he feels: "my heart is glad and my tongue rejoices; my body also will rest secure" (v. 9). He is overjoyed that God has made known to him the path of life.

When my family hikes, I like to be either in the front, leading the way, or in the back, keeping everyone safe. We have another type of hiker in our family: the one who looks for the shortcuts. He *rarely* stays on the path. Constantly looking for a quicker way to the end or a faster way to the top, he often disappears from sight. It's hard for me not to freak out! The drop-offs can be steep. There can be snakes hiding in the forest. Though it seems like the better way to him, it really is not.

START THE REVOLUTION
Plan a hike with some friends. When you're on the hike, take turns being in the front. How does it feel to lead and to follow?

Those who follow the path enjoy it! We get to see all the scenery, can spot a snake if it is on the path, and we save nature for those coming behind us to enjoy. **We experience the best** of the hike by staying on the path.

If we follow after Jesus, we experience the beauty and safety of his path. He makes the path clear, maybe not far ahead, but he is faithful to give us our next steps. He never leads us toward regret or hurt. We can trust him!

Jesus, teach me to follow you, to not look or turn in any direction other than the one you are providing. Amen.

196: Do What Pleases Him

*So Jesus said, "When you have lifted up the Son of Man, then you will
know that I am he and that I do nothing on my own but speak just
what the Father has taught me. The one who sent me is with me;
he has not left me alone, for I always do what pleases him."*
—John 8:28, 29

••••••

he perfect model—that is what Jesus is. "I do nothing on my own." "I always
do what pleases him." These were statements he made referring to his relationship with his Father God.

Do nothing on my own? Always do what pleases God? That seems crazy hard.
Maybe even impossible. How could we possibly reach this place where we only do
what pleases God?

I believe we can start by looking closely at the choices
we make, slowing down long enough to think through
each and every one. *Does this conversation please God?
Would God like my outfit today? Does my attitude bring
him joy? Do these friends point others to him?*

**START THE
REVOLUTION**
Ask yourself
today:
Does this
please God?

We start by simply asking ourselves the question,
"Does this please God?" If we do that, then we'll
be more deliberate about pleasing him. We won't find our-
selves simply watching whatever show comes on next.
We'll stop and determine whether or not it pleases God, and then make a decision.
Am I going to be like Jesus and please him or will I choose to go out on my own?

One decision to please him leads to another decision to please him. One choice
leads to another, and leads to a life that pleases God. A life that pleases God is a life
filled with peace and blessings.

*Holy Spirit, bring to my mind the question,
"Does this please God?" today. Help me to create a
habit of asking this all day long. Amen.*

197: Choose

Elijah went before the people and said, "How long will you waver between two opinions? If the LORD is God, follow him; but if Baal is God, follow him." But the people said nothing.

—1 Kings 18:21

"**M**ake up your mind." Elijah was calling the people out on their wavering faith. They claimed to be God's people, yet they spent their time and money on what dishonored God. It just didn't match up. Elijah said it was time to pick.

God doesn't tolerate those who say they are his, wearing the "Christian" label, yet their lives don't show it. For a while they may appear to be getting away with it, but they really aren't. Numbers 32:23 says, "But if you fail to do this, you will be sinning against the LORD; and you may be sure that your sin will find you out."

At some point, sin catches up, bringing ruin as its consequences. The consequences might not appear immediately, but they *will* show up.

It's like the person who keeps eating junk day after day after day and then asks, "Why do I feel yucky, and how did I gain fifteen pounds all of a sudden?" It wasn't sudden. It was a daily choice that eventually revealed its consequences.

Make up your mind. Is it Jesus or you? Who is going to call the shots? If it's you, then don't call yourself his. If it's him, then obey. Make a decision and follow through.

> **START THE REVOLUTION**
> Do your actions say you've chosen Jesus? Or do they tell a different story?

Jesus, you've said it's all or nothing. I choose you. Help me to follow you and you alone. Amen.

198: Refined

These have come so that the proven genuineness of your faith—
of greater worth than gold, which perishes even though refined by fire—
may result in praise, glory and honor when Jesus Christ is revealed.

—1 Peter 1:7

•‒•●●●‒•

Hayley's friends had encouraged her, "Come to youth group with us! You'll love it." After months of being pestered, she finally gave in. They were right; she did love it! She loved the peace, love, and joy she felt just being in a place with others who loved Jesus. She decided she was going all out. Leaving guys and partying behind, she was running hard after Jesus.

Then, something weird happened. The very friends who brought Hayley to youth group started falling away, getting pulled back into the life they had once left. It was confusing to Hayley. Not only that; it was lonely. She felt completely alone.

Sometimes it is hard to figure out why bad things happen to good people.

Today's passage in 1 Peter 1:7 explains that these tough times prove what our faith is made of. Is it based on emotions that quickly fizzle, especially when life gets hard? Or is our faith based on tried-and-true love that never lets go?

Our goal is to be girls who shine like gold, reflecting the love, joy, and purity of the King we follow. Often the way to become that gold is by going through the "fire" of hard times, when we have to lean on Jesus more than ever. When he is all we have.

When life heats up your heart, don't cool off by going back to your old ways. Let the heat prove the genuineness of your faith and make you stronger in the process.

START THE REVOLUTION

Do you have some rough spots or weaker elements in you that need refining? If you're experiencing a trial right now, try to see how God is using it to refine you.

Jesus, trials are not what I want, but I do want to shine like you. Help me to run to you—not to a quick fix—for the relief I need. Amen.

I Go After Him

199: Give and Take

The LORD gave and the LORD has taken away;
may the name of the LORD be praised.
—Job 1:21

•••●•••

"The Lord gave and the Lord has taken away." Job made quite the understatement. In one day he lost all of his sons and daughters, his business and employees; all were completely wiped out.

Job's response astounds me: "God gave it to me, he can take it away. I'm still going to praise him."

I can't imagine even responding like that! To be at such a solid place in my relationship with God that I would trust him explicitly, even when the things I love most are gone. Job trusted God completely, he knew God allowed these things to happen, and he trusted him to work for his good all the time, in every situation. That's where I want to be.

All too often, when life hits us with a deadly blow, **we blame God—we get angry.** We might think something like this: *If that is what it is like to serve you, I don't want anything to do with it.*

Why is it we think that we can take the good from God but not take the bad of life?

We need to make up our minds that we are going to follow him, no matter what. Whatever life deals us, blessings or heartache, he is our God—period. Nothing is going to make us turn back.

START THE REVOLUTION

Have you ever been angry with God? Think about how you handled that time. What would do differently?

Jesus, plant me firm. With your Word and presence in my life, solidify my relationship with you. Nothing can take me away from you. Amen.

200: What Now?

Blessed are those who have learned to acclaim you,
who walk in the light of your presence, Lord.
—Psalm 89:15

•••●●•••

*D*on't you just love worshiping Jesus at a conference or camp? Everyone is singing at the top of her lungs, going all out. It's one of my favorite places to be. It's easy to go after him there. I'm surrounded by people doing the same thing, experiencing the same emotional high.

But what about when life stinks? When you fail a test you studied hard for, what do you do then? Do you complain and ask, "Why, God?"

START THE REVOLUTION
When you ask, "What now, God?" what kind of answer do you think you will get?

My friend Lysa TerKeurst says the question isn't, "Why, God, but what now, God?" When you choose to go even harder after God, especially through praising him when life is hard, your faith explodes! Your ability to trust gets deeper. You learn how to stay off the tremulous ride of roller-coaster emotions and learn the peace that comes when we choose to praise instead. Notice David says: "Blessed are those who have *learned* to acclaim you, who walk in the light of your presence, Lord." We have to learn to praise, give thanks, and pursue God at all times.

This is a hard lesson—a tough choice. It's also the defining difference between a radical girl and a roller-coaster girl.

The end of the verse tells the result of those who learn to praise him: they walk in the light of his presence. And in his presence is peace, perspective, and purpose. Just the place I want to live!

Jesus, something is going to happen today that will try to cause me to plummet. Help me to choose not to go; help me praise you instead! I love you! Amen.

I Go After Him

> *When they had gone, an angel of the Lord appeared to Joseph in a dream. "Get up," he said, "take the child and his mother and escape to Egypt. Stay there until I tell you, for Herod is going to search for the child to kill him."*
> —Matthew 2:13

••••••

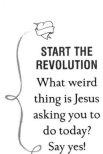

START THE REVOLUTION
What weird thing is Jesus asking you to do today? Say yes!

"Lord, I'm getting tired of this crazy stuff. First you send an angel saying I need to marry a girl who is already pregnant, and not by me! Next, we have to travel a long distance, and she has the baby in a barn. All types of people—from shepherds to star readers—show up to meet him. Now, you're asking me to get up in the middle of the night and go to another country because the king wants to kill this baby? It's just too much. I'm done!"

What if Joseph, the earthly father of Jesus, had responded this way to God? So many parts of Jesus' story might have been different! Joseph's response instead was obedience. He got up, took Jesus and his mother during the night, and left for Egypt. **Where did his obedience get him?** He was a part of seeing God's plan and Scripture fulfilled—Scripture that made a way for all mankind to have a relationship with God and spend eternity in Heaven. That's a pretty huge part!

What Scripture might God be asking you to fulfill through obedience to him today? What weird thing might he be asking you to do?

How about this one? "Then Jesus said to his disciples, 'Whoever wants to be my disciple must deny themselves and take up their cross and follow me. For whoever wants to save their life will lose it, but whoever loses their life for me will find it'" (Matthew 16:24, 25). Deny self. Take up my cross. Follow Jesus. Doesn't quite sound the same as the world's mantra: "Whatever your dream is, go for it." Key words: your dream. Jesus' radical way says his way—not yours. Only his dream leads to life.

Giving up my life? Sounds really hard, Jesus. But I want to find real life. Give me your strength. Amen.

202: Delight in the Law

They delight in the law of the LORD, meditating on it day and night.
—Psalm 1:2 *(NLT)*

• • • ● • • •

Ever have an obsession? Something or someone on your heart or in your mind that just won't go away? Dictionary.com calls *obsession* "the domination of one's thoughts or feelings by a persistent idea, image, desire, etc." This thing or person dominates—controls and rules over everything else in your life.

For you, was it a boy? a vacation? an outfit or purchase you just had to have? a book or movie that you kept enjoying over and over again?

The radical girl obsesses on God's Word.
She thinks about it constantly. She doesn't just read her Bible, she writes it in her agenda, on her mirror, in her phone. Whenever she gets the chance, she mulls it over in her mind, allowing it to trickle down to her heart.

Today's verse talks about "meditating on it day and night." Jana read a passage in her English novel and didn't get it. She read it out loud—twice even. She kept reading it over and over again, until she felt like she really understood what the author was trying to say.

That's what I think of when I picture a person meditating on the law. That's how I am with my Bible reading sometimes too. I am so intent on understanding what God's trying to say, I read it over and over and over again, even out loud, to get it.

Going after God involves us doing more than simply reading a devotional each day—although that is a good start! We need to take his Word with us wherever we go and meditate on it all day long.

START THE REVOLUTION
Take a Bible verse, type it in your phone, write it on your agenda, and meditate on it all day long. Read it over and over again, letting the truth get down deep into your heart.

Jesus, I'm going to be obsessed with your Word. Amen.

I Go After Him

211

CHAPTER SIX

203: Wake Up

You are all children of the light and children of the day. . . . For God did not appoint us to suffer wrath but to receive salvation through our Lord Jesus Christ. He died for us so that, whether we are awake or asleep, we may live together with him.

—1 Thessalonians 5:5, 9, 10

• • • ● • • •

*H*ave you ever felt excited, when you knew you were doing something completely wrong? Scary, isn't it? How quickly we can slink to doing the one thing that not so long ago we might have judged another for doing? How does it happen; how do we end up there? One small step at a time.

Susie's mom had often talked to her about remaining pure until she got married. It wasn't even a question for Susie; she had the purity ring to prove it!

That was before Jack. **Being with him always made her feel right.** And at first, the stories Susie told her mom were *small* lies: "We're going to hang out at the park." (Her parents didn't know she was at Jack's—alone.) But one lie at a time, she built a wall of dishonesty. And fun gradually slipped away, leaving shame in its place.

Have you ever found yourself in a place like Susie was in? Are you in that place now? As our passage today says, you are a child of the light and of the day. God didn't make you for condemnation; he's chosen you for salvation. He died for you so you could live with him!

START THE REVOLUTION

If you've been asleep and drunk with darkness, it's time to WAKE UP! Get up at dawn and give your heart to God.

So what do you do, now that you're awake? How do you go back to living in the light?

- Ask God for forgiveness.
- Tell someone who loves Jesus—take the secret out of the dark.
- Move—away from the person, place, or thing in the dark place.

Do it now. Before your heart can talk you out of it. Cling to the light.

Jesus, forgive me and show me who I need to share with. Amen.

*One who loves a pure heart and who speaks with grace
will have the king for a friend.*

—Proverbs 22:11

•••●•●•••

*E*veryone at the table started laughing—except Lillie. In order to get what was funny, your mind had to be "in the gutter" and Lillie's mind just didn't go there. Some called Lillie naive, but I don't think she is. I believe she has a pure heart. What her eyes saw and her ears heard came from her pure heart.

When I was a little girl, my mom taught me this song: "Oh be careful little ears, what you hear. For the Father up above is looking down in love, so be careful little ears, what you hear." We would sing it over and over again, just changing the words: "Be careful little feet where you go." You get the picture.

The revolutionary girl is careful. Her desire is to honor God, who gave up everything for her. To do that, she protects her heart. A life of honor comes out of a heart of honor. The girl who gets in on the crass joke or chooses language that's rude or disrespectful shows off the condition of her heart—and it's not pretty.

Your heart is the greatest treasure you have. If it is your desire to have the King for a friend, to truly know him, you'll guard your heart. You will go out of your way to get away from those who have no regard for their own hearts, or anyone else's.

START THE REVOLUTION

Do your words come from grace or from the gutter? Check yourself and see what your heart is speaking.

What's a girl to do if she's already muddled up her heart and lost her innocence? Second Corinthians 5:17 reminds us that we can be a new creation in Christ. New heart, new mind, new life. Ask Jesus to give you a pure heart or to help you protect the one you have—he'll do just that.

*Father, purify my heart and teach me to
protect it with all I have. Amen.*

205: Weird People

Since you died with Christ to the elemental spiritual forces of this world, why, as though you still belonged to the world, do you submit to its rules?
—Colossians 2:20

•••••••

"**W**hy does our family have to be so different?" Have you ever asked that? You want to spend the weekend with a friend, but your parents say "No, we don't know your friend or her parents well." You don't get it.

Have you ever thought that maybe your parents don't get it either? Maybe they say, "Why do we have to be so cautious? Why do I have to annoy my children?" You're not the only one who struggles with fitting in. Parents do too.

Paul could have been talking to all of us—kids and parents alike. "Why do you struggle *as though you still belonged to the world?*" Why do we do it? Why do we fight about:

- choosing clothes that are in, but are also too revealing?
- having stuff that other kids have: iPhones, laptops, designer clothes?
- wanting to do what other kids get to do (whatever it is)?

In his letter to the Colossians, Paul goes on to urge them not to be so concerned with the rules of this world, but instead to "set your minds on things above, not on earthly things. For you died, and your life is now hidden with Christ in God" (3:2, 3). He asks them to put to death things belonging to the earthly nature (check out 3:5-9 for the whole list). He then calls them "God's chosen people, holy and dearly loved" (v. 12).

In some ways, being a "chosen people" just sounds weird. But it also sounds like **weird is Jesus' idea**—both for kids and parents. Choosing to be weird can be really difficult, but it's amazing to think these weird ways are exactly what makes us set apart as "dearly loved" by our perfect God. If it comes down to being normal and not chosen, or being weird and dearly loved—I'll take weird. How about you?

> **START THE REVOLUTION**
> Check out that list in Colossians 3:5-9. Is there anything on that list that you need to "put to death"?

Holy Spirit, open my ears to hear your wisdom in all areas of my life. Amen.

206: A Heart to Know

I will give them a heart to know me, that I am the LORD.
They will be my people, and I will be their God,
for they will return to me with all their heart.
—Jeremiah 24:7

•••●•●•••

When it comes to church, youth group, or summer camp, have you ever stopped to think about why you go? Maybe it's because your parents make you go. Maybe you go because it's really pretty fun and you have some great friends there. Maybe you like how you feel better about yourself afterwards.

What does God think of these motives?

If you had friends who hung out with you because they had to, would you consider them good friends? What about if it wasn't so much that they liked *you*, but they really liked your group of friends? I'm thinking you would NOT consider them to be good friends. In fact, you would probably feel like you were being used.

How many of us have unselfish motives in our relationship with God—just wanting to spend time with him for the sake of knowing him better? I, for one, would have to say that is often not my motive.

If my heart *toward* God is not motivated by a heart to *know* God, it's no longer about our relationship. It's moved from being about him, to being about me. When it is more about me feeling good and less about me honoring the one who loves me, the relationship loses its value.

The radical girl does the things she does to know Jesus better so she can follow him better. That is really loving him with all your heart.

START THE REVOLUTION

Examine your motives next time you do something "for God." Is your heart in the right place?

Jesus, give me a heart to know you. Teach me through your Word to honor you. Amen.

207: Me Syndrome

You, my brothers and sisters, were called to be free. But do not use your freedom to indulge the flesh; rather, serve one another humbly in love.
—Galatians 5:13

•••◉••••

"The dog won't come! I think she has run away again." *Ugh. Why should I have to take care of the dog?* This was my stinking thinking one evening after spending the day doing I-have-to's. I was enjoying my few minutes of I-want-to's. And I *didn't want* to go find the dog!

Do you ever suffer from Me Syndrome? That time of the day or month when you feel that *now* is the time for you? I sure do. And during that time, if it doesn't benefit me, I don't want to do it!

Maybe that's why Galatians 5:13 jumped off the page when I read it: "serve one another humbly in love." **Freedom is given so I can serve.** I started wondering where God might want to free me up so I could serve more. Here is the list he downloaded to my heart:

START THE REVOLUTION
Do you ever struggle with ambition, jealousy, expectation, selfishness, or control issues? Ask Jesus to set you free!

- When I am free from ambition, I am free to serve with a joyful heart.
- When I am free from selfishness, I am free from irritation.
- When I am free from jealousy, I am free to rejoice in the good of another.
- When I am free from judgment, I am free to pray from a pure heart.
- When I am free from expectation, I am free to enjoy whatever comes.
- When I am freed from controlling others, I am free to see the miraculous.
- When I am truly free, I will see the kingdom of God in my life.

That's a pretty amazing list, but how can that kind of freedom happen? Only with a lot of God's help.

In order to be free, I have to be free of *me*.

Father, only you can free me of me.
I give you permission to do it! Amen.

I Honor Him

208: Fight the Pull

For you were once darkness, but now you are
light in the Lord. Live as children of light.
—Ephesians 5:8

•••●•••

I love the afterglow of camp in a girl's eyes. Getting away from it all—cell phones, TV, draining friends, and Facebook—is so refreshing! My friend just came back from camp, and she looks great.

It doesn't take long though to see the pull returning. The tug-of-war between being the radical Jesus-lover she is and the girl who doesn't want to miss what's going on. This time the pull was more than a gentle tug. Like the whipping of the Tilt-A-Whirl at Six Flags, the velocity at which the world made its play seemed stronger than she could take.

I knew that my friend needed me.

She needed me to help her set boundaries again. She needed me to hug her and remind her that rules protect her greatest treasure, her heart.

It wasn't an easy, gentle talk. No, it was a crying, snotty nose, wear-me-flat-out, lasted-for-hours type of talk. But she's worth it. She actually thanked me at the end.

Honoring God is worth fighting for.

My friend knows I love her. She knows that our goal is to be uncommon, though she desperately wants to be both—uncommon and a part of everything.

I am praying that though the world pulls, tugs, and tries to whip her around the cycle of popularity, position, and power, she will honor him.

START THE REVOLUTION

In what area do you struggle to honor God? Who's holding you accountable in your struggle? Be uncommon. Honor God.

Jesus, it is my desire to honor you. Pour into me the conviction I need today to not get pulled in. Amen.

209: You've Got Guts

If we endure, we will also reign with him.
If we disown him, he will also disown us.
—2 Timothy 2:12

•••●••

Yes, she was a Christian. She loved Jesus; really, she did! But sometimes . . . well, it was just hard! Karen knew when she received her purity ring that staying pure before she got married was something she wanted to do. It wasn't hard in middle school—most of the time. But high school was different. Kids didn't get it—didn't get her. Maybe it would just be easier to leave it at home.

Karen is in a battle! Her thoughts are trying to dictate who she is and what she'll stand for.

Peter, one of Jesus' disciples, was in the same spot as Karen. (Take a minute to read his struggle in Mark 14:66-72.) He loved Jesus; he truly did. When the time came to stand beside his friend, though, he allowed fear to overtake his love. Peter gave power to the *thoughts* of rejection in his mind, which soon were followed by *actions* of rejection toward his friend.

Standing up for Jesus isn't easy. It takes guts.

You have what it takes to be a radical girl with guts! You do, because the Holy Spirit is living inside of you. He will empower you with the moxie you need to stand up for what you believe—to say, "Yes, I love the one who loves me!"

Today's verse tells us that if we endure, we will also reign with him. If you take hold of the power the Holy Spirit brings into your life, you will have what it takes, not only to stand; you will have what it takes to influence others.

START THE REVOLUTION
Don't shrink back! He is proud to call you his. Be proud to say he's mine!

Jesus, give me guts today. Amen.

I Honor Him

210: Beauty in Clay

But we have this treasure in jars of clay to show that this all-surpassing power is from God and not from us.
—2 Corinthians 4:7

•••●•••

Does your family plant flowers in the spring? Mine does! We have a whole collection of clay pots in our garage that we fill with fresh dirt and all varieties of colorful flowers each year.

When trying to decide on the best look for our yard, what are we showcasing? Our clay pots? No! They hold the plants. It's all about the beauty of the flowers!

In today's verse we're reminded we carry the treasure of Jesus' love for us, and for the world, in jars of clay. Just as the pot is not the focus of the attention in a flower arrangement, **we're not to be the focus of attention** in our lives—the powerful love of Jesus is.

In our culture, what is the flower most often used to communicate love? The rose! It is considered the perfect flower—perfect in smell, form, and color. In history, there have been some who have referred to Jesus as the Rose of Sharon. How fitting! We are the vases that hold the beauty of the love flower!

Today focus on drawing attention to the beauty you hold; the Rose of Sharon. When your mind tries to get you to be the central point of attraction, attention, and activity, purposefully turn your thoughts, desires, and words away from the jar of you and onto the Beautiful One!

START THE REVOLUTION

Bring honor to Jesus by being aware of the needs of others. His beauty will shine through you as you carry his love to others.

Jesus, you are the beauty in my life. Through me, may others see, smell, and touch you today! Amen.

211: Without Love

*If I speak with human eloquence and angelic ecstasy but don't love,
I'm nothing but the creaking of a rusty gate. . . . No matter what I say,
what I believe, and what I do, I'm bankrupt without love.*

—1 Corinthians 13:1-3 (*The Message*)

• • ● ● • •

As the leader of her school's Bible study, she encouraged others to stand up for Jesus. "Be bold and change our school." She seemed so confident, unafraid. Somehow, though, something was wrong. She meant to be encouraging, but her approach was condescending, making others feel bad instead of bold. They left feeling they were not as good as she was—not good enough. Her words and actions didn't make others want to be like her, or like Jesus. **Something was missing.**

I was just like that girl and there *was* something missing: love. Without love, all the words and all the actions are nothing. In fact, they are worse than nothing. Not only do they not honor Jesus; they dishonor him. Pride and hypocrisy are the opposites of love, the opposites of Jesus.

There can only be one motive behind the things we do: love. Unconditional and forgiving love is what draws people to Jesus.

Love never gives up; it never puts people down. Love cares more about others than self. Love always looks for the best.

START THE REVOLUTION

Who are you having a hard time loving? Today remember when you love, you are loving and honoring God.

*Jesus, I want to honor you by
really loving others. HELP! Amen.*

212: Pridefall

Before a downfall the heart is haughty,
but humility comes before honor.
—Proverbs 18:12

•••●••

I couldn't understand why those I shared Christ with didn't come to know him. It was obviously the best way to live. I mean, look at me, right?

That was the problem. When others looked at me, they didn't see Jesus. They saw Lynn.

As revolutionary girls, in our boldness we have to be careful not to become prideful. **Pride builds walls**, creating "us" and "them" sides. Humility honors Jesus. It allows us to take unconditional love to those hurting around us and give it in a way they can receive.

Take a moment to think about your life. Why do you do the things you do? Does love for Jesus compel you? Is it because you love others and want what's best for them?

Or . . . is it to impress others? To draw attention to yourself? Maybe to make yourself look good?

All motives other than love seep through our actions and words, pointing others to us instead of to him. Paul tells us that it doesn't really matter how much we talk about God or how much we do for God, if there isn't love behind it (1 Corinthians 13:1-3). If the true motive in our hearts is that we think we're better than other people, we want to be noticed, or we're trying to hide how we really are, then all the talk, all the volunteering, and all the Jesus meetings are worthless.

START THE REVOLUTION

God says that pride comes before a fall (Proverbs 16:18). Take a look at your life. Where are you close to falling?

Jesus, I need to be humble. Help me to humble myself, so you don't have to. Amen.

213: In Which God Lives

In him the whole building is joined together and rises to become a holy temple in the Lord. And in him you too are being built together to become a dwelling in which God lives by his Spirit.
—Ephesians 2:21, 22

••••••

I n the book of Genesis, we meet Adam and Eve at the beginning of the world. They were created for the same reason that you and I were created: to fellowship with God. Genesis 2:15 says that God "took the man and put him in the Garden of Eden to work it and take care of it."

START THE REVOLUTION
How are you becoming a dwelling for God?

From the beginning of time, God designed for us to live with him and to do something good for his world. For Adam, it was to work in the garden, be a husband, and populate the earth.

Today's verse tells us that each one of us as part of the body of Christ is being built together to become a dwelling for God, a holy temple. Isaiah 43:7 tells us that we are created for God's glory.

So how do we do that—**how do we become a place where God can live**, and how do we give God glory? With our everyday lives, doing everyday things, we can cause others to see Jesus. When we do the good works God has prepared for us to do—such as being kind to those who are mean, choosing right from wrong, and honoring those in authority—we honor Jesus. When we tell others the story of Jesus' sacrifice and of our forgiveness, we show the "incomparable riches of his grace, expressed in his kindness to us in Christ Jesus" (Ephesians 2:7), and we draw others to him. And as we draw others to him, we join together with them to create a stronger, richer dwelling for his Spirit.

These good works are not to get us on God's good side. They are not to make him want us more. These good works are to honor him and cause others to want to know him. These good works are our love talk back to him. When we choose what is good, we choose to return love.

Jesus, open my eyes today to see opportunities to do good and cause others to see you. Amen.

I Honor Him

223

214: Enemies of the Cross

For, as I have often told you before and now tell you again even with tears, many live as enemies of the cross of Christ. Their destiny is destruction, their god is their stomach, and their glory is in their shame. Their mind is set on earthly things.
—Philippians 3:18, 19

•••••••

n enemy of the cross. Pretty strong language. I wouldn't consider *myself* an enemy of the cross, would you? Let's see how Paul defines an enemy of Jesus.

Their destiny is destruction. Someone whose destiny—the road to the future—is destruction. What is causing this destruction? **Destruction comes when small everyday choices are not good.** When decisions—such as what we watch, what we do, where we go—are all based on what seems good at the time, with no regard for the future. Destruction comes on the path of sin.

START THE REVOLUTION
Do your actions say "I honor him"?

Their god is their stomach. Their god—the thing they worship and follow and go to for comfort—is their stomach, their physical desires. Hunger, thirst, lust, touch.Our desires can become our idols when we are more concerned about pleasing our flesh than pleasing our God.

Their glory is their shame. Their glory—what makes them laugh or want to brag—is their shame. What stories do we repeat, what tweets do we re-tweet, what videos do we post, what language do we use?

Their mind is set on earthly things. What takes up all of our thinking? What's the thing we can't wait to do? Is it all about "here and now," with no thought of Heaven?

When I read this verse, I'm convicted. It hits really close to my heart. If I say I want to honor God, my actions will reveal whether I'm being truthful or not.

Jesus, I can handle honoring you one day at a time. I'm thankful that is all you require of me. Amen.

215: Tame Your Tongue

With the tongue we praise our Lord and Father, and with it we curse
human beings, who have been made in God's likeness.
Out of the same mouth come praise and cursing.
My brothers and sisters, this should not be.

—James 3:9, 10

••●●•••

I had a problem—I swore. I have no idea why. It must have been the thing everyone else did, so I did it too. It seems so dumb now. I said I loved Jesus, so if I did, why did I let words come out of my mouth that dishonored him? How could I praise him with that same tongue that let curse words fly?

James has some pretty strong words to say about what comes out of our mouths. He said the tongue "corrupts the whole body, sets the whole course of one's life on fire" and that "no human being can tame the tongue. It is a restless evil, full of deadly poison" (vv. 6, 8).

Wow. Harsh words. But he's got a point. It's really difficult not to pick up the talk of those around us. Slang words, fad phrases, rude jokes, and insults are so easy to adopt—sometimes they seem to roll off our tongues before we even are aware of learning the words.

START THE REVOLUTION

James says that only perfect people never make mistakes with what they say. What do you do when words you say offend others, even if it's not on purpose?

The revolutionary girl needs to **have a revolutionary tongue**. She carefully watches what she says so she can honor Jesus with her words. If it doesn't honor him, she doesn't say it. According to Dictionary.com, one meaning for *revolutionary* is "radically new or innovative; outside or beyond established procedure, principles, etc." That is what our mouths should be: radically new. Totally different from the established norm of those around us—honoring God instead of the world.

This one is pretty clear, Lord.
Keep my mouth clean. Amen.

I Honor Him

We are not trying to commend ourselves to you again, but are giving you an opportunity to take pride in us, so that you can answer those who take pride in what is seen rather than in what is in the heart.
—2 Corinthians 5:12

She had it all: the right bag, right shoes, and right jeans. Her Facebook page was full of weekend fun pics, with a huge list of friends that almost seemed made up. **Her life was picture perfect.** Or was it? Was her life really as good as it appeared?

Contrast her to Lindsey. Lindsey would tell you that she doesn't have all the name-brand this and that. Her weekends are mostly filled with time with her family and friends from church.

You know what I see each time I see Lindsey? A smile. A genuine smile of joy and eyes that sparkle. Lindsey is a natural beauty. She finds her happiness each day in the things in life that are eternal: her relationship with Jesus, her family, and her friends.

Today's verse encourages us not to take pride in the things that are seen. Bags go out of style, shoes wear out, and jeans fade. Each day comes with a choice: getting wrapped up in what ends up in a landfill or spending energy on what will fill you up eternally. What's your choice today?

START THE REVOLUTION
What things took your attention away from God today? How can you avoid that happening tomorrow?

It's so easy to focus on what I see, hear, and smell, Jesus. Through your Word and prayer, grant me the power to think bigger! Amen.

217: God's House

I rejoiced with those who said to me,
"Let us go to the house of the LORD."
—Psalm 122:1

•• • ● •••

"I really don't like to go to church. It is so boring, and I don't get anything out of it." Have you ever thought or said that?

There is a problem here. *I* really don't like. *I* don't get anything. The problem is, it's not about you; it's about *him*! I'm going to assume that if you have gotten this far in this book, you are a radical, Jesus-loving girl. If this is the case, then you know that **the focus of church is not you**—it's God.

Psalm 149:1 says, "Praise the LORD. Sing to the LORD a new song, his praise in the assembly of his faithful people." Singing together is for praising Jesus! Yes, when we worship we can feel good, but that's a side benefit! The purpose is to thank and praise him because he is perfect and good. It's all about him.

Church is also a way to gather together with "his faithful people," to learn about God, to encourage and support each other, and to reach out to those who don't know him yet. I love my church's motto: "So that those who are far from God can be raised to life in Christ." *That's* what it is about! Helping others who haven't found this revolutionary love!

So get busy! What are you waiting for? Invite your friends. Volunteer to be a greeter, a nursery worker, or a member of the sound team. Ask to sing, help with the setup, or bring treats for the worship leaders. Find your way to serve. You are not too young; your time is now! "Get the word out. Teach all these things. And don't let anyone put you down because you're young" (1 Timothy 4:11, 12, *The Message*).

START THE REVOLUTION

Make a list of all the ways you could serve at your church, and give your church a call. You'll be glad you did, and they will too!

Prayer idea: Get to your church early next time and spend a few minutes praying for the staff and volunteers, and for the people coming to seek God.

218: Gifted

Each person is given something to do that shows who God is:
Everyone gets in on it, everyone benefits. All kinds of things
are handed out by the Spirit, and to all kinds of people!
—1 Corinthians 12:11 (*The Message*)

W hat do you love to do? Write, speak, or sing? Can you create art or poetry, or dance? Does math fascinate you, or does running make you feel like you can fly? **What you love to do are God's gifts to you.**

Maybe you feel like you have no gifts. You look at your life, compare it to another's, and come to the conclusion God passed you up. That's simply not so! His Word tells us that each of us is given a gift. These gifts are then "gifted" to others! We use these unique abilities from God to point others to God.

Over the next few days, be a detective. Watch your life and see what kinds of things make you smile or laugh. What do you do well? Do you find joy when you can help another person? Do you get energy from teaching others, or from offering comfort to a friend in trouble? What abilities do you have that you can use to give God honor? Examining your life in this way can lead you to find your gift.

Look carefully for the gift he has given you; then dig it out! Make a connection between that gift and how it helps you point others to Jesus.

START THE REVOLUTION

Need help finding your gifts? Ask your parent or youth pastor what they think your gifts are. They might be able to see what you can't.

I want to use what you have given me, Lord.
Open my eyes to see what you see. Amen.

219: Respect Authority

Let everyone be subject to the governing authorities, for there is no authority except that which God has established. The authorities that exist have been established by God.

—Romans 13:1

•••●•••

START THE REVOLUTION

Say thank you to a teacher, coach, or other authority figure today.

*N*adine admits the beginning of the school year got off to a rough start. She messed around in math class, and that put her on her teacher's bad side. It also earned her a crummy grade!

But she's changed. She's pulled her grade up to a B and quit talking in class. Yet her teacher doesn't seem to notice.

Today, when her teacher picked up her homework, she simply said, "No." No explanation. She just wrote a 0 in her grade book and said, "I'm going to call your parents! This is unacceptable!" *Why? What had she done?* Nadine was fuming. She'd done her homework. It wasn't perfect, but she'd tried. Why did this teacher have it out for her? Nadine desperately wanted to talk back—telling her teacher what she thought of her unfair treatment.

What would Jesus do? came into her head. For Nadine, this well-worn phrase was a reminder that even if her teacher didn't deserve honor, she should give it. She decided to please Jesus.

I'm sure you've been in a situation similar to Nadine's—some time when you felt that someone in authority got it wrong (we're not talking about serious bullying, harassment, or abuse here—if *that* happens, tell your parents right away!). God has placed authority figures in our lives, and they are human, so they will at times mess up! When we choose to speak respectfully and respond humbly, even when they don't deserve it, we honor God, who deserves all our honor.

Jesus, I don't like it when I am mistreated, especially by those who should know better. Give me the self-control I need in these situations. I want to honor you. Amen.

220: Do Not Grieve

And do not grieve the Holy Spirit of God, with whom you were sealed for the day of redemption.
—Ephesians 4:30

here were times when Jenny just got tired of being "weird." Like the time when the new girls from her English class were coming over. They really didn't know her yet, didn't know that she loved Jesus. They might think the verses taped to her wall were weird. Maybe she should take them down, at least until they got to know her. And what if her sister starting talking to them about Jesus? She probably shouldn't have them over. It seemed too risky.

Radical girl, you are weird—there is no doubt about it! The band Mute Math says, "We are peculiar people. There is more to who we are than meets the eye." Peculiar—different in the best sort of way!

It's time to **embrace your difference, instead of being embarrassed by it**.

Have you ever had someone be embarrassed of you? It's a terrible feeling, isn't it? Is that how Jesus feels when we want to hide that we are followers of him? Today's verse tells us not to grieve the Holy Spirit. To grieve means to cause sorrow, sadness, or distress. Don't cause Jesus pain because you are scared to be bold for him. He was bold for you. He died a humiliating death for you and me. Be bold for him.

START THE REVOLUTION

Embrace your weirdness. Start with something simple—maybe share a Christian song that you really like. You may be surprised by the reaction you get.

Jesus, I never really thought about causing you pain before. Please forgive me. Give me boldness. Amen.

221: Honor Your Parents

Children, obey your parents in the Lord, for this is right. "Honor your father and mother"—which is the first commandment with a promise—"so that it may go well with you and that you may enjoy long life on the earth."
—Ephesians 6:1-3

•••●•••

*H*er parents' rule about being home at night for dinner was dumb—that was Jenna's opinion. It made her feel like she was a kid. It was only five months until her eighteenth birthday! None of her friends had to come home for dinner; they did whatever they wanted after school until late. She was just over it.

I know you've had times when you felt like your parents treated you wrongly. You've had times when you've felt like you should get to make your own rules. The tension between **gaining your independence** and still living at home is maddening at times. When are they ever going to let you grow up?

No matter if you believe their rules are dumb or that they are there for your benefit, God gives you a command: Honor your parents. It isn't based on their intelligence, character, or wisdom; it's based on their position. They're your parents.

START THE REVOLUTION
What can you do to honor your parents this week?

Here's the really cool part about today's verse: it's got a promise! God promises that if you obey and honor your parents, your life will go well and you will enjoy a long life on the earth!

I pretty much followed this verse when I was growing up. I haven't lived super long yet, but I sure can say that my life is going well. So take it from me, holding back the nasty words on the tip of your tongue and fighting the instinct to do what you want is worth a life that goes well!

Jesus, obeying and honoring my parents is definitely one of the hardest things you have asked me to do. Only through you can I do it! Amen.

I Honor Him

222: Quit Complaining

Do everything without grumbling or arguing, so that you may become blameless and pure, "children of God without fault in a warped and crooked generation." Then you will shine among them like stars in the sky as you hold firmly to the word of life.
—Philippians 2:14-16

••••••••

"**Y**ou know, I have recently discovered something. I don't like to be around people who complain." I agree with Justin. Nothing is worse than being in a tough situation and having someone complain on top of it!

So there is one good reason not to complain: if you don't stop, people won't want to be around you!

But here is another: God commands it. "Do *everything* without grumbling or arguing." He doesn't say: "Don't grumble or argue unless your teacher gives you a bad grade"; or "Don't grumble or argue except when your parents won't let you go out." There are no exclusions!

So what's the big deal? It's natural to vent a little, right?

Here's the big deal: when we don't complain or argue, we are so different, so revolutionary, **we shine like the stars**. I want to be beautiful like that, don't you? I want to be blameless and pure, without fault, as today's verse says. When we don't complain and argue, it is so countercultural, we can't help but stand out, and that opens wide the door for us to show off Jesus!

My friend Kelly has a way to help herself stop complaining. She has a bracelet on her arm. Each time she complains, she moves it to the other arm. It's a constant reminder to her not to complain!

Today, it's likely you'll have an opportunity to complain. Challenge yourself to honor God by going the whole day without complaining.

START THE REVOLUTION

Try a reminder, like the bracelet Kelly used. Take the challenge to go a whole day with no complaining!

Jesus, help me to catch myself before I complain. I know we can do this, me and you. Amen.

223: Hold Tight

To the Jews who had believed him, Jesus said, "If you hold
to my teaching, you are really my disciples."
—John 8:31

The last time I went to Carowinds, the theme park in my state, I hopped on the newest roller coaster. My favorite ones are the corkscrews. I love the thrill of twisting around and around.

At first, as we climbed up the hill, I sat there calmly. No big deal. Then came the plunge! Quickly, I grabbed the bar, clinging with white knuckles. Certain that I was going to fall out, I pictured my body as a splat on the concrete below.

Life can be like that coaster. Going along, no big deal . . . when the drop-off hits. Everything starts spiraling faster than you can take it in. How will you ever survive?

Hold on!

Jesus says that when we hold on to his teaching, it proves we really are his. Especially when life is going crazy, when we stick with Jesus, it proves to ourselves and the rest of the world that this relationship with him is not just some emotional high. By staying faithful we shout to the world that he is real. We bring Jesus true honor.

START THE REVOLUTION
Radical girl, make Jesus real to someone this week by giving love and friendship in tangible ways.

Jesus, I can't predict when the life coaster is going to plummet, but I am putting your Word in my heart so I can hang on tight when it comes! Amen.

224: Content

And I saw that all toil and all achievement spring from one person's envy of another. This too is meaningless, a chasing after the wind.
—Ecclesiates 4:4

••●●••

I t didn't matter what the temperature was outside; I put in the miles. That summer I pushed myself so I could run on the cross-country team. When I first started, I could barely run around a track. Being in that good of shape for the first time in my life felt great! Until . . .

Until I ran with the whole team. That's when I discovered I was one of the slowest people on the team. I couldn't believe that after working so hard, I was *that* slow. I didn't know until I started comparing myself to others. Then I was unhappy; I wanted to run as fast as them.

Nothing pulls joy down like comparison. *I want her grades, skin, hair, voice, body, car, wardrobe, boyfriend*—the list goes on and on.

In Ecclesiastes, Solomon tells us that all striving comes from envy—wanting what someone has. We're content until we see the "haves" of another; then *dis*contentment attacks. Before we know it, we are unhappy with this and frustrated with that.

START THE REVOLUTION

Turn the usual comparisons upside down. If you're feeling discontented, just take a look at the news stories from countries enduring war and unrest and extreme poverty.

Philippians 4:11 tells how to be free of wanting: "Actually, I don't have a sense of needing anything personally. I've learned by now to be quite content whatever my circumstances" (*The Message*).

Contentment is learned. It is learned by fighting against wanting and re-placing it with wonder. We can either choose to want more and more, never having enough, or we can choose to bask in the wonder of how good Jesus is to us, experiencing joyful contentment (see 1 Chronicles 16:11, 12).

Fight the wants. Pray this prayer several times a day: Jesus, I am in wonder of how good you are to me!

225: Healthy Fear

Then those who feared the LORD talked with each other, and the LORD listened and heard. A scroll of remembrance was written in his presence concerning those who feared the LORD and honored his name.
—Malachi 3:16

• • ● • •

Fear isn't always a negative thing; often, it's very good. Fear of fire keeps you from getting burned. Fear of snakes keeps you from being bitten. Fear can protect.

Sometimes, though, we don't fear the things we should. When told not to touch, a toddler may head to the stove as soon as her mom leaves the room. The child has no healthy sense of fear.

The more we learn about the power of a thing, the more respect we have for it. We fearfully respect fire and snakes because we understand their power. The toddler doesn't.

The revolutionary girl fears God because she understands he is all-powerful. She chooses to obey him out of love, but she also respects God's power!

I used to watch this show called *The Cosby Show*. In one episode, the dad talks to his son, Theo, about his grades. Theo delivers an earnest speech about how maybe he just isn't as smart as his parents (a doctor and lawyer) and how "maybe you should accept who I am and love me anyway, because I'm your son." There's a long pause, then his dad says, "Theo . . . that's the DUMBEST thing I've ever heard in my life! No wonder you get Ds in everything! . . . Now I'm telling you, you are going to try as hard as you can. And you're going to do it because I said so. I am your father. I brought you into this world, and I'll take you out!" (Check it out on YouTube—it is hilarious!)

Theo needed a healthy fear of punishment for his poor grades. That fear would motivate him for good. We need a healthy fear of God. He is all-powerful, holy, and mighty; therefore, we need to honor him in all we say and do.

START THE REVOLUTION

Think of times when fear has protected you. Can fear of God help you know him more? What do you think?

God, you brought me into this world, and you can take me out too! Help me to fear you because I want to do what is good for me and bring honor to you. Amen.

I Honor Him

226: Resolved

But Daniel resolved not to defile himself with the royal food and wine, and he asked the chief official for permission not to defile himself this way.

—Daniel 1:8

•••◉••

*N*ever underestimate the power of a mind resolved. When I was in junior high, I made up my mind that I was not going to have sex before I got married. Making up my mind to honor God *before* I hit that temptation empowered me to follow through.

When I was in high school, I made up my mind that I was not going to party. Finding myself in a situation where there was alcohol, I got out. I had already resolved **I wasn't going down that path**. A made-up mind is a powerful mind.

Daniel was a man of God, highly intelligent and on his way to being very successful in the king's court. The king determined each day the food Daniel would eat and the wine he'd drink. But since the choices the king was making didn't honor God, Daniel made up his mind that he wouldn't eat or drink the king's choices. He was going to honor God, no matter what. The end result was that the king found him in every matter of wisdom and understanding ten times better than all in the whole kingdom (Daniel 1:20).

Like Daniel, I want my choices to honor God. I want to make up my mind to live each day in his wisdom, so I can stand out for his glory.

What area do you need to be resolved about? Sex? Honesty? Dating? Self-control? Drinking? Cheating? Drugs? Make up your mind today and trust the Holy Spirit to give you the power to follow through.

START THE REVOLUTION

Truth time: When you make up your mind, do you stick to it? If you don't (and even if you do), find some accountability partners to help you stick to your decisions for Christ.

Holy Spirit, I am making up my mind to _____. Give me the power I need to honor God in this area of my life. Amen.

227: Benefits

But now that you have been set free from sin
and have become slaves of God, the benefit you reap leads to holiness,
and the result is eternal life.

—Romans 6:22

●●●●●●●

What's in it for me? Isn't that what we really want to know? One person asks, "Why should I volunteer? It doesn't do *me* any good." Another person groans, "I have no idea why I'm taking math class. I'll never use it."

We really don't like spending our time and energy if we don't think that it will have a payoff. And so we ask: When it comes to living a life that honors God, **what's in it for me?** How will I benefit?

Romans 6:22 tells us that being set free from sin and becoming God's slaves leads to holy living. A life that is holy is a life that I can be proud of—it's a life that's not filled with regret. Being freed from sin means not having anything in my life that I'm afraid someone will find out about; I've got nothing to hide. That brings peace and tranquility in my life. Ultimately, accepting God's forgiveness and becoming his slave leads to eternal freedom.

What's in it for you? Everything.

START THE REVOLUTION

Start a list today of all the benefits that come with being God's slave. Get a long piece of paper ... you might need it!

Jesus, "What's in it for me?" is such a selfish question to ask, but thank you that living for you does benefit me. You are good in every sense of the word. Amen.

228: In the Night

In the night, LORD, I remember your name, that I may keep your law.
—Psalm 119:55

•••●•••

What is it about the night that tempts us to do things we'd never do in the day? The revolutionary girl commits to God: "In the face of my biggest temptations, I will choose words and actions that declare who I am—a girl captured by God's love."

It was in the night that King David got up from his bed once and, walking around on the roof of his palace, saw beautiful Bathsheba, bathing. Adultery and murder followed. But here in today's verse, we see David committing that, in the night, he would remember and honor God.

I love the verses that follow: "This has been my practice: I obey your precepts. You are my portion, LORD; I have promised to obey your words. I have sought your face with all my heart; be gracious to me according to your promise. I have considered my ways and have turned my steps to your statutes. I will hasten and not delay to obey your commands" (Psalm 119:56-60).

Listen to all the choices David made: "my practice," "I obey," "I have promised," "I have sought," "I have considered," "have turned," "I will hasten," and "not delay." This sounds like a man who, no matter what has happened in the past, is now determined to honor his God, even in the night.

In the night we live out who we say we are in the light.

David says later, "My eyes stay open through the watches of the night, that I may meditate on your promises" (v. 148). Are you tempted in the night? If you find yourself in a dark place—literally or spiritually—remember the name of your Lord, and how he promises to remain faithful to you. Then be faithful to him and to his Word.

> **START THE REVOLUTION**
>
> Get some glow-in-the-dark paint or other material and make a sign: "Remember." Next time you are up in the night, remember who God is, and whose you are.

Jesus, help me to remember you, even in the night. Amen.

229: Everything and Anything

"I have the right to do anything," you say—
but not everything is beneficial. "I have the right to do anything"—
but not everything is constructive."
—1 Corinthians 10:23

••●●●••

*B*efore Jesus came, those who followed God had a *ton* of rules to live by. Rules for what they ate, how they cooked it, when they grew it, who they ate it with, and so on and so on. And those were just the rules about food!

When Jesus came, he simplified the rules: "'Love the Lord your God with all your heart and with all your soul and with all your strength and with all your mind'; and, 'Love your neighbor as yourself'" (Luke 10:27). This really changed up life for the Jewish people. Freedom!

But **freedom created a problem**. They used it as an excuse to do anything they wanted. What made this a problem? When we do anything we want, it's not always good.

Can you eat anything you want? Sure you can, but eventually you'll become unhealthy. Can you wear whatever you want? Well, I guess you *can*, but your choices may cause someone else to have sinful thoughts.

You may have the right to do whatever you want, but that *everything* might not be beneficial or constructive, especially not for the body of Christ. Your choices might not be for the common good of others to strengthen and build them up.

Before deciding to do what you want to do, ask yourself: Will my choice be good not just for me? Will it honor God and be for the good of others as well? When you can say yes to both those questions, it's a wise decision.

START THE REVOLUTION
Whenever you feel you have the right to something, ask yourself: Will my choice honor God and be for the good of others as well?

Jesus, honoring you means setting aside my rights sometimes. When faced with that decision, empower me to say yes to honor you. Amen.

230: Blameless

For he chose us in him before the creation of the world
to be holy and blameless in his sight.
—Ephesians 1:4

Are you holy? blameless? When we live lives that are according to God's Word, it is not hard for us to be set apart, or different. But it's not just a matter of not doing what others are doing; it's also **doing what others aren't**—honoring God.

Honoring God in everything:

- in my thoughts that no one can see;
- in my heart that no one can perfectly read;
- in my attitudes that I think I can hide.

That is where he calls me to honor him. Because if today I will be sanctified, holy, and set apart in my heart, in my mind, and in my attitude, my actions will follow.

START THE REVOLUTION

How are you going to live "set apart" today?

Jesus, make me your girl today! Amen.

No one has ever seen God; but if we love one another,
God lives in us and his love is made complete in us.
—1 John 4:12

••●●●••

"Y**ou're** not like that; you're not like them. Maybe that's why you shouldn't be friends with them anymore." Tonya couldn't believe Chase was giving her this advice. He wasn't even a believer! Why would he of all people give advice like this?

Chase knows her. For years now, he has watched Tonya. Seeing the things she does, the words she says, the places she will and won't go. He knows *who* she is and he respects her. Though he's not quite ready to become like her, he admires her. The kind of friend she is, authentic and truly loving, is a rarity. He doesn't want to see her spoiled.

Radical girl, you might think you are just going to school each day, doing your thing, not making a difference. But let me assure you, if you are honoring God by loving other people, it is hardly unnoticed! In a world where a *Gossip Girl* rules and *Mean Girls* are popular, a girl who practices loving others, despite how she is treated, stands out in the best sort of way. **Those around you will see Jesus when they see you.**

> **START THE REVOLUTION**
> Radical girl: Bring it! Stand out from your crowd today!

Today, when you are tempted to post that status or tweet that rude comment, don't forget: others are watching. They are looking at you and wondering, *Is it real? Is there truth in what she believes in?* They are dying, literally, to have something to live for. Will you bring it, or will you blend in?

Jesus, help me bring it—bring your love,
each and every day. Some days I want to gossip,
swear, and vent with the best (or worst) of them.
Pour your love in so I won't blend in. Amen.

I Honor Him

Finally, brothers and sisters, whatever is true, whatever is noble,
whatever is right, whatever is pure, whatever is lovely, whatever is
admirable—if anything is excellent or praiseworthy—
think about such things.
—Philippians 4:8

"She makes me so mad! Who is she to talk to me that way!" As I cleaned my house, I muddied my thoughts. Feeling pushed around, I just couldn't take it anymore. And the more my stinking thinking clouded my mind, the more my heart began to listen.

I didn't stop my crummy reasoning that day. Next time I saw my friend, my heart felt icky. Muddy meditation had soiled my affections. Dark thinking led to a dark heart.

Thoughts have the power to control our actions.

What's a girl to do when junk threatens to take over?

The Bible gives us pure wisdom: whatever is true, noble, right, pure, lovely, admirable, excellent, or praiseworthy—think about such things. It's as easy as a simple test. Does the thought in my mind fit this description? If not, it must go. If I don't get rid of it, not only am I dishonoring God with my thoughts, I will eventually dishonor him with my actions. Whatever I think about, that is what I become (Proverbs 4:23).

START THE REVOLUTION

Apply the test. Are your thoughts among the "whatevers"?

God, my thoughts are so powerful. I need your strength to stop my ugly thinking. Rid me of dark thinking so I don't have a dark heart. Redirect me today! Amen.

233: Out of Place

Nor should there be obscenity, foolish talk or coarse joking,
which are out of place, but rather thanksgiving.

—Ephesians 5:4

•••●••

Fad words constantly come and go. Unfortunately, many of them should never start. In an effort to not swear, sometimes as Christians we'll find other words to say to steer clear of cussing. *Shoot. Dang.* Those are some of the oldies, but you know what I'm talking about.

As long as they're not *swearing* they're OK, right? Not according to the Bible. "Nor should there be obscenity, foolish talk or coarse joking, which are out of place." What qualifies as obscenity, foolish talking, or coarse joking?

- Obscene: indecent or disgusting.
- Foolish: resulting from or showing a lack of sense; ill-considered; unwise.
- Coarse: lacking taste or refinement.

There's your standard. So, take your newest fad word and line it up with those definitions. Is it disgusting or indecent? Does it lack sense or is it unwise? Does it lack taste or refinement? **Is it cool or crude?**

Let's make it even simpler: Would you be comfortable using it in front of your parents, pastor, or Jesus? If you answered no, get it out of your vocabulary. The way you talk is one of the most important ways that you will honor or dishonor Jesus. Through texting, talking, and typing, your words have the power to point toward him or away from him. What's it going to be?

START THE REVOLUTION

Revolutionize your vocabulary. Which words need to go?

Jesus, your standard is high. I don't need to be cool, and I don't want to be crude; I just want to honor you. Set a guard over my mouth. Amen.

I Honor Him

243

234: By His Light

By his light I walked through darkness!
—Job 29:3

"**W**ouldn't you go back to high school if you could?" My answer is a definitive no. Not for any reason, not for any amount of money. You know why? I did it right the first time; I honored God during the hardest season of my life. I wouldn't want to have to do it again.

High school was hard! Like running a marathon in the dark with a penlight, it was difficult to see my way through to the end. I stumbled a lot. But I was never alone or without enough light, even in the very darkest of times.

I know you hate walking in the dark too. I know that standing up for Jesus and standing alone in school is beyond hard. But let me encourage you: do it right. Make your way through these years in such a way that you can look back and say, "I did it right the first time!"

START THE REVOLUTION

Are you having trouble seeing his light? What's clouding your vision?

To do this, daily spend time in God's Word and in prayer, listening carefully for his voice and looking for his light on your path. **God will give you exactly what you need** when you need it, but you have to be looking for him.

You can do it, radical girl. You can honor him today and every day. You're not going to just make it; you're going to come out with blessings, peace, joy . . . and no regrets!

Jesus, that is what I want—blessings, peace, joy, and no regrets! Thank you for your light today; open my eyes to see it. Amen.

235: Change Challenge

*That's why those who are still under the control of
their sinful nature can never please God.*
—Romans 8:8 (*NLT*)

••●●●••

"**I** just can't help it. No matter what I try, I still do it." *Cop out.* When you say you can't change, you are copping out. What you are really saying is: "It's really hard, and **it is much easier for me to say I can't change than to do what is right.** Saying I *can't* change makes me feel better."

When are you tempted to say "I just can't help it"? When you are scrounging in the pantry looking for chocolate again? (That's my personal problem.) When it's that time of the month, and you choose to be more cranky than usual? When you are in the dark with your boyfriend, at a party, or listening to depressing music?

Maybe what you need in order to help you help yourself is change:

- Change in thinking. A certain time of the month is no excuse to treat others poorly.
- Change in location. Stop being in the dark and going to those parties.
- Change in availability. Quit buying the chocolate and putting sad songs on your iPod.

Honoring God is very intentional. We have to set ourselves up to obey. If we don't, we won't.

START THE REVOLUTION
Today, what change do you have to make in order to obey?

*Jesus, I've been making excuses.
Sin is sin. Help me obey. Amen.*

236: Giving Back

"Bring the whole tithe into the storehouse, that there may be food in my house. Test me in this," says the LORD Almighty, "and see if I will not throw open the floodgates of heaven and pour out so much blessing that there will not be room enough to store it."

—Malachi 3:10

• • ● ● ● • •

*B*rittany's struggling so hard! She's got her first job, and she's loving the extra cash. So what's the struggle? Ever since her pastor preached on giving, she's felt convicted to give the first part of her paycheck to God. But she still hasn't done it.

My first job was a backbreaker! Growing up in Iowa, I joined the many teens who detasseled corn in the summer. Desperate for spending money, we walked up and down the prickly rows, pulling the tassels off the tops of the stalks. Hours later, we'd pile back into the bus, soaking wet, dirt up to our knees, and exhausted.

When it came time to give God a portion of my earnings that Sunday morning, it was a hard parting. But I did it. My parents were givers; I would be too. Giving became a part of my worship and a great habit.

When my husband and I got married, from the beginning we wanted to see how much we could give to God. We starting increasing from 10 percent to 15 percent, and up. You know what is so cool? **We can't out-give God!** As we honor him with our giving, he just keeps blessing us back. Greg and I are having a blast seeing other people's lives changed as we honor God with our money.

I challenge you. Start now. Begin with 10 percent and then see what happens. See what blessing comes pouring out of Heaven on you!

> **START THE REVOLUTION**
> Even if you don't have an income now, you can still give back to God. Give him your time, your talents, your love.

Jesus, I'm going to honor you with my money. I'm not doing it just so you'll give me more, but your Word does say that's a benefit, so thank you! Amen.

237: Cheerful

Each of you should give what you have decided in your heart to give,
not reluctantly or under compulsion, for God loves a cheerful giver.
—2 Corinthians 9:7

•••◉••

aylor has the sweetest smile. Her mom, Nedra, introduced us recently at one of my Revolutionary Love conferences.

Taylor's church hosted a conference and decided not to charge girls to come; they were going to trust Jesus to supply the money they needed. Nedra shared with everyone her hope of girls' lives being changed through this conference. As she did, Jesus provided "change" from all sorts of sources.

Approaching her mom with an envelope, Taylor said she wanted to give too. Inside was all the money she was saving for summer vacation, only it wasn't for summer vacation anymore. **She wanted to help bring change** to the girls in her school and community.

START THE REVOLUTION
Look for opportunities to bless others, just as you have been blessed.

Can you just imagine the smile on Jesus' face as Taylor gave her hard-earned money? No one asked Taylor to give, except Jesus, and when he did, she gave cheerfully.

I know that Jesus is going to bless Taylor's socks off; I hope I get to hear about it when he does. Jesus loves a cheerful giver, and I'm sure he just can't wait to return to Taylor what she has given to him.

Jesus used a fourteen-year-old to bring change to her town. You can honor God by giving your change to bring change too.

Jesus, I want a heart and a hand like Taylor's.
Make me a cheerful giver too! Amen.

I Honor Him

*Pursue righteousness and a godly life, along with faith, love, persever-
ance, and gentleness. Fight the good fight for the true faith.*
—1 Timothy 6:11, 12 (*NLT*)

•••●●•••

Spinning, spinning, spinning. Constantly trying to make everyone happy, I felt like a child's toy top. I was exhausted—just couldn't seem to do it.

Have you ever been there? Your family has planned a family night and your best friend asked you to hang out. You want to go to youth group, but if you do, what if you don't have enough time to get all your homework done? Giving to the missions project at church is pulling on your heart, but then you won't have enough money to buy your sister's birthday present.

I've come to this conclusion: **you can't make everybody happy** all the time. You'll fry yourself trying. What's a girl to do? Rely on Jesus and pursue honoring him—pursue a godly life. He promises that he has started a good work in you and he can complete it (Philippians 1:6). He works in our lives to change us so that our lives are pleasing to him—filled with faith, love, perseverance, and gentleness. That's what we really need to focus on.

START THE REVOLUTION

Take a look at your schedule this week. Consider cancelling some things so you have more time to spend with God.

While you are doing this, you might make some people happy, you might not. Just keep right on living for an audience of one—the one true God. Fight for what is good. Honoring him is what really matters.

Jesus, I don't like it when people are mad at me, but honoring you matters to me more. Help me to trust that you will work into me what pleases you. Amen.

239: What Are We For?

In order that we, who were the first to put our
hope in Christ, might be for the praise of his glory.
—Ephesians 1:11, 12

•••●••

Our purpose is quite simple: to bring Jesus praise. It's not to become famous or successful according to the standards of those around us. It's not getting into the best college that will give us the best opportunities. Our purpose is not about winning state championships or contests.

Our daily purpose is to bring him honor. Period.

We may bring him honor in all those activities, but they are the outcomes, not the goal. When honoring Christ is our goal, some of those things—honors, awards, success, trophies—may come into place, but they are only side benefits. Our purpose is greater, because honoring Jesus has eternal benefits.

START THE REVOLUTION
Read Ephesians 1 and find out about our purpose and God's power.

Jesus, those around me worry about many things—honoring you is not one of them. Burn in me the desire to make honoring you most important. Amen.

I Honor Him

Anyone who has been stealing must steal no longer, but must work, doing something useful with their own hands, that they may have something to share with those in need.

—Ephesians 4:28

•••●●•••

aybe when you read today's verse you thought, *Of course stealing is wrong; I'd never do that.* I am so glad! Because today, **stealing is easier than ever!**

It is so simple to rip off music from your friend's iPod and from the Internet. Pirated movies are everywhere—so much cheaper than paying. There are many who think nothing of stealing time from their employers by texting and surfing the Internet at work. People just don't think that these things are really stealing. It doesn't really hurt anyone, does it?

If you happen to have a friend who feels this way, give her a heads-up. It *is* stealing. When you load music and movies and books you didn't pay for, you're stealing from musicians, artists, and authors, and those who support their families by the work they do. If your friend texts or gets on the Internet at work, she is being unproductive, causing her employer to lose money—the same money the company needs to pay your friend's wages!

Paul's words are pretty clear—whoever has been stealing needs to stop it and be productive with the hands (and the minds) that God has given them.

START THE REVOLUTION

Radical girl, the easy road is boring. Stick to the high road and honor God. The climb will be worth it!

Jesus, help me to always see your perspective on current issues. Your way is the right way, even when it is hard. Amen.

241: Shut It

*Do not let any unwholesome talk come out of your mouths,
but only what is helpful for building others up according
to their needs, that it may benefit those who listen.*
—Ephesians 4:29

••••••

*I*f I thought it, I said it. Really stupid, I know, but I just didn't know any better. I lived by the philosophy that if you have an opinion, you should share it. That was being real, right? Sadly, what I "shared" was judgment and damage a lot of the time; not too God-honoring.

Through some wise advice from a friend, I've been learning to **run my words by God's Word** before I speak, because the best thing might be to just be quiet.

Proverbs 17:28 puts it this way: "Even fools are thought wise when they keep silent; with their mouths shut, they seem intelligent" (*NLT*). We have a greater chance of sinning when we open our mouths than when we keep them shut.

Take it from me: be wise and run your words by God's Word. Don't let anything that is impure or hurtful come out of your mouth. Use your mouth only to build others up and never to tear down.

START THE REVOLUTION
Practice checking your words before you speak— today and every day!

Jesus, I guess I am going to have to slow down and become a person of fewer words if I am going to honor you with my mouth. HELP! Amen.

242: Can't Be Both

He was not aware that his face was radiant
because he had spoken with the LORD.
—Exodus 34:29

••••••

*O*ver break, Janessa had been to camp; she was completely changed! The way she talked, the music she listened to, the movies she watched—none of it was the same! **Just one look, and you could see the difference.**

Someone was not happy about it—her boyfriend! Janessa no longer wanted to do the stuff they used to do. She didn't want to hang around the same people or go to the same places. "You're no fun anymore," he teased her. But he wasn't really teasing—he threatened to break up with her.

I am so proud of Janessa. She's made one wise decision: to become a true disciple of Christ, saying yes to him no matter what. But now she's staring at a truly hard decision: Jesus or her boyfriend? Because it's obvious that, in this situation, it can't be both.

Radical girl, when you are with Jesus, in his presence in worship and in his Word, you are going to change. It's going to show, and that glow is a beautiful thing! But for some people, that light in you is going to be too bright. They won't want you to be different, or to grow. They just want to keep things the way they are. But you can't be both new and old.

START THE REVOLUTION
Check your "friend" list. When you honor God with your relationship decisions, he will honor your obedience.

If this happens to you, don't let anyone dim your light. Trust that whatever you give up for God will be replaced with something so much better. Can I just say, I had to give up more than one relationship, and I am so glad I did! God's best was way better than mine!

I want others to recognize that I have been with you, Jesus. In fact, I can think of nothing more beautiful. Amen.

243: Check Your Progress

Imitate God, therefore, in everything you do, because you are his dear children. Live a life filled with love, following the example of Christ.
—Ephesians 5:1, 2 (*NLT*)

••••••

START THE REVOLUTION
You know you need Jesus. Go after him. Honor him. Be a revolutionary girl.

s we wrap up this section of "His Path for Me," I'll ask you this question: So what's the big deal about honoring and going after God?

As a Jesus follower, you have more at stake than others. When you make good decisions and are wise, you reflect Jesus to your world. Others see the consequences of your choices and make a connection to the fact that you love Jesus.

When you make bad decisions and are unwise, **you reflect Jesus to your world**. Others see the consequences of your choices and make a connection to the fact that you love Jesus.

How are you going to reflect him? What will people think about the love of Jesus that they see in you?

Honor him. When others look at your life, may it compel them to find out who Jesus is, because they've got to have what you've got.

Let's do this thing, Jesus. Amen.

CHAPTER SEVEN

We Protect Together

244: Faith, Not Feelings

The mind governed by the flesh is death,
but the mind governed by the Spirit is life and peace.

—Romans 8:6

•••●••••

*E*verything is suddenly better; you couldn't wipe the smile off your face if you tried. You even physically *feel* different. What is it?

Infatuation. Psychologist David Clarke said, "Infatuation is like a drug." Unfamiliar with the rush of the heartbeat and the adrenaline coursing through your veins, you might be blindsided when it hits and find yourself following whatever path this feeling takes. You're not alone; many girls are taken in by the high that comes from being wanted.

Don't be sucked in. Learn the power that feelings can have over your heart and mind. **Become aware of the warning signs of a crush** and make a decision *before it hits* that you will not give in to unwise choices when your mind isn't thinking straight.

When your emotions are spinning out of control, your best safeguard is to have your mind governed by the Holy Spirit. Each thought that comes into your mind needs to be tested: Is this thought honoring to God? Will it draw me closer to him? If the thought draws you further from him, ask Jesus to remove it from you immediately. Replace this thought with Scripture.

START THE REVOLUTION

Know your warning signs. Ask a friend to describe what you are like when you're crushing.

I know this sounds super weird. Who does this, right? The revolutionary girl—you who are maturing and strong in your faith. You'll not be derailed by every little crush that comes along. You will act according to your faith, not feelings.

I'm not saying that there won't come a time when you do fall for love; there probably will. But when God sends his choice to you one day, if you have been walking with Jesus, you'll know him when he comes.

Jesus, I want to live my life by faith
and not by feelings. Mature me! Amen.

245: Outfits on the Way Out

So whether you eat or drink or whatever you do, do it all for the glory of God. Do not cause anyone to stumble . . . even as I try to please everyone in every way. For I am not seeking my own good but the good of many, so that they may be saved.
—1 Corinthians 10:31-33

•••••••

Mom says, "Too low." You say, "Just fine." She says, "Too short." You say, "Just right." Why so different?

Sometimes, after spending too much time in the mall, I become desensitized. Seeing so many low-cut shirts and short skirts, I forget what appropriate is! I have to regroup and look more closely, or I'm surprised by my own purchases when I get home.

What seems like no big deal to us is a really big deal to guys! Being highly visual, they complete images in their heads. **If we are half-dressed, a guy will finish the picture** in his mind. When you dress immodestly, you can spark an inappropriate image in the head of every guy who sees you—from that guy in chemistry lab to your chemistry teacher, your coach, and even your best friend's dad!

Today's verses remind us that we are to do everything we do for the glory of God. That includes choosing your clothes—whether it's your back-to-school outfit, that wow-factor prom dress, or the swimsuit you had to order from a special catalog and wait six weeks to get. *Everything* is supposed to be for his glory.

Am I saying that next time you go shopping you have to be aware of not only the latest fashion trends, but of Jesus' standards as well? Yep! And you probably need to open those drawers and closet doors and do a little self-assessment too. It was time for a good room-cleaning anyway, right?

START THE REVOLUTION

Make a *What Not to Wear* kind of appointment with a Christian friend. Evaluate each other's wardrobes for God's glory.

Jesus, I think I've got some closet cleaning to do. Be my guide. Amen.

246: Hold Back

Above all else, guard your heart, for everything you do flows from it.
—Proverbs 4:23

•••◉••◦

Probably one of the hardest lessons for the average teenager (girl or guy) to learn is that of restraint. That it's better sometimes to hold a bit back—it's better not to give everything in your heart and mind away at once. When you don't give it all away, interest grows. There's power in holding back, especially in relationships. More important, there's safety in holding back.

I didn't learn this lesson until later. As soon as I had a boy's ear, I would go on and on, spilling all my heart. Hours upon hours on the phone, I couldn't wait for him to know all about me—right now!

No one ever told me: **don't dump all your heart and mind at once**.

The most important job you have is protecting your heart. As the proverb says, "everything you do flows from it." Emotional intimacy can be as dangerous as physical intimacy. When we expose all of our hearts, it leaves us vulnerable. And when our hearts are fully engaged, our bodies often follow.

TV shows about teen life encourage, whether they mean to or not, instant intimacy. Time is squashed in TV land. A girl and guy meet, and after the commercial, all of a sudden they've been dating for three months.

The world doesn't hold back; but remember, you are not of this world. You don't have to divulge all your deepest secrets in order to start a good relationship. It's smart to start slow—develop trust first. Besides that, though this is definitely *not* the main point, holding back is attractive. There's no harm, and a lot of wisdom, in making a guy work a little to know the best of you. Save your secrets for Jesus.

START THE REVOLUTION

Think of yourself as a castle with many rooms. Which rooms do you keep open? Which rooms need to stay locked and guarded?

Jesus, this is sure different from what I see around me! Prick my heart when I need to hold back. Amen.

Obsession with self in these matters is a dead end; attention to God leads us out into the open, into a spacious, free life. Focusing on the self is the opposite of focusing on God. Anyone completely absorbed in self ignores God. . . . And God isn't pleased at being ignored.

—Romans 8:6-8 (*The Message*)

•••◉••

Day and night, night and day—Todd was all she thought about. If she wore this outfit, would he notice? What if she changed her haircut? Why did he like that girl? What didn't he like about her? What was she doing wrong? Did he like loud girls or quiet? Lots of makeup or natural? Did he look at her in lunch today or was he just searching for a friend? Why didn't he talk to her?

> **START THE REVOLUTION**
> What do you spend most of your hours thinking about? Does that need to change?

Anne probably doesn't know she's causing herself a slow death. Using all her creative energy plotting and planning to win Todd, she's dying. Dying to the life that God created her for. Focusing on herself and ignoring the Love that has saved her, she's setting herself up for a great loss. Maybe she'll get what she wants—maybe they'll go out. But **what will she have given up?** Time and energy that could have been spent with an eternal outcome: a relationship that is closer to the Love that is boundless and without limit.

Romans 8:5-8 tells us that those who live according to their sinful nature find a dead end; they don't please God. Like Anne. Her mind is programmed to think continually about Todd and how to manipulate his attention. Not on Jesus.

You need to be smarter than Anne. Protect your heart and mind from getting crushed by another crush. Focus your attention on God. The more you guard your heart and mind and turn your thoughts away from what is not pleasing to him and toward what is, the more you will find yourself doing the things that bring joy to his heart and yours too!

Jesus, controlling my thoughts is the hardest! Help me control them so my heart and actions follow. Amen.

248: Make Up Your Mind

A time to embrace and a time to refrain.
—Ecclesiastes 3:5

• • ● • • •

Early on, I made up my mind. No guy was going to touch or see my under-the-bathing-suit parts until after we said "I do." At thirteen, with no boyfriend, it was a pretty easy commitment to make. In fact, all through middle school and most of high school too, it really wasn't tremendously difficult to stick to my plan:

1. Don't date anyone who isn't a Jesus lover (OK, so *this* was really hard, but once I kept this step, it made the no-sex thing a lot easier). Not just a Christian, but an obvious-by-the-way-he-lives Jesus follower.

2. Kissing only. If he tried more, he'd see me no more.

As long as I stuck to my plan, it was all good. Until I fell in love. I've heard it said, "You can't choose who you fall in love with, so be careful who you date." I followed my plan: he was a Jesus lover. And we were doing pretty well with number 2 for a while—it's just that the more we kissed, the more we wanted to . . . well, you know.

I'm so glad we broke up.

The "real" one came. I knew he was the real one, which made the rest of the waiting easier. If I had waited this long, I wasn't going to give up now! I knew girls who'd had sex with their fiancés and experienced the same negative effects as if they'd given it away to the *wrong* one. Timing is everything. The fact that you two are going to be together *forever* doesn't make it OK to open the gift early.

Make up your mind ahead of time to protect your purity so that, when temptation comes, you can stand firm. You know what you are going to do, and you do it.

Today, no matter what you may have already done, make up your mind that you are going to protect your purity from this day forward, and never look back.

> **START THE REVOLUTION**
>
> Write down your plan. Pull it out and pray for it—especially before going out with that certain guy.

Jesus, I'm making up my mind.
You supply the strength. Amen.

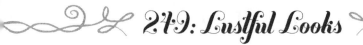

249: Lustful Looks

You have heard that it was said, "You shall not commit adultery."
But I tell you that anyone who looks at a woman lustfully
has already committed adultery with her in his heart.
—Matthew 5:27, 28

The hot August sun beat on the backs of the lacrosse boys as they swung their sticks high in the air. Sitting in my car, waiting for another practice to wrap up, I noticed that they were all shedding their shirts. I also noticed the eyes of every girl that passed by, glued to those boys. I was really glad I wasn't a mind reader.

Jesus makes a powerful statement in today's verse: **we don't have to do the act for it to be sin**. It's sin when we wish for what is not ours. Sin. Just to look and wish a little?

Yeah, sin. Serious sin. Here is just how serious it is. Jesus continues, "If your right eye causes you to stumble, gouge it out and throw it away. It is better for you to lose one part of your body than for your whole body to be thrown into hell" (v. 29). Wow, that's serious.

Dictionary.com says that the word *lust* means "intense sexual desire, uncontrolled sexual desire or a passionate or overmastering desire."

If you find yourself daydreaming of sinful things you *wish* you could do with a guy, Jesus says you've already committed the sin in your heart. You may be a technical virgin, but Jesus says it's not just the body that counts to him; he's looking at your heart as well.

Be careful what you look at. Be careful what you allow your mind to think on. Guard them both: protect your heart and mind.

START THE REVOLUTION
Establish an image in your mind to stop lustful thoughts. Maybe it's your Aunt Ethel or your dentist or Jesus. Just pick something that will work for you.

You took it up a notch today, Jesus. You don't just want me not to sin with my body; you don't want me to sin with my mind either. Keep my thoughts pure. Amen.

250: Label Swap

Flee from sexual immorality. All other sins a person commits are outside the body, but whoever sins sexually, sins against their own body.
—1 Corinthians 6:18

••••••

When the generation before mine was growing up, sex before marriage was called immoral. *If you did it, you hid it.* It was wrong. It was sin. When I was growing up, it was just called sex. Or *it.* Now, it's "friends with benefits," "sleeping with," or "hooking up." Doesn't sound so bad, right? Change the label, and we feel better.

There's this bottle of stuff I use on my furniture. Dab some on, and voilà—scratches are gone. **It's really cool stuff, when used right.** But what if I took the bottle's label off, put on a chocolate syrup label, and put the bottle in the fridge. It wouldn't be so bad to drink it then, right? No way! It's poison![1]

Sex was created by God to give a crazy amount of pleasure with the *one* man who, through marriage, commits to spending the rest of his life with you. If what you're doing with a guy involves parts of your body that should be covered up, it's sexual. It's made for marriage. God wants you to experience sex in the best way possible—you need to trust his boundaries for sex in the same way you trust what he says about love and honesty and friendship . . . and every other good thing he has given us.

START THE REVOLUTION

If this is an area you have trouble with, talk to a trusted Christian adult about it, and ask for help to stay accountable.

It doesn't matter how your friends try to define it. Some might say: "It's not sex! We aren't going all the way!" Wrong! You don't have to go "all the way" to be sexual.

Your body was created for one man one day. If you choose not to wait, you can change the label from "poison" to "chocolate syrup," but it will still eventually hurt you, or even destroy you.

Jesus, give me the desire to honor you in this area—to flee sexual immorality. Amen.

[1] Adapted from a sermon by Christine Caine, given at Elevation Church, 1/12/12.

251: Don't Fret

*Do not fret because of those who are evil
or be envious of those who do wrong.*

—Psalm 37:1

•••••••

*J*ulie looked at other kids who got away with things and wished she could too. When they partied or did stuff with guys, they just seemed to have a great time. She didn't. She couldn't, because she felt guilty. What was wrong with her?

Pastor Jentezen Franklin says those of us who have been raised in Christian homes and have praying parents are **ruined for sin**. Too many prayers have been prayed for us to be able to enjoy life apart from God. It may not seem like that is a good thing, but it really is!

In today's verse, David says we're not to be envious of those who are knee-deep in sin. Why not? They seem to be having such a great time, right? Verse 2 says, "For like the grass they will soon wither, like green plants they will soon die away."

Die away?

Sin ages you; it promises great things, but never pays up. The morning comes, bringing regret for the night before. After the breakup, painful memories are all that's left behind. There just is no coming out ahead when it comes to sin.

Verse 3 instructs us about the way we should choose: "Trust in the LORD and do good."

Simple? Yes. Easy? No, but the more often we make good choices to protect our hearts and minds, the easier the next good choices will be.

START THE REVOLUTION

Instead of feeling envious of others, concentrate on being grateful for the family and the principles you have.

Jesus, it sure looks like those doing what they want are having a great time. I need your strength to choose to do good so that I can truly enjoy life. Amen.

252: Prepare to Protect

Finally, be strong in the Lord and in his mighty power.
Put on the full armor of God, so that you can take your stand
against the devil's schemes.
—Ephesians 6:10, 11

• • ● ● • •

D o you wonder why life is so hard sometimes? Today's verse says it straight up: the devil is scheming against you—making plans to take you out. **You've got to be ready.** You've got to be strong and prepared. Preparing begins with putting on God's protection: his armor.

I love movies that take place during the time of knights and jousting. *Knight's Tale* is one of my favorites. The character William's armor is not strong enough against the knights with modern, expensive protection; his doesn't even fit right! As a result, he gets seriously hurt in a contest.

START THE REVOLUTION

What strategies have helped you deal with temptation in the past?

You can't go about life without having strong spiritual armor that fits you right. One way you get this armor is by knowing what God says in his Word. When you know his Word, it will come to your mind in the heat of a temptation battle, giving you the strength you need to overcome that temptation.

When you have a test coming up, you prepare by going over your notes, memorizing what the book says, and making sure you know the material.

Prepare for the test of your faith the same way. Go over God's notes, memorize what his Word says, and make sure you know his material.

Lord, it sounds a bit freaky to think that
I am in a battle with the devil. I know what
you say is true; please help me prepare. Amen.

Stand firm then, with the belt of truth buckled around your waist,
with the breastplate of righteousness in place.
—Ephesians 6:14

•••●••

"I get so tired of being alone." I've known that feeling; I think many who truly pursue Jesus do. The enemy of our hearts is hoping we will get *so* tired of the battle to serve Jesus, we'll quit. He doesn't want us to stand anymore!

That's why Paul says, "Stand firm then." Stand firm when you feel the weight of fighting against the plans of the devil. Stand firm when it seems no one is standing with you.

He tells us what we need to stand firm. First, there's the belt of truth. **Truth is the belt that holds the rest of you up!** When the enemy tries to whisper lies to you about who you are, what others think of you, or what your future holds, truth holds you up. "I am beautiful" (Song of Solomon 4:7). "I belong to Jesus" (2:16). "He has plans of good and not evil for me" (Jeremiah 29:11). You fight off lies with truth.

Paul also says to have the breastplate of righteousness in place. Righteousness— right standing with God—is a gift that has been given to us, through forgiveness of our sins, by Jesus. When we receive right standing with God through Jesus, our hearts are cleansed. This breastplate, the piece of armor strapped directly to the chest, protects our hearts from the enemy's attempt to damage our relationship with Jesus. The only reason we have this relationship with Jesus is because he first loved us. This right standing, purchased with love, protects our hearts.

START THE REVOLUTION

When you stand firm, you help others not to fall down. Pray for a friend today who needs to be held up with truth.

Knowing I'm in a battle explains why life can be so hard, Jesus. I need you to help me use truth to protect my heart and mind. Amen.

254: Your History, His Story

In addition to all this, take up the shield of faith, with which
you can extinguish all the flaming arrows of the evil one.
—Ephesians 6:16

•••●•••

We've been getting our armor on; preparing for the daily battle with the enemy of our hearts, Satan. Paul says, in addition to the belt of truth and the breastplate of righteousness, take up the shield of faith.

A shield, in Roman times, was placed on a soldier's forearm and was held in front of him during battle. These shields would take the first brunt of the enemy's fire.

I love that faith is our first defense against the enemy's attack. **Faith is the fuel behind our belief** in Jesus and his love for us. Faith empowers us to hope when we can't see what God is doing, and it is the evidence in our lives for what he has already done (see Hebrews 11:1)!

Our faith is personal—it is our story of Jesus' love living in us. Other people may be able to argue about whether they believe Jesus is real or who he says he is, but they can't dispute your story. It's yours.

Your history, his story in your life, is faith that quenches the fiery arrows of the evil one. When the evil one tries to tell you God is not going to come through, you simply recount all of the times that God has been faithful in the past. He can't argue with that!

A knight's shield would also tell who he was; his shield was decorated with his family emblem, crest, or motto. Your shield of faith is decorated too! Right across the front it says, "Beloved of the King of kings"!

START THE REVOLUTION

Design a simple symbol to represent your faith. You could make the symbol into a sticker or a patch for your backpack.

Jesus, thank you for giving me everything I need to
fight the enemy of my heart. Thank you too
that you are always with me! Amen.

We Protect Together

265

255: Guard Your Head

Take the helmet of salvation and the sword of the Spirit,
which is the word of God.
—Ephesians 6:17

••●●••

The first step to taking the helmet of salvation is knowing where our salvation comes from. Through Jesus, we are saved from our sins—we are delivered from the penalty and judgment that we deserve, and are given forgiveness and eternal life instead.

Next, we take the thoughts we have and get rid of any that are not his, replacing them with the sword of the Spirit, his Word.

The mind is our greatest battleground. The devil fights hard, using his minions to place all types of thoughts against us and our God, causing us to think that these thoughts are our own! Thoughts against our self-worth: thoughts of fear, worry, confusion. He'll use any thought that is in opposition to God's Word.

Ephesians 6 says that on one arm you have the shield of faith. This is your defense against Satan's arrows. In the other hand, you have the sword of the Spirit, your weapon of offense. The sword of the Spirit, which is the Word of God, is what you will attack the enemy with, if necessary. Jesus demonstrated how to do this.

Read Matthew 4:1-11. Notice how each time the devil came after him, Jesus used God's Word to back him off. He didn't mess around with the enemy; he just gave him the truth. Radical girl, **to use God's Word, you have to know God's Word** for yourself. You can't rely on this book or your pastor, small group leader, or mom. It's not enough! When you are in the middle of a battle, they might not be there. But if you know God's Word for yourself, it will be just what you need to fight and win!

START THE REVOLUTION
What methods do you use to memorize facts for classes in school? Apply those same methods to memorizing the Bible as well.

Jesus, today I will teach myself to use the sword,
your Word, to fight the enemy in my mind. Amen.

256: Be Alert

And pray in the Spirit on all occasions with all kinds
of prayers and requests. With this in mind, be alert
and always keep on praying for all the Lord's people.
—Ephesians 6:18

••●●•••

When do you pray? Before you go to bed? Before your supper? When does God tell us to pray? All the time! "On all occasions with all kinds of prayers and requests . . . always keep on praying." Wow, that sure is different than a few lines once a day, right?

What's the big deal? Why pray so much and in so many different ways?

This verse follows up all the verses we have been reading about protecting our hearts and minds with the armor of God. **Prayer is part of our defense and offense.**

Paul told the followers of Jesus to pray on all occasions: times when we are excited, sad, happy, ticked, ecstatic, frustrated.

He says we are to pray all kinds of prayers. Prayers of petition are when we ask for things. Prayers of thanksgiving simply express our gratitude. Prayers of lament are when we cry out to God, brokenhearted. David prayed these types of prayers in the book of Psalms, and so did Job. Prayers of intercession are prayers for others.

All these kinds of prayer are ways of communicating with God, which brings us closer to God.

Paul says we are to be alert—on guard for the scheming plans of the enemy. When a person is alert, she is not caught off guard; she is not surprised. An alert girl is a girl who is serious about protecting her heart and mind. The enemy is not going to catch her unaware.

START THE REVOLUTION

Today, pray one-line prayers throughout the day. Talking to him all day keeps you connected, helping you be protected and aware.

Jesus, please remind me today
to talk to you all day long. Amen.

257: His-Appointment

How great is the goodness you have stored up for those who fear you.
You lavish it on those who come to you for protection,
blessing them before the watching world.
—Psalm 31:19 (*NLT*)

••●●••

isappointment. What a struggle for me, when I'm steeped in expectation. Missionary Todd Guckenberger recently told me, "Expectation is premeditated resentment." That smarted!

No one wants to be disappointed. Programmed to believe we can be and do anything and all our dreams will come true, we're stunned if they don't. But Jesus said, "In this world you will have trouble. But take heart! I have overcome the world" (John 16:33).

START THE REVOLUTION
Think of some appointments you've had with God lately.

You're going to get cut from the team. You're not going to get an invitation to that party. The lead part will be given to someone else, and that boy will not ask you to prom. When these things happen, are we being ripped off and treated unfairly? Or do we really believe that God is in control of everything?

How do we protect our hearts from resentment? from becoming angry with God? We see our situation not as a disappointment but as his-appointment.

Yesterday, vacation plans fell through, things broke, and friends let me down. Thankfully, the Lord helped me handle it well then, but today, the bummed-out feelings came with a vengeance. Then I read Psalm 31:19. **The Love who gives to me is the same Love who keeps from me.** He is good, and he prepares goodness for me when I trust him. I can trust his protection and partner with it.

Each day is a new day to see my world as his-appointments and not disappointments. Why didn't I make the team or get the lead? Maybe I struggle with pride. Why wasn't I invited to the party? Maybe God has other friends for my good.

The Love who gives to me is the same Love who keeps from me.

Jesus, I love that I can trust you. Help me not to feel disappointment, but to see your appointment. Amen.

258: Devil's Next Meal

Therefore Jesus said again, "Very truly I tell you,
I am the gate for the sheep."
—John 10:7

••●●●••

My dog's name is Oreo, but it could be Houdini the Magician Dog. I lock our gate, put a rope around the top too! It doesn't work. Oreo's desire to escape compels her to find new ways out.

Oreo doesn't know I keep her in our backyard for safety. Is she a bad dog—doing rotten stuff when she gets away? No! I keep her safe because she's been picked up by the dogcatcher, and if she's picked up again, she won't return home.

I wish Oreo knew why I want her safe—that I don't want her caught by the "enemy."

Jesus says he's the gate for the sheep. That's us. A shepherd in those times would make a makeshift pen for his sheep by building a rock wall around his flock. Then at night he would lay his body across the only entrance to the pen, keeping harm—bears, lions, and wolves—out and sheep in.

Like Oreo, sometimes we're just plain dumb! We think that Jesus' rules are holding us back. **We want to experience everything beyond the yard**—what others say is fun. We believe the lies and fail to trust the love of the Shepherd. But God's Word says the enemy is a roaring lion looking for someone to devour (1 Peter 5:8). That someone is you!

Be wise. Don't become the devil's snack. Embrace God's protection; avoid damage just beyond the gate of his love.

START THE REVOLUTION

What does it mean to you that Jesus laid down his life for you so you could be protected from the enemy?

Shepherd, I don't want to be dumb and be the devil's next meal. Your gate is your love. Empower me to choose to stay in your protection. Amen.

259: Using Discretion

Discretion will protect you, and understanding will guard you.
—Proverbs 2:11

•••••••

If someone told you today, "You're getting ready to make a really bad decision, one you'll regret for years, but I can help you." Would you listen? That's exactly what Solomon is telling us in Proverbs 2:11-13 (*The Message*). He says: "Good Sense will scout ahead for danger, Insight will keep an eye out for you. They'll keep you from making wrong turns, or following the bad directions of those who are lost themselves."

Discretion is the power to make decisions with your own judgment. That's power! You aren't relying on someone else, someone who may or may not have your best interests in mind. Discretion doesn't come from friends who are making dumb decisions; discretion comes from the wisdom of a God who knows everything.

And what about understanding? How does it guard you? The girl who understands the choices in front of her also gets the consequences of those decisions.

You have a choice: smoke pot or stay sober? Discretion says: What's wise? What does God's Word say about my body? It is the temple of the Holy Spirit; God lives inside me. Understanding says: Drinking may alter my personality, cause me to hide my actions, and take away my motivation. **Is that the turn I want to take?**

What is the area you're having trouble with right now? Internet abuse? Boys? Honesty, fear, or worry? An eating disorder or cutting?

START THE REVOLUTION

Do you have a group of people you trust to talk with about the choices you make? How do you hold each other accountable?

Use wise judgment from God's Word. Understand the consequences of your steps. Plan how to escape. Put boundaries in place. Tell an adult who can help you. Don't delay; don't be too late. Let discretion and understanding protect you now!

Jesus, protecting my life is an all-consuming task. Reveal to me the best plan to protect the life you have given me, and empower me to follow that plan. Amen.

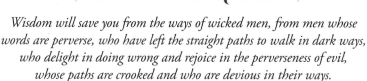

Wisdom will save you from the ways of wicked men, from men whose words are perverse, who have left the straight paths to walk in dark ways, who delight in doing wrong and rejoice in the perverseness of evil, whose paths are crooked and who are devious in their ways.

—Proverbs 2:12-15

I travel a lot, doing Revolutionary Love conferences all over the country. Most times, I'm in a city I've never been before, so before I go, I get directions from a source I trust. Directions from the airport to the hotel, from the hotel to the event. I'm prepared, because the worst possible time to find out something doesn't work is when it doesn't work.

The worst time to find you're not where you want to be is when you have no way to get out.

Wisdom looks ahead. The smart girl anticipates what could happen and asks, "Where will this path take me? What's happened to others who have taken it?" She asks herself the hard questions and makes the hard decisions. She checks her sources of information and doesn't blindly follow a crowd, especially a crowd whose path is crooked.

Have you found yourself in situations lately you know you shouldn't be in? Have you followed people who love God or people who love doing wrong? Protect yourself. Make plans ahead of time with girls who do make wise choices. Make a change.

Have you been getting caught up in gossip in the locker room before practice? Pick a new spot to get dressed. Have you been sleeping in late and getting in an argument with your mom? Move your alarm clock across the room; get up to shut it off.

Wisdom plans ahead to protect herself. Wisdom will save you from going down a path to nowhere.

START THE REVOLUTION

Are you a planner or a procrastinator? Be honest with yourself and take steps to keep out of temptation's way.

Planning ahead takes work, Jesus. Teach me to care enough about myself to do the hard stuff. Amen.

We Protect Together

261: Don't Fool Yourself

*The prudent understand where they are going,
but fools deceive themselves.*
—Proverbs 14:8 (*NLT*)

•••●••

At our high school, the police are going through the parking lot for the next month, checking for unlocked cars. It's not like it's against the law to leave your car unlocked. Students have a right to not lock their cars if they want to, right? Are the police infringing on privacy?

Not at all. By having random checks, police are reinforcing the best way to avoid theft—lock your car! Locking your car keeps stuff from getting ripped off. You take your valuables with you or hide them from onlookers and lock your car. **You make a plan, then work the plan.** This plan keeps what's yours, yours!

START THE REVOLUTION

In what areas do you need to make a plan and then work your plan? Do it today.

If you just listen to the police talk about the plan, but don't do it, the plan won't protect you. If you make a plan but then don't do the plan, the plan is worthless. You have to make a plan and carry it out.

So what's your plan to protect yourself from being used by a guy? First, plan to never be alone with a guy. It's harder for a guy to make moves on you when you're surrounded by people. Second, surround yourself with people who are like you, who want to live right. You won't find yourself bombarded with as much temptation when you hang around those who want to please Jesus.

Jesus, it seems weird that I can't just live my life, taking on what comes when it comes. But I don't want to be a fool. Help me to make good plans. Amen.

262: Barricades or Boundaries

What shall we do for our sister on the day she is spoken for?
If she is a wall, we will build towers of silver on her.
If she is a door, we will enclose her with panels of cedar.
—Song of Solomon 8:8, 9

••●●●••

God's Word is so interesting—woven with stories explaining the richness of our relationship with him. In Song of Solomon 8:8, 9, the picture is painted of a woman, the beloved, surrounded by a family who had definite plans to prepare for her marriage—on "the day she is spoken for." If she displayed good character, making good decisions and resisting temptation, her protectors would allow her a large measure of freedom and reward her. That's what is meant by "if she is a wall"—if she protected herself. The reward referred to as towers of silver could be an expensive head ornament, like a crown.

START THE REVOLUTION

Mind your boundaries— do you know where your lines are drawn?

Just as her virginity and purity were valuable, her reward would be valuable too![2]

But if she was unwise, made poor decisions and gave in to temptations, especially relating to men (she's a door—lets anything in), they would restrict her freedom (enclosing her with cedar panels). Think of the way people board their houses shut when a hurricane is coming; they do all they can to keep the storm out.

Needing more boundaries or less all had to do with how she conducted herself. If she was constantly drawing a man's attention, she needed more. On the other hand, if she was modest, friendly but not flirty, and confident in who she was as a child of God, she could have more freedom. She would have demonstrated maturity.

Barricades needed or boundaries already in place? Which describes you?

Jesus, give me the wisdom and power I need
to set my own boundaries in place,
for my sake and your glory. Amen.

[2] Explanation of verses from J. F. Walvoord, R. B. Zuck & Dallas Theological Seminary, *The Bible Knowledge Commentary* (Wheaton, IL: Victor Books, 1983)

263: Purity and Contentment

I am a wall, and my breasts are like towers.
Thus I have become in his eyes like one bringing contentment.
—Song of Solomon 8:10

••●●●••

Barricades needed or boundaries in place? The beloved answers: "I am a wall." She is keeping her life pure, her boundaries are in place where they should be. Though her brothers love her and are ready to jump to protect her, she doesn't need extra restrictions from her family. She is protecting herself by her own choice.

What a huge relief this girl is to her friends and family! **When she goes out on Friday night, they don't have to worry.** She's demonstrated she cares about herself and knows her worth, that she is making wise choices to protect her life for her own sake.

The second part of this verse describes her reward. Having grown up and matured not just physically but spiritually as well, she's ready to experience the joy that comes from having a husband. She has waited to share her body and heart with one man, and it brings them both pleasure and happiness.

You were designed to bring contentment and pleasure to you and your husband one day. The revolutionary girl knows what she is protecting herself for and why she is doing it. And she follows through on her promises to her friends, her family, and her God.

START THE REVOLUTION
Does your family worry about you when you go out, or do they trust you? If you don't know for sure, why not ask them?

Lord, I want to protect me for me. Grow this desire in my heart, giving me strength and wisdom to wait for your best. Amen.

264: Be Careful

So be careful how you live. Don't live like fools, but like those who are wise. Make the most of every opportunity in these evil days.
—Ephesians 5:15, 16 (*NLT*)

• •●●●• •

A brand-new pair of white Ugg boots is probably not the smartest fashion choice for a football game, but boy was she careful! When someone passed her in the stands, she tucked her feet under the bleachers to protect her boots. If someone was carrying a drink nearby, she asked them to be careful; she didn't want a stain. Whatever it took, she did her best to keep those boots clean.

START THE REVOLUTION

Be aware today; see each decision as important.

Your heart is a lot more valuable than a pair of Ugg's, but take a tip from the girl: **no matter what it costs**, protect and keep a pure heart. Be careful. Be very careful. Don't be a fool. Be wise.

A wise girl doesn't live carelessly. Paul went on to say in his letter to the Ephesians (v. 17): "Don't act thoughtlessly, but understand what the Lord wants you to do." Constantly aware of her surroundings, the revolutionary girl doesn't allow herself to get pulled into compromising situations. She isn't naive either. Understanding that the enemy is always against her, she doesn't walk blindly into his traps of temptation to sin. Although her heart may beg her to overlook "small" indiscretions, she doesn't give in. No matter how big or small the decision, she makes each a wise one, knowing that all decisions affect her relationship with Christ. She is always seeking to do what God wants her to do.

The radical girl thinks through her steps because she knows every opportunity counts.

Lord, often I do things without thinking. Let's make that change. Speak to me each time I am making a choice and teach me to be careful and wise. Amen.

265: He Can't Make You Do It

No test or temptation that comes your way is beyond the course of what others have had to face. All you need to remember is that God will never let you down; he'll never let you be pushed past your limit; he'll always be there to help you come through it.
—1 Corinthians 10:13 (*The Message*)

•••●•••

*T*he devil made me do it. When I was a kid, this saying was plastered on T-shirts with a little, red, horned creature on the front. I never thought too much about it at the time, but that saying is completely ridiculous. The devil can't make you do anything. In fact, he can't tempt you to the point where you can't resist. Jesus says he won't allow it.

The temptations you and I face are the same temptations humans have dealt with since the beginning of time. Take jealousy. The very first set of brothers struggled with jealousy, to the point where Cain killed Abel. He could have resisted. If Cain would have humbled himself and confessed his sin, God would have given him all the power he needed to put down the green-eyed monster. But that wasn't the choice he made. When his emotional volcano began to boil, he allowed it to erupt.

Emotions are powerful. They can push us up to the very brink of sin, which is why we have to protect our hearts so carefully. At the first sign of temptation, run. When you first sense your heart is being pulled down a wrong path, cry out to Jesus. Turn your thoughts to all you have in him. Make your heart obey, even if you don't feel like it. You can do this. You don't have to allow sin to rule. This is when the confident girl discovers where her confidence comes from—from God's power and love.

START THE REVOLUTION

When was the last time you felt God helping you to face temptation?

God, when I face temptation on my own, I get worn out. Teach me to allow your power to give me the strength I need, not just to resist temptation, but to become more like you. Amen.

266: Doesn't Fit

But among you there must not be even a hint of
sexual immorality, or of any kind of impurity, or of greed,
because these are improper for God's holy people.
—Ephesians 5:3

•••●••

They just don't fit. Your dad won't bring the lawn mower into the house. Your youth pastor doesn't criticize your performance on the soccer field. A friend doesn't wear a swimsuit to a job interview at the day-care center.

They don't fit together.

Neither do the revolutionary girl and impurity.

The girl who has been radically changed by the love of Jesus doesn't tolerate sin in her life—not greed, not sexual sin, no known sin—because it doesn't fit.

What does fit is a heart that seeks to honor God and to get rid of even the slightest hint of sin. She doesn't want anything to come between her and her relationship with Jesus.

You won't get it right every time. Some days you'll slip and act in a way that is not fitting for a girl who is madly in love with Jesus. Don't beat yourself up. Don't let stinky thinking take control: "I've gone this far. I've messed up this bad, so I might as well keep going." That's not true! Jesus can forgive. He'll cleanse your heart. Then you can begin again, making choices that fit with a heart renewed in the strength that comes from God—the strength you need to protect yourself from impurity.

START THE REVOLUTION
What doesn't fit in your life today? Confess it as sin, asking the Lord to remove it.

God, forgive me for allowing _____ in my life. It doesn't fit who I am in you. Set me free to obey and protect in every area of my life. Amen.

We Protect Together

All of us also lived among them at one time, gratifying the
cravings of our flesh and following its desires and thoughts.
Like the rest, we were by nature deserving of wrath.

—Ephesians 2:3

••●•●••

*D*ressing inappropriately is a selfish decision. When we do this, we put guys in a place where they have to fight not to think wrong thoughts. It's also selfish because it's an effort to draw attention to ourselves, taking the limelight away from others.

When we are so full of the awareness of Jesus' love for us, we will not feel this need to be in the limelight. As girls who are loved by a God who loves perfectly and unconditionally, we need to desire his attention and his praise.

This thinking is really radical. Girls are known for being attention seekers. The world places a lot of pressure on girls to groom themselves to gain more attention, not less.

More attention = more value.

But this equation doesn't hold true for the girl revolutionized by love. She knows what Jesus says: "All those who exalt themselves will be humbled, and those who humble themselves will be exalted" (Luke 18:14).

Sometimes though, we need reminders to help us with this; it so goes against our culture. I've got just the trick! Pop over to my website at www.LynnCowell.com and click on "freebies." There you will find a closet card reminder! You can download this handy door hanger and place it on your door. Each time you see it, ask yourself: "Am I protecting guys with my choice today?"

> **START THE REVOLUTION**
> Get your closet card and make a good choice today.

Jesus, your standard is high because your standard is true love. Teach me to love the way you do and protect myself and the guys. Amen.

266: Temptation Test

Jesus answered him, "It is also written:
'Do not put the Lord your God to the test.'"
—Matthew 4:7

••●●●••

"It will be all right; Brenda is with me." My sophomore year I was the new girl at Cedar Falls High School. Well, not completely new. I had gone to elementary school with most of the kids. Since returning to public school after going to a private school for junior high, I was desperate to find my place.

One night, I was so fearful and uptight, having never been to a real party before. I thought to myself, *I'll be OK. Brenda doesn't drink either. Together we'll be fine.*

Once I got there, I was anything but fine! Of course, there were no parents in sight. The drinking terrified me. *What if the police come? What if someone offers me a drink? What if I fail?* I knew I had to leave—immediately.

I was one stupid girl that night. I knew what was going to be happening there. I was testing God and my faith. Not smart.

I passed that night. The lesson I learned was more than the fact that I could pass up drinking. I learned to never put myself in that position again.

Did I earn a reputation that night? Definitely. For the rest of high school, Bren and I were labeled Jesus Freaks. It's a label we wore proudly then and still do today!

START THE REVOLUTION

Don't give yourself a temptation test! Protect yourself and turn away from temptation before it ever starts.

Jesus, sometimes I don't know temptation is coming, but often, if I am really honest, I do. Help me to make the decision to protect before temptation even comes. Amen.

We Protect Together

269: Conquerors

No, in all these things we are more than conquerors through him who loved us.
—Romans 8:37

••••••••

What will be the thing that compels us to get through this life, winning the daily battles of protecting the heart and mind God has given us? Paul says in our verse for today that it is "through him who loved us."

Jesus, the one who loves us deeply, will give us the power and strength to not give up. He will be the one who daily gives us the hope that our wise decisions will lead us to peace, joy, and his best—instead of to shame, sadness, and a life of regret.

In order to be a conqueror, you have to position yourself in a place to conquer. The girl who continually allows herself to be in compromising situations can't hope not to compromise. Jesus will strengthen you, but you must do all you can to avoid circumstances that pull you into sin.

Don't fool yourself. Many girls think they can have it all: **popularity and purity**. Don't be deceived. If you continually hang out with those who are doing wrong, you'll eventually get a crack in your shield. And that's not good for a conqueror. We're all human; we are all weak and frail on our own.

Follow Jesus' path and find the peace and joy and victory you long for.

START THE REVOLUTION

Read Romans 8 and find out what "all these things" are that Paul is referring to.

Jesus, my heart lies to me. It tells me I can have it all when that simply isn't true. May I be true to you. Amen.

270: Find a Friend

The righteous choose their friends carefully,
but the way of the wicked leads them astray.
—Proverbs 12:26

•••●●•••

"*I* feel so alone. Everybody is smoking weed and having sex—everybody! It's all they ever talk about at lunch, along with what party they went to and who they did what with. It just makes me wonder what I'm missing."

I've been where Mary's been. Sometimes when you're making choices to protect your mind, heart, and body, it feels like you're the only one.

But everyone *isn't* doing it!

According to SADD, Students Against Drunk Driving, 46 percent of high school students have sexual intercourse (http://sadd.org/stats.htm). That's less than half! Yes, it may be very hard to find another girl who believes like you. The question is, do you really want to find her? Have you been seeking her out?

START THE REVOLUTION
Get real. Who's influencing you? Who are you influencing? Protect your heart.

A huge part of protecting yourself is choosing carefully your traveling buddies in life. You have got to find a friend who also wants to protect her mind, heart, and body. Without her, it may be a long and lonely road, and a lot harder to stay on the right path. Pray and ask Jesus to bring into your life another girl who loves him like you, and then hold tight to each other!

Lord, I know I need to choose my friends carefully, because I will become like those I hang around with. Help me choose wisely. Amen.

271: Safety

So I say to you: Ask and it will be given to you;
seek and you will find; knock and the door will be opened to you.
—Luke 11:9

• • • • • •

Relationships with guys terrify Casey. As a little girl, she was sexually abused, so she really doesn't want anything to do with guys now. Though she is well on her way to being healed, she still has a cautious heart that says "What if?" What if the relationship appears safe, but really it's not?

So Casey takes steps, maybe not on purpose, but subconsciously, to protect herself. She avoids guys; she just doesn't trust them. **Fear keeps her world very small**—she hopes it's small enough to keep her from getting hurt again.

Is this God's best for Casey? Shutting herself off from others and missing friendships? It doesn't seem like it to me. If Casey will just take that first step, asking Jesus to help her be brave and reach out to meet new people, he will be there for her. She needs to know that he will protect her, but she won't know that until she takes that step of faith. "Ask and it will be given to you."

Do you know a Casey? Are you a Casey? Share your pain with a trusted adult. Ask Jesus for the courage to find friends who will support and love you.

START THE REVOLUTION

When you see someone who is hurting or afraid, ask God for the courage to reach out to her. You never know what hope you might bring.

Jesus, relationships can be so scary. Guide me and help me to recognize safe ones. Amen.

272: If Only or You Wholly?

Again, the devil took him to a very high mountain and showed him all the kingdoms of the world and their splendor.
—Matthew 4:8

•••●•••

"If only I had_____, then I'd be happy." How would you fill in your blank? Maybe it's this: If only I had a tight family where everything goes right and nothing goes wrong. There's nothing wrong with wanting that, right?

Actually, there is. When I focus on what I *don't* have, it makes me discontented and ungrateful for what I do have. This kind of wanting in my heart dishonors God.

Satan came to Jesus with **the temptation to have it all**. He does the same with us. Boyfriends, great grades, and the newest electronics. A great college, a new car, and a wonderful career. A handsome husband, a big house, and the latest fashions. In each season of life, it is the same—we're never satisfied. Once we get what we want, we move on to something different. Bigger. Better.

A discontented heart dishonors God because it is not looking wholly to him to become full. We need to look to him for contentment. We need to protect our hearts from ingratitude.

Make a deliberate attempt to turn your heart and mind toward the one who loves you.

> **START THE REVOLUTION**
> When you think "If only," turn to Jesus. Say "In you wholly, I have all I need."

Jesus, when I have an "if only" thought, I will turn to you wholly. Amen.

273: Beware

*Now the serpent was more crafty than any of the wild animals
the LORD God had made. He said to the woman,
"Did God really say, 'You must not eat from any tree in the garden'?"*
—Genesis 3:1

•••●••

START THE REVOLUTION
Practice your listening skills today. What messages are you picking up?

here are qualities that are great to be known for. Kindness to others. Being a loyal friend. Having a great throwing arm. Then there are *other* qualities—things that should alert you to avoid people's company.

Today's verse tells us, "Now the serpent was more crafty . . . " No, it wasn't super-skilled with a glue gun. It was crafty as in skillful in underhanded and evil schemes—not the type of creature a wise girl should be around.

Now, Eve at this point did not know about good and evil, so she maybe didn't know about this creature's particular skill. However, there was a moment when she should have recognized something was wrong. A few words that were out of place. **A truth that was twisted.** "Did God really say, 'You must not eat from *any* tree'?"

The serpent had it wrong. That should have been Eve's first clue. One of the best ways to protect your heart, mind, body, *and reputation* is to pay close attention to the words people say, and what those words say about them. Eve should never have kept talking with the serpent. But certainly, once this creature actually suggested she disobey her Creator, she should have run as far and as fast as she could.

When a girl engages in a conversation with a deceiver, it's hard to come out the winner. Whether it's a guy who wants to date you ("I'm really not that bad"), some friends who want to party ("Don't act so serious all the time!"), or the Enemy whispering to your heart ("You aren't good enough")—the girl who engages in these conversations opens the door to destruction. Don't engage; protect your heart. Just because someone speaks to you, it doesn't mean you have to talk back.

God, I'm afraid of being thought of as a wimp. Help me to only care about what you think of me. Amen.

274: Honor over Dishonor

*Honor your father and your mother, so that you may live
long in the land the LORD your God is giving you.*
—Exodus 20:12

"My parents are so dumb! For the past six months,
every time I've told them where I am, I'm not
even there." I couldn't help overhearing this girl as she let all
her friends know she really had her parents fooled.

Who really is the dumb one? Her parents for
trusting her, or is she dumb for choosing to dishonor
them? According to today's verse, it sounds like she's
not that bright—or else maybe she just doesn't want to
be around that long.

The revolutionary girl will avoid dishonoring her parents
because she wants to be blessed with their protection. She
wants the promise that goes with honor.

Whether you live with your birth parents, foster parents, adoptive parents, grandparents, or guardians of
some other sort—the people who care for you and feed
you and clothe you every day are also the people who know quite a lot about protecting you. And if you deceive them, you're only making their job harder. Seriously, do
you really think it's smart for the people who look out for you the most not to know
where you are or what you're doing? It may seem like a pain to be honest and open
with your mom and dad, but the alternative could be a LOT more harmful.

So next time your brain says, "They have no idea what they are talking about!"
speak back to yourself: "I will honor my father and/or mother." If your friend says,
"Why do you always tell your mom everything?" you can say, "I honor my mother."

You want to stick around a while? Increase your odds; take hold of God's promise.
Honor your mom and dad with the truth.

**START THE
REVOLUTION**
When disre-
spect is cool, be
hot for Jesus:
choose honor
over dishonor. Is
there anything
you need to
reveal to your
parents today?

*Jesus, help me to catch each dishonoring thought and
stop it from growing. I need humility, Lord. Amen.*

We Protect Together

285

A heart at peace gives life to the body, but envy rots the bones.
—Proverbs 14:30

•••◉••

She had always been happy with whatever her parents were able to give her. That is, before Lacey moved to a bigger city. Now, she felt she *needed* the manicures, bags, and shoes all the other girls had. She had to have them. She'd stick out if she didn't! Her mom informed her it just wasn't in the budget; her family didn't make that kind of money. Lacey was mad and embarrassed. If she could just have the fashion—or the family—the other girls had, she knew she would be really happy!

I feel sorry for Lacey. She's got a lot going for her. She's a talented artist, and her heart is so kind. And up to this point, she'd really enjoyed life. But now I see that slipping away. I see her losing her carefree self to envy.

Today's verse tells us envy rots the bones. How gross! But that is what envy does! It ruins us all the way to the core of who we are. Once we give in to envy, there is never enough. You can't buy enough clothes, lose enough weight, or get enough friends to satisfy envy. **There is only one word in envy's vocabulary:** *more*.

Check your heart. Have you protected your heart and chosen a life of peaceful contentment? Or is envy rotting your bones? It's not too late for a bone transplant! Ask Jesus to forgive you for your sin of discontentment that's leading to envy.

START THE REVOLUTION

There's nothing like a good dose of reality to cure a bout of envy. Take a good look at the people you want to be like. Does all their stuff really make them happy?

Jesus, envy makes me miserable. Help me to spot it immediately when it tries to creep into my heart. Amen.

276: Before

At this, the administrators and the satraps tried to find grounds
for charges against Daniel in his conduct of government affairs,
but they were unable to do so. They could find no corruption in him,
because he was trustworthy and neither corrupt nor negligent.
—Daniel 6:4

•••••••

ick and tired of Daniel being King Darius's favorite, the other dudes on the king's staff began scheming to find a way to get him fired. There was one major problem: they couldn't catch him doing anything wrong! In everything Daniel did, he was trustworthy; he had the king's back. He was never dishonest or lazy. Daniel knew what he needed to do, and he did it. Since he was careful to do what he was supposed to, the government guys had no ammunition to take him out. They had to create a situation instead.

START THE REVOLUTION
If you don't have a regular routine in place for feeding on God's Word, plan one out today. Then make up your mind to stick to it.

Daniel knew he was being trapped, so he protected himself the best way he knew how: "Three times a day he got down on his knees and prayed, giving thanks to his God *just as he had done before*" (Daniel 6:10, emphasis added).

The time to start protecting your heart is not when trouble begins, but way before it starts. Daniel was already in the practice of praying and giving thanks to God. He already had **a history of relying on God** and asking for help; this was just another chance to see his God be faithful.

The time for you to prepare for temptation in your life is not when you are in the middle of it; it is way before. You have to make up your mind that you are going to honor God. This is the best protection you can get.

Jesus, I need to prepare for temptation by praying and reading your Word. Please remind me to walk away from my computer, phone, and TV, and get on my knees like Daniel. Amen.

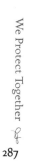

277: Listen to the Spirit

*Now the one who has fashioned us for this very purpose is God,
who has given us the Spirit as a deposit, guaranteeing what is to come.*
—2 Corinthians 5:5

•••●•••

She felt it in her spirit: "Say no and tell them you'll just go home." Just as if he were standing next to her, speaking to her, Carley knew the Holy Spirit was giving her the guidance she needed, as temptation glared in her face. She hadn't anticipated she would find herself in this situation; she simply said yes to spending the night with a friend. Yet, even if she hadn't known it was coming, the Holy Spirit had.

The Holy Spirit was sent to us as **God's gift to us**. Jesus sent him from Heaven to teach and remind us of his teachings after he was gone.

Your job is to be sensitive to his voice. The more you protect your heart through obeying his voice, the more often you will hear him speak. He has your best interests in mind every time. Listen and obey!

START THE REVOLUTION

When you hear a direction in your heart and it lines up with God's Word, follow it— every time!

Holy Spirit, make me sensitive to your voice no matter where I am: at school, playing sports, or hanging out with friends. Help me to listen and obey! Amen.

278: Rule

If you do what is right, will you not be accepted?
But if you do not do what is right, sin is crouching at your door;
it desires to have you, but you must rule over it.

—Genesis 4:7

•••●••

She kept telling herself it was wrong; she had to stop. Each time he called her, though, she said yes. Having him want her made Marley feel so good, she just couldn't say no. What is it with sin that drags us in, even when we know it's wrong? Cookies every day, smoking weed, copying homework—all of it is bad for us. Bad for our health, our brains, our future. Yet we keep going back, again and again and again.

I like what Kelly once told me, "I know me. I know that I just can't even try some things once, because I am the type that will want it again and again."

Kelly is one wise girl. She may not know what it says in Genesis 4:7, but she knows that **the best way to protect your heart is to never start**. "If you do not do what is right, sin is crouching at your door; it desires to have you, but you must rule over it."

Crouching. I picture a starving lion, hiding in the African grasses, preying on an unsuspecting deer.

Sin. I picture a worldly-wise upperclassman, checking out new freshman girls, looking for one who appears extra eager to be accepted. As the girl makes her way through the crowd, looking for new friends, she suddenly finds herself the object of his affection, and so much more.

START THE REVOLUTION

Rule over your heart and rule over sin. Radical girl, you rule!

I have watched this exact scenario more times than I wish. Sin is longing, just waiting for an opportunity to pull you into its grasp, radical girl. Don't let your guard down. The best way to protect your heart is never to start. You must rule over it; don't let it rule over you.

Jesus, I know I am vulnerable. Every human is. Give me the strength to protect my heart and never start in the areas where sin is just outside my door. Amen.

279: Revolutionary or Ordinary?

Turn my eyes away from worthless things;
preserve my life according to your word.
—Psalm 119:37

••●●●••

*P*am's favorite time-waster is the game Angry Birds. Kathleen loves *Glee* reruns. Most everyone has something they love to do that is worthless, not good for anything. We think that it's no big deal. Apparently, that's not true!

In Psalm 119, David has been contemplating what he needs:

- Teach me to follow you.
- Give me understanding.
- Direct my paths.
- Turn my heart not toward my selfish ways.

Then . . . "turn my eyes away from worthless things." This little request is a big deal. If we will turn our eyes from worthless things—time-wasters, mindless activities, junk food for the heart and mind—we will leap instead of walk forward in our relationship with God. To choose to spend time only on people and things of value according to God's standards takes maturity and catapults us in our pursuit of protecting our hearts and becoming more like God.

Every one of us has the same twenty-four hours to spend; no one has more, no one has less. What you do with those hours shows what kind of girl you are and determines what kind of girl you will be. Revolutionary or ordinary? What girl are you?

START THE REVOLUTION

Keep a tally of hours you spend on activities in one typical week. How many are spent on worthless pursuits?

Jesus, I want to be revolutionary. Help me to recognize when I am wasting my mind and my time by looking at worthless things. Amen.

280: The Cost

*Again, the kingdom of heaven is like a merchant looking
for fine pearls. When he found one of great value,
he went away and sold everything he had and bought it.*
—Matthew 13:45, 46

•••●●••

*L*ike the merchant in the Bible, I sold everything I had to buy it—God's best for me in the choice of a guy and in my sex life. It wasn't cheap.

I had to give up being a part of the really popular crowd. Think about the popular kids you know. Are they protecting their purity or doing the opposite? I don't have to tell you that in most high schools in this country, it's not popular to wait until marriage. I'm not saying that, if you wait, you won't have friends or school will stink. I am saying waiting is not popular, and chances are, you might not be either if you make up your mind to go after the best.

START THE REVOLUTION
What would you sell to get God's best for your life?

What did I gain? True friends who really loved me for me. Friends who valued the same thing I did and helped me to follow Jesus with them.

I had to give up dating guys who were not Jesus followers. This was the most expensive thing I gave up; the guys who asked me out were the guys who didn't follow Jesus. But what I lost in dates could never compare to what I gained.

Putting this protection plan in place put me in a place to get God's best. He wants his best for you too!

*Jesus, help me to be like the merchant looking
for fine pearls. I want to give up everything
to get your very best for me. Amen.*

281: Waiting for the Best

"For I know the plans I have for you," declares the LORD, "plans to prosper you and not to harm you, plans to give you hope and a future."
—Jeremiah 29:11

•••●•••

When I was crushing on Greg, I just could not see why God would not let us get together! I could just picture us together, and I knew it would be so good! Why would God not say it was best for me?

Greg was a Christian, so it wasn't because he wasn't a Christ follower. I was living a life that was honoring him; as far as I knew, there wasn't sin in my life that I was ignoring.

What was the deal?

If we go back and check out the last part of this verse, we'll find our answer: "to give you hope and a future."

When it comes to what is best for you, **God is looking way beyond today**. He's looking past next week, next month, and next year. He's looking past middle school, high school, and college. He's looking at your entire future, and unlike us, God has perfect patience. When it comes to our best, he doesn't have issues with wanting everything now. He gets the value of delayed gratification.

Waiting is often the limousine that takes us to his best. Since his very best is the place he wants to take you, he's going to use the very best vehicle to get you there.

START THE REVOLUTION

How do you see waiting for sexual intimacy in your life until you are married? Do you feel deprived, or is it a privilege to get God's best? Ask God to give you his perspective.

God, all I know is that sometimes waiting seems beyond hard. Help me to keep in mind that you're preparing for me a future with hope! Amen.

282: Catch and Toss

Those who live according to the flesh have their minds set on what the flesh desires; but those who live in accordance with the Spirit have their minds set on what the Spirit desires.

—Romans 8:5

••●●●••

"**W**here's your head?" Ever have that yelled at you? I have! It's a short way of saying, "You're not doing what you should!"

Where your head is determines the outcome of your actions. If you are up to bat, you can't keep your thoughts on that guy staring at you in the stands. If you do, chances are, you'll strike out!

The principle here is true when it comes to all of life. If you allow your mind to fantasize about what you shouldn't do—like things with a guy outside of God's marriage boundaries—you'll find yourself doing those things.

"Come on!" you might be saying. "I'm just daydreaming!"

That's not what God says! If it's explicit daydreaming, he says, "Those who live according to the flesh have their minds set on what the flesh desires." **Your thoughts lead to actions.**

Thankfully, this can also work for our good! If we control our thoughts and make them line up with God and his Word, our actions will follow! We'll think thoughts and live lives that honor God, not lives that bring regret and pain, shame and embarrassment.

Throughout your day, check yourself. What are you thinking about? That girl's ugly outfit? How you wish he'd ask you out? What it would be like to try _____? Catch and toss. Catch those thoughts and toss them toward God, asking his Spirit to replace your desires with his.

START THE REVOLUTION

Do you know what the Spirit desires? Read in the Word to find out.

Holy Spirit, my thought life is a tough battleground. Teach me to catch and toss my thoughts to you today. Amen.

You are the salt of the earth. But if the salt loses its saltiness,
how can it be made salty again? It is no longer good for anything,
except to be thrown out and trampled underfoot.

—Matthew 5:13

"*I* can influence him, Lynn, I just know I can! He's so open to hearing about Jesus. If I date him, I'll be able to spend lots of time telling him more about the Lord."

Dating to lead a guy to Jesus? I'd love to tell you it works, but the truth is, it doesn't.

When you like someone, you may do anything to please the other person. It's not that that guy you're interested in is deceitful; if he comes to know Christ, it may very well be genuine. The problem is, his motive is likely to be messed up. He needs to come to the conclusion that he is a sinner and needs a Savior on his own. Instead of coming to Christ because he wants Jesus, he may be coming to Jesus because he wants you.

That spells trouble. I have more than one friend who

START THE REVOLUTION

Be picky in your dating choices. Be realistic too. If Jesus isn't the guy's center before you date, chances are he won't be after.

led her husband-to-be to Jesus. Once they were married, the motivation for following Jesus was gone. Those guys had given their lives to Christ to get the girl. Now that they had their wives, they didn't need Jesus! Even if they did need him, their faith was young, just developing. They didn't have the **spiritual maturity** it took to lead their marriages, as God calls them to do.

Jesus has called you to be the salt of the earth, but when your motivation for sharing your faith is all mixed up with feelings, you just may lose your saltiness.

Don't be deceived. Protect your heart and choose to date only a guy who loves and follows Jesus because he knows that without him, he is nothing.

Jesus, it's so tempting when a guy I like wants to learn more about you. Give me the wisdom to not mix sharing my faith and dating. Amen.

CHAPTER EIGHT

284: Get Mad

For we are not fighting against flesh-and-blood enemies, but against evil rulers and authorities of the unseen world, against mighty powers in this dark world, and against evil spirits in the heavenly places. Therefore, put on every piece of God's armor so you will be able to resist the enemy in the time of evil. Then after the battle you will still be standing firm.
—Ephesians 6:12, 13 (*NLT*)

•••●●•••

What's your biggest problem? Your parents? Your algebra teacher? That mean girl who plays second base? Your boyfriend who's always pushing you to go too far? It's easy (and normal) to think when we have trouble in our relationships with people that it's all about them. But it's not really about them.

Paul wrote a letter to his friends in Ephesus, where he'd planted a church. He told Jesus followers that the source of their problems was not "flesh-and-blood enemies." In other words, it's not people. Our real struggle is with what we cannot see: evil rulers and authorities of the unseen world, mighty powers, and evil spirits.

Our enemy, Satan, uses whatever means possible, even people, to drag us away from Jesus. He's got a goal, and nothing is off limits when it comes to reaching it.

START THE REVOLUTION

Stand up against evil schemes and deceitful plans. Look in the Word. Look beyond your relationship struggles and stand your ground.

We can't stop the devil's scheming and planning, but we can work to protect ourselves. Being aware that he can use our relationships to cause us to struggle, we can look at arguments, disagreements, and even put-downs differently.

Next time you experience tension in a relationship, **consider the source**. Could the enemy be trying to bring hurt and pain to you and he's simply using this person as his pawn? Don't get mad at your friend or loved one; get mad at your real enemy!

Jesus, I've never thought of my relationship troubles from this angle before. Before I blow up at others, I'm coming to you for insight. Amen.

285: Exclusive

My beloved is mine and I am his.
—Song of Solomon 2:16

•••●••

*T*here is a new fad. At least I hope it's a fad, because it's just plain dumb. Two people *act* like a couple—flirting, holding hands, and way more. Are they a couple? No. At least that's what they say. "We don't want to be exclusive."

I'm just saying, it's weird. Why wouldn't this girl want to say he's her boyfriend? Is she ashamed of him? If so, why is she acting like he's hers?

Is the guy wanting to keep his options open? There is no way I would even hang out with a guy like that! There is no way I'd let a guy use me like that, even if it is just for "casual" flirting. **Do you really want to be just another option?** When you put yourself in a relationship like this, you're making yourself vulnerable, with absolutely no safeguards or trust in place to keep you from getting hurt. My heart is way too valuable for me to do that—and so is my time.

If you're going to give up even a little bit of your affections, do it knowing that the guy is proud to say you're his, because you know what? You're worth that much, and more!

Once again, Jesus is the perfect guy. He says it loud and says it to everyone: she's mine. You know my response? It's the same as the girl in Song of Solomon 2:16—Jesus is mine and I am his. I'll say it to everyone and anyone.

Why waste time on a relationship that isn't real? Life's too short. And your heart is too precious. Don't let it be used for nothing.

START THE REVOLUTION

Watch out for guys who are just looking to skip the hard stuff of a relationship to get your affection. And keep an eye out for friends who fall into this trap too!

Jesus, thank you that you are proud to say I am yours. May I never attach myself in any way to someone I am ashamed of or who is ashamed of me . . . for any reason. Amen.

286: Prized

He never changes or casts a shifting shadow.
He chose to give birth to us by giving us his true word.
And we, out of all creation, became his prized possession.
—James 1:17, 18 (*NLT*)

••●●●••

Your shoulders sag. Your eyes are dull. A tear appears in the corner of your eye. The problem? That guy doesn't like you.

Here's the secret: If a guy doesn't like you, it doesn't mean there's anything wrong with you! What it most likely means is that you and this guy are probably very different. Or it means that this guy is just looking for something different. Or it means he just wants something different . . . today. **Tomorrow could be another story.**

People change. Teens have a habit of changing a lot. There's so much growing that goes on in those years—physically, mentally, and spiritually! I'm glad God never changes. To him we are always his prized possession.

A lot of teen guys have one thing on their minds. I'll give you a hint—it's not sports. Ask yourself some questions about this crush of yours: Do you have a lot in common? Are his values your values? What type of girl is he attracted to? You may not like the answers, but you may find that the reason he's not the one for you is more about his maturity and less about you! Instead of drooping into despair, stand up and become a magnet.

START THE REVOLUTION

Become a magnet by spending time in God's Word. Live out magnetic characteristics such as love, confidence, and unselfishness.

What? Yes, I said a magnet. Think about it: What type of guy do you want to attract? One who honors and fears God? If you want to attract this type of guy, you will have to be this type of girl. Live like the prized possession that God made you to be. Be the magnet and leave the guy thing up to God!

Jesus, together let's make me a magnet. Amen.

*People went out to him from Jerusalem and all Judea
and the whole region of the Jordan. Confessing their sins,
they were baptized by him in the Jordan River.*
—Matthew 3:5, 6

··●●●··

For some reason, people felt compelled to dump their stuff on Julie: boy stuff, drinking stuff, drug stuff. When Julie's friends unloaded on her, they felt better. She wouldn't reject them, and their burdens were lifted just by telling someone. Did they change? No, but at least they didn't feel so bad.

For Julie, **it felt good to be needed and wanted**. But at sixteen, her maturity and life experiences were still being developed. Though her friends lightened their loads, Julie became sad carrying their burdens. Sometimes it was too much, especially with Becky.

Becky had talked to Julie, sharing only the surface of her hurts. Julie knew Becky needed help, but didn't understand the depth of Becky's anguish. After Becky killed herself, tremendous guilt swept into Julie's heart. She felt like God had put her in Becky's life and she had failed.

She took on guilt that wasn't hers to take on—her job wasn't to heal Becky.

Julie might have been helped by looking at the example of John the Baptist. People came to him to be baptized, to be made clean. John didn't try to solve all their problems. He wouldn't allow them to think *he* was great—he pointed to the Great One.

Feeling wanted and needed is a wonderful thing. God made us nurturers. *We* cannot, however, fill the love gap and needs in others' hearts. We can be a good friend, but even the best friend doesn't make a Savior. Only Jesus can be that. When we allow others to look to us to meet their needs, we are helping them to commit the sin of idolatry. This sin keeps them from what they truly need—Jesus.

START THE REVOLUTION

Be the best kind of friend by not just listening to others' burdens, but by pointing them to the solution.

Jesus, I need to introduce my friends to you. You had the answers then; you have the answers today. Amen.

288: Use Is Abuse

Do nothing out of selfish ambition or vain conceit.
Rather, in humility value others above yourselves.
—Philippians 2:3

••••••••

Marley's never had a boyfriend. Not because she didn't want one—she did! The guy she likes never seems to like her back. Until now. Derek was flirting with her, hard. He was a great friend, but she had never thought of him as a boyfriend. But maybe she could? It would be fun to finally have a guy like everyone else.

Marley needs to check her motives. Why does she suddenly like Derek, thinking he might make a good boyfriend? Is it because Derek has the character she's looking for in a guy? Is he kind? patient? respectful? a disciple of Jesus?

Or does Marley just like the idea of having a boyfriend? The idea of having a guy to do stuff with on the weekends, a guy who wants to hang out with her?

START THE REVOLUTION

Look up uses of the word *humility* in the Bible. Remember to set your value meter by this standard.

Philippians 2:3 says we are not to do anything out of selfish ambition or vain conceit. If Marley begins dating Derek now, it seems like it will mostly be out of selfish ambition, don't you think? She doesn't care that much about Derek and what is best for him; it's all about Marley and what she wants. She'd be using Derek.

Using is abusing.

Paul reminds us in Philippians to "in humility value others above yourselves."

Is Marley valuing Derek if she goes ahead with this relationship? No way. Marley is valuing how she feels and what others think of her. This would be a totally selfish move and definitely not the way of a girl who's been revolutionized by Jesus. Radical girls don't use.

Jesus, I don't like admitting when I'm selfish. Open my eyes to see when I am tempted to use others. I choose love instead. Amen.

289: Not in Secret

It is shameful even to mention what the disobedient do in secret.
—Ephesians 5:12

•••••••

nna hated being stuck at this table during lunch; their conversations made her so uncomfortable. The things they did with guys, the dumb things they did when they were drunk—she just wished they could hear how they sounded. They thought they were so cool; really they were so dumb.

Sin dumbs.

If we get caught up in what everyone else is doing, we grow numb to things that are totally degrading! We grow dumb. If we realize just how foolish we've been, we're embarrassed. We'll want to hide; keep it a secret.

Don't just do what you see other people doing. Look at what is going on around you from a different perspective. Put on the glasses of the girl you will be in just a few short years. How about your twenty-one-year-old self? Does she want to look back and see what you did with that guy you no longer speak to? Does your twenty-four-year-old bride self, walking down the aisle to her new life, want a flashback of that night behind the school? Does your forty-four-year-old self want to say no when your daughter asks you, "Mom, did you wait?"

Make decisions today that will make you confident tomorrow. Live your life out in the open, not in secret.

START THE REVOLUTION

Pre-decide that you will not do shameful things in secret. Make decisions today that will make you confident tomorrow.

Jesus, I know how I feel at night when I crawl in bed after I have been dumb. I want nothing to hide. Help me live a life that I'm not ashamed to put out in the open. Amen.

290: Plan to Honor

Commit to the LORD whatever you do, and he will establish your plans.
—Proverbs 16:3

START THE REVOLUTION
Commit all your plans to God. Do it for real and wholeheartedly, and he will really and wholeheartedly be behind you every step of the way.

She had been planning her outfit to the Sadie Hawkins dance for weeks. Sam had the dress, shoes, necklace, purse, earrings, and headband. They were even laid out on her floor, a daily reminder of the great time she was going to have. The tickets were bought, rides lined up. Everything was set.

Sam planned every detail of her special night, except one. She failed to plan how she was going to honor God that night.

Those who fail to plan, plan to fail.

Sam is bound to run into something that night. A conversation of criticism, a drink offered, a move by her date. Just as she has invested hours planning to look just right, Sam needs to plan how she will handle tempting situations in her relationships, and how she will honor Jesus with her words and actions.

Sam can plan to honor God, and God will honor her plan.

Jesus, I don't want to make a choice that dishonors you and shames me. I'll prepare to honor you. Amen.

291: Decide and Declare

To him who is able to keep you from stumbling and to present you before his glorious presence without fault and with great joy.
—Jude 1:24

•••●••

*P*art of her was psyched; the other part terrified. Dannie had been asked to prom by a really sweet guy; there shouldn't be anything to be afraid of. But what if he tried something?

Here was my advice to Dannie before the big day (and to you too): Decide now. Dannie needs to decide now that she will not, under any circumstances, do something that dishonors her true love, Jesus. Then, she needs to make this clear ahead of time to her date. Hopefully, he already knows that she is a revolutionary girl, so this conversation won't come as a surprise.

Don't ever assume anything. Don't figure that he knows you don't drink, smoke, or hook up with guys. Set the record straight—be up-front and clear. Then, as you make wise decisions, trust Jesus for the rest. He is able to keep you from stumbling! He is able to work in your life, fashioning you into a girl without fault and one who brings him great joy.

Be bold in your relationships, revolutionary girl. You're his. Make sure others know.

START THE REVOLUTION
Decide what you're going to do and declare your decision. Guys may actually appreciate you being straight with them more than you know!

Your love in and through me drives out fear in me, Jesus. I know that you are able to keep me from falling. Make me faultless and a bringer of joy to your heart. Amen.

292: Overcoming Power

I have given you authority to trample on snakes and scorpions
and to overcome all the power of the enemy; nothing will harm you.
—Luke 10:19

•••●••

As Lauren walked by, she became the topic of conversation at the lunch table. "She says she isn't having sex until she gets married. Be real! Like anyone nowadays can really do that!"

They can! I've met the girls who have waited and heard their stories. I *am* a girl who waited. I know it's possible.

Not only do I know it is possible to protect your heart and body because I have heard it and experienced it, **I know because Jesus said it!**

In Luke 10:19 he said that he has given us all the power we need to overcome any and every temptation you face, even sexual temptation. We can rely on this power, the same power that raised the widow's son at Nain (Luke 7:11-17), Jairus' daughter (Matthew 9:18-26; Mark 5:21-43; Luke 8:40-56), and Lazarus (John 11:1-44) all from the dead; not to mention Jesus. If his power is enough to raise someone from the dead, it is enough to keep you from sin!

Get into the habit of calling out to Jesus for power. Don't wait until you are in a tough situation. Ask him for help in everyday matters, so you are ready for the big ones!

START THE REVOLUTION
Maybe you don't have snakes or scorpions, but call on God's power to control your problems today!

Talk about confidence, Jesus. I've got some incredible power flowing through my life. Help me to tap into it, calling out to you for strength and wisdom in my relationships. Amen.

293: Crushing Crush

I have considered my ways and have turned my steps to your statutes.
—Psalm 119:59

••●●••

It lasted for too many years! My crush on Greg was absolutely ridiculous—unhealthy too. I wish that someone would have stepped into my life and told me to just get over him.

Do you have a crush crushing you? Let me be the voice I wish I had heard in my life: this crush is not good for you, and you can do something about it.

I believed that I was stuck, that I couldn't quit. I was so wrong.

Getting over a crush is a choice. It's my choice what I choose to obsess over. Yep, it's your choice too.

Was my obsession good for me? good to me?

No. Not having him as my boyfriend just made me sad. It made me miss what was around me because I was caught up in what wasn't around me. My obsession drew me away from really good friends. It drew me into myself and my selfishness. It made me just plain annoying! Those around me got so tired of my complaining!

Obsessions rarely honor God; unless of course you are obsessing on him!

Make a choice to move on. Then do it! Change the way you think. Change the route you drive. Change the kids you hang out with. Change who you follow on Twitter and who you friend on Facebook. Change whatever you have to change to move toward God and away from your unhealthy obsession. As you change, just watch. Your heart will become healthy once again.

START THE REVOLUTION

What do you need to do get over that crush? Tell someone what you need to do, and ask them to help you follow through with it.

Jesus, I like my crush, even though he's crushing me. Help me want to get over him. But until I do, help me make the changes I need to make. Amen.

294: What's Wise?

Yet I am always with you; you hold me by my right hand. You guide me with your counsel, and afterward you will take me into glory.
—Psalm 73:23, 24

••●●●••

*E*veryone was making plans to go to the beach over break, but Carley felt uneasy. Allie's advice: "Tell your parents you're going with me; that's the truth! You don't need to mention that some guys are going too." But was that really OK?

Overnight in a house with guys? Even if Allie's parents were there, stuff always happened in those situations. She didn't want to be a prude, but just thinking about getting stuck with nowhere to turn made her anxious inside.

START THE REVOLUTION
There's one question you can never ask too much: What's wise?

Carley's got every reason to feel uneasy. And she should listen to those feelings. **That's wisdom talking.** The Holy Spirit is our guide, holding our hands and directing us in the right path—*if* we will choose to be led. He is always with us; we'll sense him *if* we will choose to be aware of his presence.

Wisdom asks the question: What's wise? Then it does it. No matter what someone else says or how it affects our relationships. Wisdom knows that although it might not feel good now, doing the right thing always leads to a good place. Following wisdom brings joy and peace instead of sadness and regret. Following wisdom brings glory to God.

It seems so serious to constantly have to analyze all my relationships and actions, Jesus. I'll take your hand, listen to your counsel, and allow you to lead me to good every time. Amen.

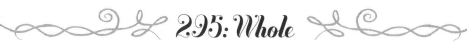

295: Whole

There's more to sex than mere skin on skin. Sex is as much spiritual mystery as physical fact. As written in Scripture, "The two become one."
—1 Corinthians 6:16 (*The Message*)

••••◆••

here it is, in black and white: sex is more than a physical act. It is a mysterious thing that connects two people spiritually and emotionally as well.

I guess that explains why Debbie was having such a hard time getting over Josh. She had dated other guys; breaking up hadn't been so hard before. But it was different with Josh. Everything was different with him. So many boundaries she had crossed. Now she was regretting every one. It had been months, but Josh was still all she ever thought of or dreamt about. How long was it going to take to get over him?

If you rip this page out of this book, it's going to have a tear down both sides—the edge where it was torn out and the edge of the separated page. Each part will be impacted; the page will no longer be a part of the book, and the book will be missing a page.

But that's not how it's supposed to be. When I wrote this book, I intended for this page to be right here. This page makes the book whole.

Your heart isn't meant to be ripped out either. That is why God created sex to be an intimate part of a marriage that's made to last your entire lifetime. Sex brings a husband and wife closer together. But when it is experienced outside of that covenant, it is a sure setup for damage down the road.

Wait for the best sex; don't have your heart ripped out.

START THE REVOLUTION
If you've already experienced the heartache of sex outside of marriage, you can start anew. Renew your mind in Christ, and he will make you whole again.

Lord, I've seen the heartbreak in those who have given themselves through sex without the commitment of lifelong marriage. I'm making up my mind now to wait for your best. Amen.

We Relate Together

I want women to be modest in their appearance. They should wear decent and appropriate clothing and not draw attention to themselves by the way they fix their hair or by wearing gold or pearls or expensive clothes.
—1 Timothy 2:9 (*NLT*)

••●•●••

*W*hat is it that makes us want to draw attention to ourselves? As women, we like the looks, the compliments. But sometimes, we can really cross the line. We need to do the opposite; we've got to protect the guys.

What? That's what you're probably saying. **Why do I have to protect guys?**

If you leave half of your body undressed, a guy's brain will automatically finish the picture. All of us are intrigued by what we see, but for most guys, what they see can be a strong trigger to physical desire.

If the goods are not for sale, don't dress as if they are! The instructions in 1 Timothy to the women were not just about personal preference for Christian guys at the time. There were women who went around with much adornment but had very bad reputations. Paul's instruction was to guard the female followers of Jesus from giving the wrong impression by how they dressed.

START THE REVOLUTION

You can dress well and still be fully dressed. You'll feel more confident in clothes that keep you covered. And that confidence is beautiful!

If you choose to dress improperly, you'll attract guys who have the impression you act improperly!

It's a guy's responsibility to handle the thoughts that come into his head, but it's yours to help not put the thoughts there. It is no small task for guys to fight against the natural desires of their bodies and the images in their minds—why would you want to make that struggle harder for them?

Lord, dressing can be a real challenge! Help me not to make any excuses. Help me to be responsible and to feel the need to protect the guys. Amen.

297: Nothing Less Than Best

Marriage should be honored by all, and the marriage bed kept pure,
for God will judge the adulterer and all the sexually immoral.

—Hebrews 13:4

•••●••

My heart was spinning, making me dizzy. I never believed that this day would come. Greg wanted to look at engagement rings! Since he was in college and didn't have a lot of money, I gravitated toward the small ones—a plain band with a wee little diamond.

The jeweler said, "Go ahead and pick out a small one now. Later on, when you have more money, you can trade it for the big one." That made sense to me.

Not to Greg!

"She needs to get the best now," he corrected the jeweler, "because she's going to wear it for the rest of her life." I loved that!

START THE REVOLUTION
What do you want to give the love of your life? Commit to giving him the best.

Get the best the first time.

Do you want the best? When you go shopping, do you look for the best? The best prom dress? The best softball cleats? You take your time, checking out all the options, and then get the best.

One of the best things life has to offer is sex. Yep, sex. Sex within marriage.

Get the best sex—sex with one who has committed to being the man who loves you like Jesus loves you, unconditionally and for the rest of your life. Don't settle for less than best.

Jesus, I don't want to settle for less than best. This is too big of a deal to not get the best the first time. Amen.

We Relate Together

298: Choices

Choose life, so that you and your children may live and that you may love the LORD your God, listen to his voice, and hold fast to him.

—Deuteronomy 30:19, 20

•••●●•••

We don't like waiting, do we? When making choices about what to do with a day, we often opt for whatever the easiest and fastest option is. We want what we want when we want it!

If you don't want a boyfriend right now, that's great. Relax and enjoy this time getting to know yourself and your God. But if you do want a boyfriend, I know it's hard not to want one to appear—right now!

All too often girls go after guys, no matter what the cost. Pastor Kevin Gerald says, "Choice is our greatest power." That wrong boy at the wrong time will pull right up to your heart—and you'll have to decide. Say "No . . . I'm listening to the wisdom of radical perfect love." Or "Yes, I want the thrill of the ride now."

START THE REVOLUTION

Remember that rushing to a bad choice can be far worse than waiting for the right one.

That's the beauty of perfect love. **Love offers choices.** Nobody wants forced love, because forced love isn't love at all. Forced love is manipulation in disguise.

To get what we want faster, we'll look for the first thing to take us there. Instead of waiting for a limousine, when the garbage truck of infatuation pulls up, we ignore the fumes—the regrets of those who didn't wait—and hop right in the cab and go.

Other times, because God is aware of just how weak we are, he doesn't allow the garbage truck to pull up at all. He protects us by not allowing that boy to notice us or return our feelings. He knows that our vulnerable hearts would not make the right choice and out of his wise love, he shelters us from wrong opportunities.

We have choices. But thankfully, we have a God who loves us enough to save us from our choices and to give us wisdom to make the right choices too.

Jesus, I think I'm one of those girls who needs your shelter. Please protect me with wisdom to make the right choices. Amen.

299: Shelter

It will be a shelter and shade from the heat of the day,
and a refuge and hiding place from the storm and rain.
—Isaiah 4:6

•••●●••

When we are in the heat of temptation, our God can be the shelter and shade we need—a refuge and hiding place. That's exactly what I needed. God knew that if Greg liked me back, Greg would have all of my heart. I hadn't fallen in love with Jesus yet, and because my heart was not full of Jesus' perfect love, I would not have protected my heart. I might have made some really dumb decisions.

Sometimes, though, we don't see God's protection this way. We're crushed by our crush and even mad at God.

I know that this is really a revolutionary thought, but **shouldn't we be thankful for his protection?** It is easier to have no choice than to have the option and make the wrong one. I know that seems crazy—to be thankful when the guy we like doesn't like us back. But that is what a revolutionary girl does. She recognizes Jesus' crazy love protecting her, and she is grateful.

My friend Tracey is learning this. For years she has been crushing on the same guy, but he always seems to like someone else. She has felt jealousy, anger, and insecurity. But this year, radical love has gotten hold of Tracey's heart. Her eyes have been opened, and she is seeing exactly why God has not allowed Jack to like her back. She knows that all these years Jack has had first place in her heart, and Jesus loves her too much to let that continue. Now, Tracey is taking steps to move on.

START THE REVOLUTION

Love can make us do some crazy things. But revolutionary love will make you do even crazier things in the eyes of the world. Go for it!

Jesus, I too want to have my eyes opened to see you loving me by protecting me. I want to be a radical girl, thinking radically. Amen.

300: Rejection Protection

For where you have envy and selfish ambition,
there you find disorder and every evil practice.
—James 3:16

•••●•••

Often, when God provides protection in our relationships, we're not grateful. When we see our best friend in a relationship based on infatuation, we feel jealousy and envy, when maybe what we should be feeling is concern.

Here's the difference between the girl who has been filled by God's perfect love and the girl who is still empty: the revolutionary girl recognizes that man's rejection, that boy not liking you, equals God's protection for you.

I didn't say you have to like it, but if you will at least recognize that God's perfect love is protecting you from heartache and possibly lifelong regret, you can protect your heart from bitterness and from believing something is wrong with you just because some boy doesn't like you. There is nothing wrong with you! Let me say that again: **THERE IS NOTHING WRONG WITH YOU!** Your King, the one who is crazy about you, is protecting you because he loves you!

Now, if you'd told me in high school that man's rejection equaled God's protection, I would've screamed. I was so over rejection. I didn't like not having a boyfriend.

I only got asked out by guys who didn't live the way I did—guys who were not Christ followers. Thankfully, my fear of God kept me from dating guys who didn't love Jesus. I had a very healthy fear of the consequences that came from disobeying his command to not be partnered with unbelievers.

As much as I didn't like it at the time, man's rejection was God's protection for me.

START THE REVOLUTION

Remember this message and repeat it to a girl you know who is struggling with rejection. Let her know about the God who loves her enough to protect her.

Jesus, help me to remember when I am struggling
with rejection, that man's rejection is your
protection for me. Amen.

301: Date Jesus

I love those who love me, and those who seek me find me.
—Proverbs 8:17

•••●•••

You might be thinking, *So what am I supposed to be doing when everyone else is dating?* This is the time to be investing in your perfect love. Date Jesus! Take the time that you'd like to be talking with a boy and talk to Jesus. When you wish you were reading love notes from your crush, read God's love letters to you.

There might never be another time in your life when you have less responsibility than you have now, so **this is the perfect time to get to know him**. Practice listening and learning what his voice sounds like by reading the Bible and sitting quietly, listening for his whispers. Sing songs of love through worship to him. Listen to sermons—learning what others know about him.

Mara is doing this! She told me the other day she has loaded sermons by her favorite speakers on her iPod to start listening to. Last week she told me she had switched to only listening to Christian music in her truck.

Whenever church has a service, Tracey is right there. In fact, she's been sitting on the front row so that she can focus 100 percent of her attention on Jesus! She's not just talking about moving on, she's doing stuff to do that. She is using God's Word to replace the thoughts about her crush. You know what I am seeing in Tracey? Joy! Her heart is becoming happier because she is not focusing on what she can't have and is paying attention to the one she does have!

> **START THE REVOLUTION**
> Be patient and wait on God. There is a time for everything.

All this time you are investing in relationship with Jesus will have great benefits. You will become a wiser girl, and a wiser girl makes wiser choices. A girl who makes wiser choices is a girl with fewer regrets and many blessings. Your life will have more joy, less regrets, and less heartache. Keep seeking Jesus—you will find him.

Jesus, I want to spend time with you. Thank you for your love that teaches, protects, and stretches me. Amen.

Indeed, the very hairs of your head are all numbered.
Don't be afraid; you are worth more than many sparrows.
—Luke 12:7

•••●●•••

Vikki has liked a guy since the beginning of this school year. She's heard he thinks she's cool. She's wondering what she should do. They've been in carpool at the same time, but he doesn't talk to her.

At the baseball game recently, they spent the whole night talking and getting to know each other. Vikki was ecstatic. But when the night ended, he never asked for her number. Her friends tell her she should get *his* number and text him. Should she?

Based on my experience, if a guy likes you, he'll let you know. If he doesn't, he's either not that into you, or he has issues with confidence and courage.

If he doesn't like you, face it. Move on. Stop stalking his Facebook. Quit following his tweets. Skip his hall or bypass Starbucks when he works. Don't look desperate! You're not. You're a girl who is madly loved by the King of all, perfectly and unconditionally. You don't need a guy to notice you in order to feel valued. There is one who notices you so much, the Bible says he knows how many hairs are on your head!

> **START THE REVOLUTION**
> You don't have to despair. You have hope in Jesus.

If this guy doesn't have the courage to at least talk to you, he needs to get some! You can't do it for him! You can't make him notice you or like you. Are you so desperate for a boyfriend you'll settle for a guy that you have to lead and call all the shots for? Not me. My man is a man's man. He treats me like a lady and I love it! I know I may sound harsh, but it's only because I have been there and I know it's true. If a guy doesn't know his own mind, he may have a hard time making wise choices.

There is no reason to be desperate; you already have a guy who *is* that into you!

Lord, this guy thing is hard and confusing. I really want to trust that you have my best in mind, but it's a struggle. HELP! Amen.

303: Friendship Zone

A time to search and a time to give up,
a time to keep and a time to throw away.
—Ecclesiastes 3:6

••●●••

So often my relationships got stuck in the friendship zone. Have you been there? You want to be more or you think he wants there to be more, but you're just not sure. What are you supposed to do when you're stuck?

Wait. There is a season for everything. Wait to see if this is the season for you to date this guy. Maybe it is, maybe it's not. Don't be in a hurry. Either way, God will let you know, and the guy will let you know if he likes you.

There's nothing worse than saying you like a guy friend, but he doesn't like you back. Awkward! That can make the friendship really weird, or even destroy it.

While you are in the friendship zone, enjoy it! There are a lot of great things there that you can learn. You can learn how to communicate better with the guy (they speak a different language you know!). You can figure out how they think (I can't say I get how they think; it's really different than us, I do know that!). And you can give the guy some lessons in understanding women too.

START THE REVOLUTION

Enjoy the friendship zone. Guys can be great friends, if you give them a chance.

When you are friends with a guy, concentrate on the same things you need to work on in any relationship. Work on learning to give and take. Learn how to be unselfish. Think about how you can care for your friend.

Enjoy the friendship zone, because things change. Once you're out of it, there's no going back.

Thanks for the guys in my life that are friends, Lord. Help me to enjoy the relationships for what they are and help me learn to be an amazing friend. Amen.

We Relate Together

304: Choose Carefully

I discipline my body like an athlete, training it
to do what it should. Otherwise, I fear that after preaching
to others I myself might be disqualified.
—1 Corinthians 9:27 (*NLT*)

Once you start dating, there are only two ways that a dating relationship can go. Just two. You'll either get married or you'll break up. If you break up, chances are you won't be able to get back to the great friendship that you started with. So don't push or rush into anything. Be wise with your next step. Ask yourself this question: **Can I see myself marrying this guy?**

"Come on! I'm only fourteen!" Yeah. So was I!

If you can't see yourself marrying this guy, stay friends. Remember the probability of you ever being friends after dating can be slim to none.

START THE REVOLUTION
Train yourself so you're ready when those emotions come rushing in. Don't get swept too far away!

Since you can't choose who you fall in love with, choose carefully who you date. We can't always control who we are attracted to. One day, you're walking down the hall, and then you notice him! Six-foot-two, built like a brick wall, dark curly hair . . . Whatever you think gorgeous looks like, you see him! Immediately your heart starts thumping. You want to scream, but instead you dart into the bathroom so no one sees you freaking out.

You couldn't control that, right? You didn't tell your heart, "Let's pick that one guy in German class, first row, two seats over, and flip over him!" Nope. It just doesn't work that way. You can, however, control what you do after you experience that first feeling. That's when your wise side needs to step up.

Jesus, I know that I can make wise decisions about controlling my thoughts and feelings, but sometimes it seems like I can't. Remind me, when my mind is spiraling, to get it under control. Amen.

305: Be Honest

I searched everywhere, determined to find wisdom and to understand
the reason for things. I was determined to prove to myself that
wickedness is stupid and that foolishness is madness.
—Ecclesiastes 7:25 (*NLT*)

••●●●••

When your heart starts crushing, it's time to ask some questions: What do you know about this guy? Is he a Christ follower or not? What is he known for? Does he make good choices, or is he known for partying hard, smoking pot, or going as far as he can? The answers to these types of questions are going to determine where you allow your mind to go next.

If you know this guy well, know that he's a Christ follower, and his life reflects that, then just maybe this is God's best for you and the time is right.

If you either don't know the answers to these types of questions or you do know the answers and they are bad, you have to be honest with yourself. This guy is not God's best for you, and you need to redirect your thoughts. **Refocus. Don't delay.** Don't allow yourself to focus on what you know is not God's best for you.

I have so often heard girls say, "But I just can't help it!" Really? You choose NOT to focus on the guy who sits right next to him, don't you? Yeah. It's a choice, right? Our greatest power is our power to choose. It may not be an easy choice, but it is your choice. This choice not to focus on this guy will make the next step—not to date this guy—easier.

Again, since you can't choose who you fall in love with, you had better choose very carefully who you date. If you're honest with yourself, you know, deep in your heart, whether you should date this guy or not.

START THE REVOLUTION
You'd tell your best friend if the guy she liked wasn't good for her, wouldn't you? Then tell yourself too.

Jesus, I never really thought of it as lying to myself, but that is exactly what it is when I don't admit the truth. Help me to choose right. Amen.

Do not be yoked together with unbelievers.
For what do righteousness and wickedness have in common?
Or what fellowship can light have with darkness?
—2 Corinthians 6:14

•••●•••

If you ask most girls who follow Christ whether they want to marry someone who follows Christ or not, they would say of course! If this is the case, then why do so many Jesus-loving girls marry guys who don't love Jesus?

They failed to put this one rule in place. Are you ready? Seriously, if you will live by this rule, **it will make a HUGE difference in your life**. Here it is: I will not date a guy who doesn't follow Christ and have the actions to prove it. Let me say that again: I will not date a guy who doesn't follow Christ and have the actions to prove it.

Here's the benefit of this one rule in your life: If you never date a guy who doesn't love Jesus, you will never marry a guy who doesn't love Jesus. Which leads me back to our point, since you can't choose who you fall in love with, you had better choose very carefully who you date. Are you getting it?

If you have good friends who are Christians and friends who aren't, you'll see the problem here eventually. No matter how good people are, if they don't have Jesus as Lord of their lives, you won't be able to get past a certain point in your relationship. There will be a spot where a wall comes up. Light is light, and dark is dark. When the two mix, all you get is gray.

START THE REVOLUTION

Dating can be super fun. But don't kid yourself. It's serious business too! Don't get partnered up in this business with someone who doesn't share your goals. It just won't work.

I guess this dating thing is more than just a cute game, Jesus. I want to be determined to honor you and protect myself in my dating choices. Amen.

307: Sustained

Cast your cares on the Lord and he will sustain you;
he will never let the righteous be shaken.
—Psalm 55:22

•••●•••

*M*y new friend Kayla e-mailed me, telling me the great stuff God is teaching her on relationships. Since she's sixteen, I knew you'd love to hear her:

"Ever heard, 'You deserve the best, so never settle for less?' That's so hard to believe! So many times I feel I'm not good enough. I start believing I'll never be pretty enough or thin enough for that certain guy. But the thing about being pretty or 'thin' (however that's described), is those things are only outward. Looks may be important to the world, but God sees our hearts.

"Recently God has put me through some trials and has gotten me through them too! I thank him for these tough experiences because without them I wouldn't be as strong as I am today. He has shown me a whole new perspective. What he's really shown me is a better outlook on the type of guy he wants me to have. Not one who sees my flaws and all the things on the outside, but a guy who loves my heart.

"Now, I'm learning what it means to honor God in every decision. . . . By putting God first in every decision, I can build a stronger relationship with him. I need God over any guy out there; he is my Prince of Peace and knight in shining armor. He will never let me go and loves me unconditionally. God's will is best, and when he's ready for me to start a relationship with a guy, he'll send me the guy he's chosen for me.

"So **there is no need to rush**; God will bring you just the right guy at just the right time. All us girls have to do is be the God-fearing, Proverbs 31 girl we should be, and love and laugh and be ourselves every day. Know God is in control."

> **START THE REVOLUTION**
>
> Relax in the sustaining love of Jesus. Cast all those dating worries on him. He won't let you fall.

Jesus, my heart often wants to take control, but I want to trust you. Help me today to just be the me you created and let you take care of the rest. Amen.

308: All About You

You can be sure that using people or religion or things just for what you can get out of them—the usual variations on idolatry— will get you nowhere, and certainly nowhere near the kingdom of Christ, the kingdom of God.

—Ephesians 5:5 (*The Message*)

• • • ● ● • •

Have you ever stopped to think about why you like the guy you like? What do you say about him?

- "I like the way he makes me feel."
- "I feel more confident when I'm with him."
- "It is so good just knowing someone is there for me."

What do these statements all have in common? It's all about you. The way he makes you feel, the confidence he gives you, that someone is there for you.

What about him?

When it's all about you, you're really just using someone. Using them to make you feel and look better. That's a form of idolatry—making something your god. That is offensive to God and will get you nowhere when it comes to growing in your relationship with him and becoming more like him.

START THE REVOLUTION

Don't use people. Use God's Word to love people his way.

It's time to grow up . . . in God. It's time for you to make Jesus the most important thing in your life and make your relationships with others unselfish—about the other people and their good. It's time to know love, not that mushy-feeling stuff that is here today and gone today, but true love that comes from God. That kind of love is unselfish (1 Corinthians 13). Be mature. Love God's way.

Jesus, I want my life to be all about you and loving others the way you do—unselfishly. Amen.

309: True Love

It does not dishonor others, it is not self-seeking,
it is not easily angered, it keeps no record of wrongs.
—1 Corinthians 13:5

•••●●•••

*F*our. That's how many different words for love I found in the Greek language that the New Testament was written in. In the English language, when we use the word *love*, it can range from the love I have for peanut butter and chocolate to the love you have one day for a husband—and everything in between!

One way we can protect our hearts is by understanding what kind of love we are experiencing.

Storge is family love—love between family members or people who are like family.

Philia is personal affection or fondness for something, often the love of friends. It is a highly subjective feeling of attachment or amity. You love because the object of love appeals to you—creates warm fuzzies.

> **START THE REVOLUTION**
>
> Do a love study. Read 1 Corinthians 13.

Eros is passionate, highly sensual, even intoxicating. It desires something—it's a craving, lust, passion, or a seeking of fulfillment.

Agape is love rooted in the mind and will of the subject and means to value, esteem, prize, treat as precious; to be devoted to. This kind of love may feel less personal or emotional than *philia*, but it's not less. *Agape* love sticks; it is a choice rather than a feeling. It loves for the benefit of the object loved rather than for the way it makes us feel. Movies and TV rarely show *agape*, even though this is what true love is.

To protect your heart, **when you think you love a guy, define it**. Are your feelings based on an attachment or attractiveness? Is it "hot"—making you feel crazy inside? Is your love because you want to care for and about him? Check your motives. Mature love cares more about the other person and less about you.

Jesus, help me to learn about and understand the love you have for me, and to love others with that kind of love. Amen.

310: Intentionally Friends

"Come, follow me," Jesus said, "and I will send you out to fish for people."
—Matthew 4:19

••●●••

Some of the friendships in your life have absolutely nothing to do with you and everything to do with God. He orchestrates peoples' paths to cross in unlikely means, just so they can hear the truth of his love for them.

Tammy, my running partner in high school, was one of those people in my life. She shares the power of intentional friendship: "Lynn was weird, in a good way! She impacted my life every morning at six o'clock, as we trained for cross-country and track. She was devoted to the sport; I was devoted to chatting! To put your body through torture just for time with a friend was crazy, but Lynn filled me up every morning. That's exactly what got me out of bed to run ten miles in the freezing cold winters of Iowa.

"Lynn listened to my drama, most of which I created myself, praying out loud for me as we ran. She never judged me. Believe me, she could have!

"People couldn't believe we were friends; we were totally different from each other! I appeared to have it all together. I was the loud, obnoxious girl, who was crowned Miss Congeniality—always fun, but looking for a challenge. Fearless, I didn't mind looking foolish, all in the name of a good time. What people didn't know was I needed Lynn to feel accepted.

"I still shake my head, thinking, *It is amazing God put Lynn in my life*. I accepted Christ on a run, in a lightning storm, at fourteen. Lynn planted the seeds in my heart, showing me how to be sold out for Christ.

"God brings people into your life for a reason, even if only to show you a glimpse of his inexhaustible love, his forgiveness, and his fun side. Sharing her faith every day for three years, I saw this, and I am grateful for her stepping out for Christ and for me!"

> ### START THE REVOLUTION
> You don't need an evangelism plan for your friends. Just be a real friend first, and let them see Christ in you.

Lord, what friends need me? I won't hold back. They need your truth! Amen.

311: Mercy Maker

Blessed are the merciful, for they will be shown mercy.
—Matthew 5:7

••●●••

er tender heart is always drawn to those struggling. Ever since she was a little girl, Mandy has looked for ways to reach out to the disabled. Mentoring at camps, being a date to a special "prom," she sows kindness and value where it is often missed.

There is a special blessing Mandy will reap in her life. God promises that those who show mercy will be shown mercy. When Mandy herself needs forgiveness, gentleness, and kindness, she will receive it.

Every person on this earth has been created in God's image (Genesis 1:26). **Not one of us was made better than another**; not one of us has been created "less than." As his girl, you show the world that you believe in the equity of your Creator by the way you treat others. Every person is lovable.

START THE REVOLUTION

See that person in the wheelchair. Observe the girl heading to her special class. Be the friend she needs. Extend kindness. Be Jesus with skin on.

Jesus, often I worry about what others will think, or worse yet, I am too wrapped up in myself to see those who are neglected. Make me like you. Amen.

Blessed are the peacemakers, for they will be called children of God.
—Matthew 5:9

••●●●••

Rita couldn't take it anymore. Any opportunity she got, Tori talked behind Rita's back. *What was her problem? Why was she so mean?* Everything within Rita wanted to stab her right back, but she knew that was the wrong way. For now, the best she could do was just to be quiet.

Rita might feel being quiet is not much. She might even feel like a wimp, but choosing not to retaliate when you are put down is anything but wimpy! She's being a peacemaker; she's being like God.

People are watching you—constantly. You may think you're invisible; nobody sees you. But you aren't, and they do. Others are aware of the big things and often the little things you do.

Deanna talked with me about a kid in her math class. When she drops her pencil, he picks it up. When her chair needs to be moved, he moves it. He doesn't wait; he does the kind thing every opportunity he gets. I wonder if he knows Jesus?

START THE REVOLUTION

Having trouble finding peace? Learn from the Prince of Peace.

Then there is Lindsey. When others are circling around, eyes big with the newest story of who did what this weekend, Lindsey goes the other way. She doesn't want to be a part of seeing another girl's reputation flushed away, even if what they are saying is true.

When we refuse to be a part of the newest and juiciest gossip, that's radical. That's different. It takes courage and strength and self-control. It's part of being a peacemaker.

Lord, I want others to see you, so I'll try hard to be like you. Help me make peace. Amen.

313: Something to Talk About

Blessed are you when people insult you, persecute you and falsely say all kinds of evil against you because of me.
—Matthew 5:11

••●●●••

armie couldn't believe they called her *that*. The group of girls had no idea she was standing close by. They couldn't see her, but she could hear them. The descriptors they used didn't fit her at all. That was the part that made her so mad.

When she told me about it after school, I had to laugh. It's one thing when people say bad things about you, and what they say is true. I mean, what can you say if it's true? But when they have to make up things to say about you, that's great! **It is a true indication that you are a revolutionary girl!** When they look at you and can't find anything bad to say about you because you are living a life that is honoring God, well . . . it just doesn't get any better than that!

START THE REVOLUTION
Next time you hear someone saying something mean about you, smile. Remember that Jesus is proud of you.

Jesus says when other people insult us, persecute us, or say false things about us, we are actually blessed. *Blessed* means "divinely or supremely favored."

Why would we be blessed or happy, even when others put us down? Because they see Jesus in us. How much better is that than if those ugly words were actually true!

Today, give someone something to really talk about! Show kindness to the one insulting or saying unkind things about you. *That's* something to talk about!

Jesus, I want to be blissfully happy when others insult me. It sounds impossible, but you said it can happen, so I want it and I believe. Amen.

317: Turn It Around

*For God has not given us a spirit of fear and timidity,
but of power, love, and self-discipline. So never be
ashamed to tell others about our Lord.*

—2 Timothy 1:7, 8 (*NLT*)

•••●••

ear. When it came to telling others about Jesus, Michelle felt fear. That was until her eyes were opened to the depth of Jesus' unconditional love for her: "Knowing that Jesus loves me unconditionally opened my eyes. Why should I be afraid of mentioning him in everything I do? I'm sure that if he were on earth, he would mention me at all times, simply because he loves me that much. I want people to know how great Jesus is, and how he loves us even if we are constantly making mistakes. . . . To know that they do not need to keep searching for another human being to fill them with love.

"I would like for people to know that they are never alone. I hope that when I mention Jesus to people, I'll save them from doing something they'll regret in the future. A couple of days after reading *His Revolutionary Love*, I received some terrible news about a friend. She took her own life because she felt alone and unloved. The first thing that came to my mind was, 'I wish she could have read *His Revolutionary Love*.' I'm sure she would not have felt alone if she'd realized that Jesus loved her that much. I just wish she had realized that God had a bigger plan for her."

You are part of a bigger plan. Jesus used me in the life of Michelle to help her see that Jesus was crazy about her. He wants to use you in someone's life too!

> **START THE REVOLUTION**
> Who around you needs to hear about Jesus' love? Don't be afraid to talk about it—God has given you a spirit of power, love, and self-discipline. You can do this!

*Jesus, someone in my world is lonely and
without hope. Show me how to reach out to
her today with the truth that you are wild about her.
You can turn it all around. Amen.*

315: Outside of the In-Crowd

Samuel did what the LORD said. When he arrived at Bethlehem,
the elders of the town trembled when they met him.
They asked, "Do you come in peace?"
—1 Samuel 16:4

• • ● ● • •

Inseparable. Where Lexi was, Noelle was—at least last year. This year, things changed—Noelle changed. Dumb stuff last year was important to her this year: popular kids, expensive clothes, and "in" parties. Last year, she didn't care what she looked like; this year she wouldn't be caught dead without makeup.

That was just the outside things. Noelle's heart was different too. Being around the popular crowd meant doing what they did. Knowing Lexi didn't approve of things she was doing made Noelle not want to be around Lexi. This left Lexi brokenhearted. She wasn't judging Noelle, so why did Noelle feel this way?

In our verse today, Samuel, God's man, obeyed God. Whatever God asked him to do, he did, and others knew it. When Samuel went into a city, the officials of that city felt uncomfortable. *Why was Samuel coming? Would he call them out on the sin in their lives?*

Maybe this has happened to you. It has happened to me, a lot. When you live life trying to please God, **you are going to make some people uncomfortable**. I hope it's not because you are judging them. Light and darkness just can't be in the same place at the same time. I know it hurts; you feel rejected. I won't tell you that there isn't a price to pay—there is. But the benefits of peace, positive self-worth, confidence, and joy far outweigh the price of being on the outside of the in-crowd.

START THE REVOLUTION
Whether you are outside or inside the popular crowd in your school, keep an eye out for those around you. Make sure you are being true to God and kind to others.

Jesus, I believe it's worth it, but I still feel a loss. Comfort me. Help me move on and enjoy your best! Amen.

We Relate Together

316: Standing Out, Standing Up

Arise, shine, for your light has come, and the glory of the LORD rises upon you. See, darkness covers the earth and thick darkness is over the peoples, but the LORD rises upon you and his glory appears over you. Nations will come to your light, and kings to the brightness of your dawn.

—Isaiah 60:1-3

•••●••

I know you get tired of being different. You wonder when you'll ever fit in. Every day, going against the crowd wears you out. Maybe you can't see your own beauty—the beauty of Christ living in you—but they do. **Those around you see you.**

Some see his beauty in you and are intimidated by it. Others feel jealousy. Some are drawn to you. They see your confident peace and they want to be like you, but they don't know how. Since they see the light of Jesus so little, they don't know what it is that makes you different.

Don't be afraid of this gift that's in you. Don't despise the way that it makes you different. Embrace it. Look for ways to share it. As Isaiah said in today's passage, others "will come to your light."

START THE REVOLUTION

If you are a follower of Christ, you're going to shine. That's just who you are. So shine bright!

Jesus, on the days when I am weary from standing out, remind me that because of you I stand up. Amen.

317: Keep Away

And now, dear brothers and sisters, we give you this command in the name of our Lord Jesus Christ: Stay away from all believers who live idle lives and don't follow the tradition they received from us.
—2 Thessalonians 3:6 *(NLT)*

•••●••·

I could see them, looking like they were sharing a secret. "Who're you talking about?" I asked, as I approached my friends. Suddenly, they became very quiet. "Nobody." "Nothing." They sounded like parrots. I had already caught bits and pieces of their conversation. I shouldn't have been nosing around. It was none of my business.

The girls had been talking about a guy we'll call "Tom." Tom really used girls, especially the younger ones. Making them feel important by flirting with them, he'd get them all high on his attention, and then get them to do whatever he wanted. They played right into it.

You'd think these girls would get it, that they would know better. But **the power of the flirt** can be hard to fight off. The power of a flirt who claims to know Jesus is even worse.

Paul commands us in today's verse to "stay away from all believers who live idle lives." The word *believer* refers to someone who claims to follow Christ. But if this person not only doesn't display evidence in his life that he follows Christ, but also models a heart against God's commands, we are to keep away from him.

If someone says he is a disciple of Christ, he needs to act like one. Don't put yourself in a position where you are the next one compromising.

> **START THE REVOLUTION**
> Be selective. Know who it is you are hanging around with, what they believe, and what they do.

Jesus, I'll keep away from those who say they belong to you, but don't show they belong to you. Amen.

318: Speaking the Truth

Instead, speaking the truth in love, we will grow to become in every respect the mature body of him who is the head, that is, Christ.
—Ephesians 4:15

•••●••

Dishonesty is my greatest weakness. Not wanting to make others mad at me, I've been known to go to great lengths not to offend someone. But the truth is (no pun intended), I'm really lying. When I am dishonest about how I feel or what I see, I'm really just lying.

Today's Bible verse tells us that when we speak the truth in love, it's a step toward becoming mature—growing. That's what we want! Imagine if you were still the same girl you were when you were ten. How awful! There is nothing beautiful about a girl who is stuck, a girl who won't grow. Every day, in your relationship with Christ and in your other relationships, you have the opportunity to mature. **Being truthful with others is a huge part of that maturity.**

START THE REVOLUTION
You can't love without truth, and it's not good to deliver truth without love. Measure your words carefully.

The mature girl talks to the person she is upset with instead of talking to others about her. She is honest about the real reason she is angry, quiet, or sad, instead of causing others to play the ask-me-a-million-times game. The mature girl lovingly tells her friends what they need to hear, not just what they want to hear.

Speak the truth in love. And make sure you are loving, because truth, when not spoken in love, just brings pain.

Lord, this is really countercultural. Honesty is just not something I see a lot of! I want to be mature. Make me truthful! Amen.

319: Check Your Clothing

Therefore, as God's chosen people, holy and dearly loved, clothe yourselves with compassion, kindness, humility, gentleness and patience.
—Colossians 3:12

•••◉•••

There are days when I just feel like quitting. When it seems too complicated—it just takes so much work to get along. I've noticed a pattern with me. **The more I focus on me, the harder relationships are!** When I try so hard to get things to go my way or try to make someone see my side, it doesn't help. Things only get worse.

Today's passage helps me get why my relationships are so difficult: often it's me!

God says I am to be compassionate, kind, humble, gentle, and patient. When I act like Jesus, choosing these traits, it's hard not to get along with me! Compassion, kindness, humility, gentleness, and patience settle fights; they calm disagreements. When I act like Jesus, it sets the other person at ease, making it easier to talk and harder to yell.

In the relationship you are in, take a moment to analyze the way you act or react toward the person. If you have been uncompassionate, mean, prideful, harsh, or impatient, make a trade. When your friend is upset, calmly listen, and try to understand. If you've been tempted to retaliate when you are feeling neglected by your boyfriend, turn it around. Be kind to him. Choose the action that is opposite of what you have been doing, and see if it doesn't make a difference!

> **START THE REVOLUTION**
>
> If you're consistently having trouble making relationships work, it's time for some self-assessment. Try doing the opposite of what you usually do.

Jesus, so often the answer to my troubles is me changing. Give me strength to choose actions that you call me to do and help me to see the changes that can be made. Amen.

320: Independent Spirit

Fear the LORD and the king, my son, and do not join with rebellious officials, for those two will send sudden destruction on them, and who knows what calamities they can bring?
—Proverbs 24:21, 22

••●●••

"Hiding the beer from my parents so we don't get caught. #promproblems." What a crazy caption under the Instagram picture!

When we're young, we have an amazing gift—the belief that we can do anything! We feel we're invincible, able to go anywhere and face whatever comes. This is a gift from God. It's the very thing that empowers us to leave our family, go to college, or move out and start our own life. It gives us the *umph* we need to go for it!

But if it is not harnessed and not forced to work for us within the context of respect for God, our parents, and the law, it can also get us in a lot of trouble!

Bethany had started smoking a little weed here and there with her new boyfriend at the beginning of high school. One thing led to another and now she found herself in trouble with the police. **She had never seen that coming!** What started out as a little "fun" now and then had become a pit that she was caught in.

Don't be foolish! When the drive for independence steers you away from the Lord and those in authority over you, force yourself in the other direction. Making choices that disrespect God and the law will never turn out well. As today's verse says, "those two will send sudden destruction . . . and who knows what calamities they can bring?"

START THE REVOLUTION

Are you full of spirit or just rebellious? If you are itching to go, make sure you're not headed the wrong direction. Check with your parents, a mentor, your pastor, and God's Word.

Jesus, give me wisdom beyond my years when it comes to relating to those in authority over me. Empower me to choose to relate in wisdom. Amen.

321: Don't Overdose

Unfriendly people care only about themselves;
they lash out at common sense.
—Proverbs 18:1 (*NLT*)

•••●••

I'm a big fan of hot sauce! When I moved to Texas after high school, I worked in our school's dining room. Hot sauce was served with everything from eggs at breakfast to tacos at dinner. A meal just wasn't complete without it! The more I used hot sauce, the more I wanted to use it. Each time I would increase my "dose." Until the day . . .

Greg and I were newlyweds and I wanted so badly to impress him! Taco pie was going to be the meal to convince him that I was a great cook. Thinking **if a little was good, a lot would be great**, I doubled the hot sauce. Bad, bad idea! The pie was so hot, we had to throw it out!

In a dating relationship, the more you are around your crush, the more you can lose sight of what is best. Too often I see girls who want to spend tons of time with their new guys; they just love the way they feel when they are with them. So, if a little time feels great, more will just be wonderful, right? But as they increase the time with their guys, they are losing their appetite for their friends. And when the day comes (as it usually will) when their crushes are no more, they may find their friends are also gone. People have moved on, grown, and formed new groups, while the girls who spent all their time on their guys are now left alone.

When it comes to spending time with your guy, a little goes a long way! Hold a bit of yourself and your time back not only to keep the relationship fresh, but also to allow balance in your life with your other relationships as well.

START THE REVOLUTION
Check your schedule. Too much time blocked out for your guy and no room for anyone else? Make some other appointments. Start with time with Jesus.

Jesus, the rush of a crush feels so much more exciting than friends I have known forever. Help me to remember that I need balance in my life. Amen.

We Relate Together

322: Two Made One

Haven't you read . . . "For this reason a man will leave his father and mother and be united to his wife, and the two will become one flesh"? So they are no longer two, but one flesh.

—Matthew 19:4-6

When I was trying to decide about waiting to share my body with a guy before marriage, I heard a lot of reasons not to wait:

- If I wait, no guy will ask me out.
- Everyone else is having sex.
- If I wait until I get married, I might not know what to do when I get married!
- Marriage is just a piece of paper. What matters is that you love each other.
- If I don't have sex with a guy, he'll dump me.
- Sex isn't a big deal, so why make a big deal out of waiting?

Yet, when I compared these reasons to God's Word, Jesus made it plain to me that they were off the mark. **Sex is more than a physical act**— emotional and spiritual connections occur as well. Sex without commitment, outside the union of marriage that God established, leaves us lonely because there is no "becoming one"; no intimate relationship, just intimate bodies. Sex before marriage is a sin that violates the Holy Spirit inside us.

We are to let others see Jesus in us, even when it comes to our sexual choices. For the revolutionary girl, it is not a matter of waiting or not waiting, it is a matter of obedience. You have to decide to honor Jesus in all your relationships—especially when it comes to your relationships with guys. No other choice will affect your future like this choice.

START THE REVOLUTION

Tune out the voices of people telling you about sex, and tune into the one who created sex.

Jesus, no other choice makes me stand out like this one. You say that with you all things are possible. Make this possible for me. Amen.

323: Submit

In the same way, you who are younger, submit yourselves to your elders. All of you, clothe yourselves with humility toward one another, because, "God opposes the proud but shows favor to the humble."

—1 Peter 5:5

Parasailing looked so fun, but boy, was I scared! I had never done something so adventurous. What if the driver ran into the side of a hotel? What if he dumped me hard into the ocean? Was it worth the risk? To find the answers, I asked people at the front desk and those who had parasailed before. Only then was I able to make up my mind.

Maybe you have never dated before. It looks so fun, but like me, you're scared! Don't feel bad. There is usually some fear when you're about to do something you have never done.

Today's Bible verse says those who are younger should submit to those who are older. *Submit* can mean "to subject to another's influence." God knows that if we will be humble and ask godly people who have dated before for some advice, it can help us to make wise decisions instead of mistakes.

Be wise. **Learn from other's experiences** rather than having to experience things yourself. Listen to advice on how to date wisely, if you date at all, and avoid the pain of figuring out things on your own.

START THE REVOLUTION
Want to avoid mistakes? Learn from some experts. Talk to some people older than you who have been where you are. You might be surprised how much you learn.

Lord, please show me who I can ask for godly advice when it comes to relationships. I want to be wise. Amen.

We Relate Together

CHAPTER NINE

327: Seize It

*So if you ignore the least commandment and teach others to do the
same, you will be called the least in the Kingdom of Heaven.
But anyone who obeys God's laws and teaches them
will be called great in the Kingdom of Heaven.*
—Matthew 5:19 (*NLT*)

••●●••

Taking in the crisp fall air with a steamy Starbucks, Mary Ann shared her story: "It was my senior year. I had just graduated from drug-rehab where I spent the last eighteen months for my substance abuse/addiction and severe emotional problems. At my worst, I became anorexic, weighing 74 pounds at age eleven. I often cut myself, ran away from home, and nearly overdosed on cocaine and alcohol by age fifteen. But there I sat, in drama class, staring at the chalkboard in horror at the wavy and almost indecipherable question: WHO ARE YOU AND WHY ARE YOU HERE?

"My answers would have been: 'Mary Ann Rosina' and 'I have no idea.'

"Cheryl was called up by the teacher to answer. . . . It was as if she and I were the only two in the room. Hearing about Christ's love and sacrifice for me through her bravery and conviction rendered me speechless. All I knew was that *I WANTED WHAT SHE HAD!* Afterwards, I thanked her with my heart pounding, tears brimming. She then invited me to her church youth group where I received salvation that night. We became inseparably close, and each of us still serve Christ to this day.

"Years later, Cheryl shared with me how she was very tempted NOT to testify that day because she had been doing that throughout her young life, with much persecution and many people not seeming to listen or care. . . . But she remembered the voice of pastor Keith, our youth leader, saying, '**Always seize an opportunity** to share Christ. Don't wait for a second chance.'

"My life has never been the same, thanks to Cheryl."

START THE REVOLUTION

Imagine having a conversation about your faith with someone. Be ready for when the opportunity comes. Seize it!

*Jesus, help me to be brave, like Cheryl. Help me
always to seize an opportunity to share Christ! Amen.*

325: Words Hurt

You're familiar with the command to the ancients, "Do not murder."
I'm telling you that anyone who is so much as angry with a brother or
sister is guilty of murder. . . . The simple moral fact is that words kill.
—Matthew 5:21, 22 (*The Message*)

•••●••••

Seven thousand a day. That's the average number of words a girl says in a day (compared to two thousand for a guy), according to some studies. That's a huge number! Add to that the amount of words we text, tweet, and post—who even knows what that number would be!

Jesus says we must be responsible *never* to use our words to tear a person down.

I'm not a name caller, I just never really went there. But what about those digging remarks made in jest?

I've done it. I've hidden behind the "just kidding" cover-up. Isn't it just a way to get around saying something rude and offensive by putting a joke blanket on top? The truth is, it's still mean. It still hurts. In fact, it might possibly hurt even more; no one likes to be the brunt of a joke.

Maybe one way for us to be more careful is to talk less. **The less we talk, the fewer words we have to be responsible with.** When we take time to think before we speak, we can more easily weigh each word that might have a profound impact.

START THE REVOLUTION
Talk less.
Think more.

Be a student of your words today, carefully watching what comes out. Are you the jester bringing pain with the laughs? If so, change your ways.

Jesus, I never really thought it was a big deal to tease others, but it is. You didn't hurt with your words, I won't either. Amen.

326: Hurt or Heal?

The words of the reckless pierce like swords,
but the tongue of the wise brings healing.
—Proverbs 12:18

•••●●•••

As we stood waiting for a table in our favorite restaurant, I heard voices escalating behind me. "You've been putting me down all day and I am sick of it!" one girl said in a sharp tone. I wasn't quite sure what was going on, but I was thinking, *They're going to ruin our dinner!*

Turning around to get a glimpse, I saw tears running down the other girl's eyes. Minutes later, they were hugging. I wondered, *What is going on?*

Then I overheard the crux of the problem. The family had spent the day looking at colleges, and one sister was grieving her up-and-coming loss. The way she was dealing with her pain was with cutting words.

This girl is not alone. Often, **when we're in pain, words fly** that are hurtful to those around us. Failing to properly process our feelings, we spew them on those closest to us. Since we know that our family loves us and won't reject us, we feel comfortable letting whatever crosses our mind fly out of our mouths.

Proverbs 12:18 gives us so much wisdom: "The words of the reckless pierce like swords, but the tongue of the wise brings healing."

In the next couple of days, when you are upset, stop long enough to process what's going on in your heart. Before you speak thoughtlessly or rashly, put the dagger back in its sheath. Share calmly with those in your life how you are feeling. Use your words for good.

START THE REVOLUTION

Every word you speak today will either hurt or heal. Which is it going to be?

Lord, words are so powerful. Please help me to choose mine wisely. Amen.

327: Listen Up

Love is patient, love is kind.
—1 Corinthians 13:4

•••●••

*E*ver have one of those days when your friend's emotions are so unstable, she goes from crying to laughing faster than you use up your cell data plan?

At moments like these, we think *Here we go again!* We just want her to *calm down*. In an effort to move this process along we might even say "It's going to be all right" or "This isn't that big of a deal."

When we hurry our friend past the emotions she's feeling, we're saying "I don't really care. You're annoying me." We're saying her feelings are invalid. Our friend will feel like we don't care about the things she cares about. She might feel alone and unloved.

START THE REVOLUTION
Remember: what you sow, you reap. Listen today—you might need to be heard tomorrow.

If, instead, we choose to listen and learn, we can hear the heart of our friend. Beyond the tears and raised voices, there might be pain, rejection, anxiety, or excitement. **Listening past the words to hearing the heart** will open doors for you to encourage her and to show her real, unconditional love.

Give me patience and compassion, Jesus, for those who need to be loved by me. Amen.

328: Weird Kindness

For you know that we dealt with each of you as a father deals with his own children, encouraging, comforting and urging you to live lives worthy of God, who calls you into his kingdom and glory.
—1 Thessalonians 2:11, 12

••●●●••

I'm always a bit nervous the first time someone joins us for dinner. Dinnertime conversation can be really interesting at our house and I'm never quite sure what's going to fly out of someone's mouth—even when it's my own!

Amy joined us at the last minute, so when I served her the portobello mushroom and turkey burger, I was already feeling she might think we were weird. I started feeling better when Mariah shared a kind act she did at school that day. Amy piped up next: "I invited the new kid at school to sit by me at lunch, because he didn't know anybody."

Even though Amy was new at our house, she felt proud that she had shown kindness and knew we'd think it was cool too.

Acts of kindness during our day speak loudly of the one we love and serve. These actions stand out because they are weird in the world we live in. **Normal is rude.** Normal is selfish and cares only about making yourself happy. Normal doesn't do anything that requires me to go out of my way for another person. It's not normal to love.

Look for the opportunity in your community to give to those who have no way to give back to you. Be the only Jesus someone is going to see today—be love.

START THE REVOLUTION

Look around you today to find someone to love. Be aware of the kid who has no friend, the kid who gets picked on, or the kid who is just having a bad day.

Jesus, it is so easy to get my whole day wrapped around me and my problems. Open my eyes to see the world of those around me and empower me to make a difference with your love. Amen.

329: Sticky Friends

One who has unreliable friends soon comes to ruin,
but there is a friend who sticks closer than a brother.
—Proverbs 18:24

•• ● ● ● ••

They didn't keep your secret. She wore that dress to the dance—the one you told her you were going to wear. You left your Facebook open, and they wrote an embarrassing message for your status. She said something unkind about you to your boyfriend. They posted a picture online of you dancing in your bedroom.

There are thousands of ways to ruin a friendship.

Let's face it. People are unreliable. Even the most virtuous person on earth has been guilty of letting someone down at some point. Knowing no one is perfect, we should be able to overlook minor offenses and unintentional hurts.

But if you find yourself in a group of friends who are untrustworthy, unfeeling, or ungodly, there's only one thing to do. Get out! They will bring you down in one way or another.

Stick to the friends who are true. The friends who stick by you, no matter what people do or do not say about you. The friends who stick up for you through very hard times. The friends who are stuck on you, even when you mess up. These are the kinds of friends who stick closer than family.

START THE REVOLUTION

Remember you have a friend named Jesus, who will stick with you forever. Be the kind of friend to Jesus that he is to you.

Jesus, I'm so glad you stick by me, no matter what. Please help me be a sticky kind of friend to others. Amen.

330: Carried Away

Carry each other's burdens, and in this way
you will fulfill the law of Christ.
—Galatians 6:2

••●●●••

irls can be catty. Girls can exaggerate. Girls can turn tears on and turn them off. Girls can be just hard to understand!

If you're having a hard time figuring out a friend of yours, try looking for patterns:

- Does she consistently stir up problems?
- Does your friend struggle over and over with jealousy?
- Is this the first time she's broken down crying in school?

By looking for patterns, you might be able to determine how you should respond.

Your friend may be going through some tough stuff at home: her parents arguing, a sibling on drugs, or family financial stress. She may need extra encouragement and support to just make it through. A crisis in her self-worth means she needs you to **pour truth into her heart**. Just knowing she is not alone is often all it takes.

Other times, the silent goal of erupting emotions is simply to gain attention and create a reaction. In this case, you just need to let it go and move on, and help your friend move on too.

START THE REVOLUTION

Carrying each other's burdens doesn't mean just picking them up, but trying to understand them too.

Girls will be girls, and often just being in the center of the mix fuels behavior. By looking for consistent behavior, you can determine which friendships are ones that are healthy for you, which are ones you should invest in, and which relationships are better left alone.

Jesus, I want to be a good friend. Show me when my friend needs me, and when my friend needs to change. Amen.

We Love Together

343

331: Greater

He must become greater; I must become less.
—John 3:30

•••●●•••

*I*t's not all about you. I know that might come as a bit of a surprise, but as a girl being radically transformed every day by revolutionary love, your life will become more and more about Jesus, and less and less about you.

Tammy helped me to see this in a whole new light recently. "I love it when people get to meet me," she shared. "I love me some me and I love getting attention! The feeling of everyone in the room wanting me is a rush. I am that girl who can command a room not because of physical beauty, but because of my personality. I have the ability to draw people to me, even people that should not be drawn to me. Often people tell me stuff they shouldn't."

Do you recognize any of Tammy's traits in you? Being able to relate to people is a gift. Do you use that gift for God, or do you give Satan a foothold by flirting, making other girls feel inferior, or commanding a room just because you can? Attention-seeking is a heart issue; it often reveals a longing to fill a deep void of insecurity. Only one person can fill that void.

God wants you to want *him* as much as he wants you. He wishes you would command *his* attention with love, joy, peace, patience, kindness, goodness, faithfulness, gentleness, and self-control. He longs to spend time with you each day and to remind you that he can give all the attention you need, even if you don't physically feel it.

When you are getting all the attention you need from your Love, you make others the most important people in the room. Look for that person who needs love and be Jesus' spotlight today.

Make your prayer today a prayer of action. Find that girl who needs attention and make it all about her.

332: Weighty Words

The tongue has the power of life and death,
and those who love it will eat its fruit.
—Proverbs 18:21

••●●•••

*I*n our home, we have a pact. It's not something we've actually talked about, just something we do. If we catch each other gossiping, we call it out. It's a good way for all of us to stay on guard about the words we say. We hold each other accountable.

We know our words have the power to empower or implode, or as the Bible says, "the power of life and death." That's some pretty amazing power.

We can empower a girl with confidence by saying: "Your smile makes others want to get to know you!"

Or we can cause a girl to implode, sliding deeper into her insecure heart: "Couldn't your family afford braces?"

Thoughtless words often are damaging words.

Don't allow yourself to speak without thinking. If you had a loaded gun, you wouldn't just start shooting it off. That's exactly what your mouth is—a loaded gun. It can help or hurt; it's up to you.

> **START THE REVOLUTION**
> Think before, during, and after you speak. Watch the effect of your words.

I shoot off my mouth without thinking
all the time, Lord. For the sake of others,
teach me to weigh my words. Amen.

333: Take Cover

A perverse person stirs up conflict, and a gossip separates close friends.
—Proverbs 16:28

••●●●••

*J*ust too easy. A comment made about *those* shoes quickly spins, growing into a full-blown gossip tornado. It never ends well; it just can't. Tearing up everything in its path, gossip injures both the carriers and the target.

Gossip has a rotten root: comparison. You look at her, compare yourself to her, and decide you don't measure up. What's a girl to do when she doesn't measure up?

One action you could take is to cut others down. You may think, if you can just get that other girl to feel bad, cut her down to be as low as you feel, then you will feel better about yourself. And maybe you will even climb a few steps up the social ladder as well.

But does it really work that way? Not so much. Instead, after you get finished chopping someone down to size, you will most likely feel downsized too. Why? Because we were meant to build up, not tear down.

Ephesians 4:29 tells us only to say what is helpful for building others up. That cuts out a whole lot of our conversations, doesn't it?

Let's be girls who repair instead of rip apart close friendships. Be smart: Take cover and get out of the path of gossip whenever you can.

START THE REVOLUTION

Whenever you are faced with gossip, imagine the object of the gossip is your sister or your very best friend.

Lord, when the gossip storm starts brewing, help me to walk away. Instead of exciting me, cause it to sicken me. Amen.

334: Radical Friends

Oh, the joys of those who do not follow the advice of the wicked,
or stand around with sinners, or join in with mockers.
—Psalm 1:1 (*NLT*)

•••●••••

reshman year stunk, Madeline thought. She had just begun to make new friends in middle school, and now that they were in high school, everything was changing. Some were making choices she couldn't agree with, doing things she couldn't go along with. Madeline had already decided: she wasn't changing.

Madeline followed the advice given in Psalm 1; she wasn't following others. She sure didn't feel joyful, though. She felt lonely and discouraged. She felt left out.

START THE REVOLUTION

Analyze your inner circle today. Choose wisely. Choose godly.

When we make right choices, the blessings of God are not always immediate. That can be hard for the revolutionary girl. In many situations, we're used to getting things right away. We pop our mug of powder and milk in the microwave for a minute, and *ding*! We've got hot cocoa. If we're bored, we can turn on the computer or the TV and within seconds find a show to watch, pictures to view, or friends to connect with. No delays, no waiting necessary.

God's economy rarely works that way. God's plan often involves making right decisions today and getting the rewards for those right decisions a long time later. Can you wait for the rewards of being blessed? **Can you put off instant happiness today in order to have lasting joy?** Endure the uncomfortable feelings of going against the crowd to experience the comfort of Jesus' best in your future.

I know most people say they have to learn from experience. Learn from mine: it is worth it to have your inner circle be girls who are also radical about Jesus. There is no getting around it. Look at your five closest friends. If you stick together, you'll be like them in five years. Is that a good or bad thing for you?

Jesus, there are definitely some friends close to me who shouldn't be. Help me to take steps toward good friends and away from those who aren't. Amen.

335: Out of the Heart

*A good man brings good things out of the good stored up in his heart,
and an evil man brings evil things out of the evil stored up in his heart.
For the mouth speaks what the heart is full of.*

—Luke 6:45

•••●••••

"**L**ynn, why do you bother wearing a bra? You are so flat, you should just wear Band-Aids!" I remember it like it was yesterday. Of course, after seeing my mortified face, he probably added something like: "I didn't really mean it!"

"I didn't really mean it" is just a cover-up; the cutting remark reveals the truth. This isn't just my opinion, Jesus said it too (check out our Bible passage for today).

When our hearts are full of kindness and love, kindness and love naturally spill onto others. If our hearts are full of jealousy, anger, and insecurity, our mouths will give us away. It happens so easily . . .

Trying to win the approval of others, you point out someone's bad hair day, or that guy's silly math mistake, or another person's goof in gym. **Their faults become your fun**.

START THE REVOLUTION

What do your words today say about what's in your heart?

You know what Jesus thinks about that? He thinks it stinks. After these words in Luke 6:45 he went on to say in verse 46: "Why do you call me, 'Lord, Lord,' and do not do what I say?"

There's the question of the day: Why would we say we're his, yet not show Christ's love? The revolutionary girl has a revolutionized tongue.

*My heart reveals my secrets, Jesus.
Erase my insecurity, remove my jealousy,
and make me your mouthpiece. Amen.*

336: From Mean to Meaning

Be kind and compassionate to one another,
forgiving each other, just as in Christ God forgave you.
—Ephesians 4:32

E ver heard the saying: "Wounded dogs bite"? Most mean people are people who are hurting. Often those who caused the hurt are those they thought were their friends—people who were supposed to love them.

When we hurt, we have options. We can run to Jesus and allow him to heal our wounds and restore our hearts, or we can allow the pain to fester, creating a heart that oozes ugly stuff.

The next time someone hurts your feelings, switch your thoughts over to thinking about the person who hurt you. What was their motive for hurting you? **Maybe your offender has a damaged heart.**

Do they get picked on? This could be why they picked on you.

Do you know anything about their family life? Possibly things are falling apart.

Do they struggle to make friends? Maybe they're lonely.

The answer to some of these questions just may contain the reason they pick on others.

While this person has used her tongue to damage, we can turn it around. With the power of God's love, we can love this person! We can use our words to heal where she has been damaged. We compliment the girl who is using her sharp words to cry for help. We smile at the one with the glaring eyes. If we have the guts to ask him, the Holy Spirit can give us ideas on how we can influence for good.

START THE REVOLUTION

Do you have what it takes to turn a mean girl into a girl with meaning? Maybe not, but the Spirit living inside of you does. He can use the radical girl who says yes.

Help me to see that mean girl as a girl with meaning, Jesus. Give me your heart. Amen.

Love your enemies. Let them bring out the best in you, not the worst.
When someone gives you a hard time, respond with
the energies of prayer for that person.
—Luke 6:27, 28 (*The Message*)

••●●●••

eople will often "bite" at those they are jealous of, those they wish they could be like. Are you smart? successful? well liked? You might find yourself a victim of mean girl tactics.

James tells us in 3:16 (*NLT*), "Wherever there is jealousy and selfish ambition, there you will find disorder and evil of every kind." The mean that comes out of girls when they are jealous can be vicious.

START THE REVOLUTION

Be radical about praying for your enemies. You might just find new friends!

Hopefully, knowing you are wildly loved by Jesus has given you confidence, purpose, and hope. Others, though, might see these qualities and feel jealous. If jealousy is the cause of harassment from a mean girl in your life, the safest thing you can do is simply walk away and don't say a word. Don't retaliate or fight back.

A radical girl though, will go one step further. **The radical girl will pray for her.** In our verse today, Jesus commands us to do just that.

There is nothing more loving you can do than pray. Your prayers are very powerful. Your prayers may be the door opener to sharing with your mean girl the source of your confidence, purpose, and hope.

Jesus, you know why she picks at me. I ask you to reveal yourself to _____ and help me to reflect your kindness and love in all I do. Amen.

338: Don't Mind the Mockers

Whoever corrects a mocker invites insults; whoever rebukes the wicked incurs abuse. Do not rebuke mockers or they will hate you; rebuke the wise and they will love you.
—Proverbs 9:7, 8

••●●••

*D*o you often find yourself the target of a mean girl? It's just possible you are provoking it. Hard to believe, I know. But slow down and take a look at what is going on.

Are you correcting the person? Do you annoy the offender by being right all the time? Sometimes, we miss the fact that we might actually bring some of the mean behavior on.

Remember, it is a rare girl who likes to be corrected. When you point out someone else's faults or make them feel "less than," you're asking for trouble. As today's proverb says, correcting people who just don't have any respect for anyone invites insults and abuse—hatred even. Offering words of advice to those who are wise, on the other hand, results in them loving you.

START THE REVOLUTION
Radical girl, don't try to fix those who don't even know they need fixing yet. Let Jesus do the work on them.

So what do you do with someone who continually mocks you or picks on you, but has no respect for you? Don't try to correct them—**your words will fall on deaf ears**. Instead, forgive them and move on. Show them kindness when you can—give them respect as a fellow creation of God. Who knows? Maybe someday they will see something in you that they want to get closer to, to find out about.

Jesus, a humble girl doesn't have these types of struggles—she feels no need to correct others. Make me humble, Lord. Amen.

We Love Together

339: The Only Thing

The only thing that counts is faith expressing itself through love.
—Galatians 5:6

••••••••

Ready for a challenge? Define yourself in one word. *Judgmental* or *self-righteous* would have defined the high school me. Not words to be proud of. How about *loving*? I doubt it.

Since I didn't grasp I was loved unconditionally, I only projected what I thought: *If you get it right, you are accepted. If you mess up, not so much, so you better not mess up!*

I thought God was hard to please, so in a weird way, I became hard to please. The heart that was empty of love was empty to give away love as well.

See, **we can't give away what we don't have**. If you don't know that Jesus loves you perfectly, you'll never be able to share with others that he loves them perfectly. You will pass on what you believe, whether that belief is true and healthy or is messed up.

Paul tells Christ followers that the only thing that counts is faith expressing itself through love. The only thing. That's pretty clear and very narrow. The only way others will be able to believe that Jesus is what they need is when love is backing it up. Without love, we are just wasting our breath. Worse yet, we're actually damaging his name and his message.

I sure was missing the one thing—love. I can only imagine what type of impact I could have had back then if I had shared the truth of Jesus, wrapped up in the love of Jesus.

> **START THE REVOLUTION**
>
> How does your faith express itself? Through judgmental words or a gentle example?

Jesus, fill me with love so I can pour out love. Amen.

34℃: Before You Type

We love because he first loved us. Whoever claims to love God yet hates a brother or sister is a liar. For whoever does not love their brother and sister, whom they have seen, cannot love God, whom they have not seen.

—1 John 4:19, 20

••••••

The media attention lately almost makes bullying sound like a new thing. It sure isn't. In 1 Samuel 1:1–2:10, Hannah was bullied by Peninnah. Hannah couldn't have a baby; Peninnah could. So when they went to worship, Peninnah taunted her. (Imagine that—getting bullied on your way to church!)

In today's Bible passage, John made it clear that hatred, which bullying is a form of, is wrong. It's not OK to call someone names—not at school and not on the Internet. Not in a text, not in a tweet. Not to a friend, not to an enemy. Not about what's true, not even for a lie.

I think that since the Internet has expanded and become available everywhere, we have become outspoken in the worst sort of way. People think they are being brave, when actually they are acting like cowards—saying things they would never have enough guts to say to someone's face. Proudly typing hurtful messages on a screen from the safety of their own bedrooms, they feel justified in doing it.

> **START THE REVOLUTION**
> Every word that comes from you—spoken, written, typed, or texted—needs to honor him. Let it be love.

Think twice before you speak and before you type. Literally, read your words twice and before you hit "share" or "send," ask yourself this question: Could I post that on Jesus' Facebook page? If your text accidently went straight to Jesus, would that be all right? If your answer is no, delete. Then think about why you are wanting to hurt someone and what you need to do instead. Because no matter what you do, you can be sure Jesus is getting your message.

Loving others is more than hard, Lord.
The mean me wants to bite back when bitten.
Help me forgive and love. Amen.

341: It's All on You

Therefore, if you are offering your gift at the altar and there remember that your brother has something against you, leave your gift there in front of the altar. First go and be reconciled to them; then come and offer your gift.

—Matthew 5:23, 24

•••●••

"If she has a problem with me, she can just come to me!" Ever heard that one? That's definitely not the way Jesus operates. In fact, he says, if you remember that your brother has something against you, *you* are the one who needs to get it taken care of. Even if you're in the middle of something very important, and you remember that someone has something against you, go and get it resolved.

Are you the type of girl who can't stand to have someone mad at you? By the sound of this verse, that's a God gift. Unresolved conflict only does one thing: simmer. The longer it sits in a heart stewing, the more likely it is for unforgiveness to grow. Left unresolved, bitterness is produced. **Bitterness makes for one very ugly girl.**

Notice that in this verse, Jesus says it is up to *you*. It is up to you to go to the person when they have something against you, not the other way around.

START THE REVOLUTION
Don't be the conflict creator; be the conflict solver. Go to your sister first and get whatever is in the way, out of the way!

It's embarrassing, Lord, to ask for forgiveness. Nobody does it! I guess that is one reason you ask me to—to show that I am really yours. Amen.

342: Space Needed

So Abram said to Lot, "Let's not have any quarreling between you and me, or between your herders and mine, for we are close relatives."
—Genesis 13:8

••••••

*E*ven best friends need space. Tonya and Anna were besties—together all the time. Between classes, at lunch, after school—always together. When their parents would allow it, they even vacationed together.

But sometimes . . . it wasn't pretty. Like dogs broken loose from their leashes, they could really go at it. It wasn't even always over something important. It might be a flippant comment about an outfit or about waiting too long to text back that would set one of them off.

Often their arguments brewed from just spending too much time together. Sometimes silly disagreements piled up until the two were like firecrackers, just waiting for someone to spark the fight.

Abram had this happen too in Genesis 13. His family was spending too much time together in cramped spaces. Fights broke out everywhere; it was no good. He came up with a plan: let's plan some space apart.

In order to keep your relationships healthy, spend some time alone, time apart from each other. When we are together 24/7, we begin to lose our appreciation for each other and can take each other for granted.

START THE REVOLUTION
Embrace space. Use time away from your friend to get more perspective on your best friend, Jesus.

There's some truth to the old saying, "Absence makes the heart grow fonder."

If you and your best friend find yourselves often on edge, do yourselves a favor: **take some time apart.** See it as an opportunity to save your friendship and restore the reason you're best friends to begin with!

Jesus, thank you for my friends. When we need space, remind me of this devotion today and help me plan to save our friendship. Amen.

We Love Together

343: Just Visiting?

The Word became flesh and made his dwelling among us.
We have seen his glory, the glory of the one and only Son,
who came from the Father, full of grace and truth.

—John 1:14

Going to visit Grandma and Grandpa was not on my top ten list of things to do. Let's be honest. It didn't even make the top fifty. The drive was way too long, there was nothing to do there, and they didn't even have cable—all making a visit more painful.

Pretty selfish, huh? Since when was visiting another person about me anyway?

Jesus sure got that it wasn't about him. When he came to earth, he didn't just pop in for a visit. When compared to his heavenly home, I'm sure this place wasn't the ideal vacation destination, especially when most of the people hated him.

START THE REVOLUTION
Love like he loves us.

It seems to me he could have found a more convenient way to come and die for our sins. Isn't it possible he could have shown up on Good Friday and left after he rose from the dead?

But he didn't. In fact, for over thirty-three years, he made planet earth his home with the full experience: birth, growing pains, puberty (weird, right?). He went through the awkward stage of gaining independence while still being respectful to his parents. He learned a skill, got a job. He made friends and found a good temple.

Unlike me, too selfish to even pay attention to my grandparents, Jesus came and engaged. He wasn't too good for the place or the people. **That's powerful, unselfish love in action**; love that invested all the years of his life on earth just to die for us.

Are there some places in your life where you are "just visiting"—tolerating what's going on instead of really loving people? At school, at work, in sports, or at home? Open your eyes today to see with love the value in people that Jesus saw.

What a challenge today, Jesus. Help! Amen.

344: Be Genuine

Therefore each of you must put off falsehood and speak truthfully to your neighbor, for we are all members of one body.
—Ephesians 4:25

•••●●••

Real guts. That's what it takes to be truthful. People putting up a front might say these things: "Nothing's wrong!" or "I'm not mad!" or "It's no big deal!" Yet inside, they are crying, seething, and aching.

Genuine friends tell it like it is. They aren't hurtful; they aren't hateful. They're honest. True friends recognize truthfulness as the foundation to long-lasting relationships. Where there is no honesty, there is no real friendship. The whole friendship is based on falsehood and when hard times come, the relationship crumbles.

Believe me, I know how hard it is to be honest. I have gone to many lengths to get around telling those closest to me how I really feel. Fear of rejection whispered to me that "the truth turns others away." It wasn't until I felt the Holy Spirit challenging me on my lying ways that I began to make changes.

Paul challenged followers of Jesus to "put off falsehood and speak truthfully." Follow this command and build relationships that last a lifetime.

START THE REVOLUTION
We're all part of the body of Christ. Be honest with each other and yourself.

Jesus, I am terrified to be honest. What if they reject me? Help me to trust your way. Amen.

345: Sunset

"In your anger do not sin": Do not let the sun
go down while you are still angry.
—Ephesians 4:26

•••●••

Behind the closed door—better yet, *locked* door—Mindy finds comfort. She hates arguments with her dad, but he never sees things her way! The fights are always the same—him telling her what she's doing wrong. Her favorite weapon, hiding in her room, gives her the last word. At least she wins . . . or so she thinks.

Mindy couldn't be more wrong.

Notice in today's verse, Paul didn't tell Christ followers "never be angry." When kids get picked on or justice isn't served, it's legitimate to get angry.

What Paul did say was, "Do not let the sun go down while you are still angry." **Going to bed mad gives evil a whole night to work on both of you.** Hours and hours pass as your heart and mind simmer in the boiling fury, making it harder for forgiveness to bring peace to the broken relationship.

It's OK, healthy even, to take a break when tempers flare. Time-outs can prevent unwanted words from flying out of an unchecked heart. But don't let the break last overnight. Agree to disagree, if need be. Ask for forgiveness, say you are sorry. Decide to talk about it when you're both calm and can reasonably listen and discuss. Just don't go to sleep with an angry heart.

START THE REVOLUTION

Before you lay your head down on your pillow, lay your anger down at Jesus' feet. Go and forgive, and be forgiven.

Lord, I don't like to be the one to go first, to say I am sorry and make amends. Help me to humble myself like you did when you died for me. Amen.

If your brother or sister sins, go and point out their fault, just between the two of you. If they listen to you, you have won them over. But if they will not listen, take one or two others along, so that "every matter may be established by the testimony of two or three witnesses."
—Matthew 18:15, 16

••●●•••

She was the bonfire at camp; you could practically see the smoke spiraling out of Tina's head. Fuming, she was going to make sure everyone heard the tale of what Allie had done.

Who is this problem between, anyway? Tina and the entire drama team? Jesus says the problem is between Tina and Allie. Nobody else.

He explains in Matthew 18 that when someone sins against us, we are to *go to that person*. Not to your best friend. Not your sister or your boyfriend—just the offender.

Why would Jesus not want us to blow a little steam off to our friends? When we choose to pull others into our drama, **we go from being the offended to being the offender!** We become the gossip spreader (even if

START THE REVOLUTION

Don't fall for being the enemy's helper. Keep your troubles between the three of you: you, your problem maker, and Jesus.

it's true, it's still gossip if we are talking about someone who is not there to defend herself). With our story, we can cause others to look at our offender differently, which may not be fair at all.

That's exactly what I'm hoping for! you might be thinking. You want everyone to know the type of girl she is!

But wait a minute. Are you really sure *you* know for certain what type of girl she really is? You've probably lost all possibility of being objective at this point, don't you think? If you go with your assumptions and spread destructive words against this girl, you'll not only be being mean, you could end up being dead wrong.

Jesus, when someone has made me mad, sometimes I want everyone to know! Help me first face my offender on my own, and not spread gossip. Amen.

347: Best Friends

Two are better than one, because they have a good return for their
labor: If either of them falls down, one can help the other up.
But pity anyone who falls and has no one to help them up.
— Ecclesiastes 4:9, 10

Having the absolute worst day of her life, Madi just wanted to be with Dianna. She wouldn't even have to tell Dianna all the details. She just knew that if she could be around her friend when her heart was breaking, she would feel calmer. Dianna just understood her; she would set her heart at ease.

Do you have a Dianna? A friend who understands you—your quirks, your annoying habits, your sensitive side? If you do, you are a blessed girl!

Are you a Dianna? **Are you the type of friend who keeps secrets secret?** The girl who sets everything aside to lift a friend up?

Friends you can goof around with are a blast; everyone needs some. Friends you can go to the mall, play sports, or watch movies with are fun too. But the best friends are those who can sit and talk—the friends who don't have to be doing anything, just enjoying each other's company.

Find a girl you have things in common with. Do you both love Jesus? (That's a great place to start.) Do you like the same sport, music, or hobby? Do you seem to laugh at the same things and have similar priorities?

START THE REVOLUTION

Make a special day for your friend. Set aside time to go to dinner, have coffee, go to a movie, or whatever she likes to do.

Once you've found her, invest in your friend. Listen to her. Go out of your way to show her you care by texting her encouraging words, remembering her birthday, writing her a card. When she is down, lift her up. The seeds of unselfish giving that you sow will come back to you. You'll find yourself having the type of friend that you have been.

Jesus, this type of friendship is rare.
I want to be a rare friend. Help me to
be that for someone today. Amen.

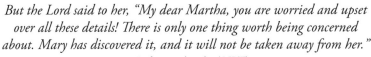

348: Complaint Killer

But the Lord said to her, "My dear Martha, you are worried and upset over all these details! There is only one thing worth being concerned about. Mary has discovered it, and it will not be taken away from her."
—Luke 10:41, 42 (*NLT*)

••●●●••

Think of that one girl who drives you crazy and is completely annoying. Is it your sister? The girl in front of you in chorus? The left fielder in softball?

What is it about her that pushes your buttons? One thing that pushes me over the edge is a complainer. Complaining takes a hard task and makes it nearly impossible.

Jesus had a complainer friend: Martha. Mad that she was making dinner all by herself, she told Jesus, "Tell her to help me!" (Can you believe she had the guts to tell Jesus to do anything?)

Jesus, of course, answers her perfectly, encouraging her to calm down and see what was really important.

When we're annoyed, our response needs to look like Jesus' calm one, encouraging without slamming. He is love, and love is patient and kind. **Kindness kills complaining.** Today, when you hear complaining, kill it with kindness. Speak calmly to your friend, helping her to see the bright side of her dark corner.

START THE REVOLUTION

Remember to kill your own complaints with kindness too. Instead of complaining about someone, do something nice for them.

Lord, the last thing I want to do is be kind when someone is complaining! "Kindness kills complaining" will be my motto though, today. Amen.

"Leave her alone," Jesus replied.
—John 12:7

• • • • • •

S he couldn't quit staring at it. The chocolate diamonds in her new purity ring were so gorgeous; she still had a hard time believing her parents had given her such an extravagant gift. She would never take it off!

At least during Christmas break. Now that school was back in session, the ring was bringing a lot of stress! The first day back, he spied it—the guy who always looked for a reason to pick at her. "What's that, Lara? Your little 'Do Not Touch' sign?" Others chimed in to give her grief.

Let's say you're sitting at the table too, listening. Are you going to do something, or **do you play the safe game and keep quiet?**

In John 12, Jesus' friend Mary was getting picked on. Take a couple of minutes and read the short story; it'll give you the whole picture.

START THE REVOLUTION

Radical girl, defend your friend and be the friend you want to have.

To show her crazy love for Jesus, Mary had taken the most valuable thing she had, perfume worth a year's wages, and poured it on his feet. I know it sounds weird, but sometimes love is over the top! Judas, one of Jesus' followers, jumped all over her. "What a waste of money!"

Jesus didn't stand for it. Immediately, he stood up for her. "Leave her alone." He didn't hesitate or wait for someone else to come to her rescue. He defended his friend.

Now Jesus did a lot of things we will probably never be able to do. Calming storms, healing sick people, rising from the dead. But here is one thing we definitely can do to be like Jesus. It's not that hard. When you see someone taking a verbal beating, defend that person. Don't leave her stranded. Who knows? One day you might be the one who needs defending.

Jesus, I don't like to stand out. What if others turn on me? Give me courage and enable me to defend my friend. Amen.

350: Kind Correction

Whoever loves discipline loves knowledge,
but whoever hates correction is stupid.
—Proverbs 12:1

••●•••

I love to be corrected! It makes me absolutely happy when someone points out my flaws, helping me to mature and become more like Christ.

Ha! You didn't actually believe I meant that, did you? I wish I could say the above statement was true! I'm working on it; but it's hard seeing those who correct me as doing me a favor. I'm afraid I fall more often in the "stupid" category from today's verse than on the loving knowledge side.

When we receive correction, immediately our hearts can become defensive. Instead of seeing it as a help up, we see it as a put-down. A true friend, though, is one who doesn't allow you to get stuck in bad habits or keep heading down a path leading to pain. **She loves you enough to say the hard things** in order to see good things come your way.

Who are the people in your life who are brave enough and love you enough to correct you? Often, at least one of those people will be a parent. It's easy to want to tune a parent out, especially if you hear that voice of correction a lot! But do a new, revolutionary thing. Actually listen. And listen without talking back, without trying to defend yourself. Just listen. Don't be stupid. Be a lover of knowledge.

START THE REVOLUTION

Be radical: next time someone corrects you, be it a friend, a parent, teacher, or coach, say thank you! (Be forewarned—you might give them a heart attack!)

Jesus, give me new eyes to see correction
as a help up and not a put-down. I can't wait to
see the woman I'll become as I embrace the
change others see I need! Amen.

351: Sharper

As iron sharpens iron, so one person sharpens another.
—Proverbs 27:17

••◦●◦••

heir names are Laura and Samantha. If I didn't love them so much, their names could be pain and misery. You see, Laura and Samantha take each word I write and tear it apart. That's how I saw it at first. Laura and Samantha are my editors; they are in my life to help me become a better writer. Being sensitive and touchy, though, I would look at the new sentences they created and get upset; offended even. I mean, what was wrong with the way *I* said it?

Do you have a Laura and Samantha? Does your mom always ask to read your papers for school and then offer "suggestions"? Does your dad come behind your chores, "teaching" you how to do them better?

It's easy to see these suggestions and teachings as slams. Our minds can hear: "You didn't do it right the first time." "You can't do anything right!" Before we know it, we've got this little seed planted in our hearts. If left on its own, quickly it sprouts into a plant of bitterness.

After many years of writing, I have learned that friends like Samantha and Laura are very good friends, because without them, I would be stuck. Stuck writing the same old way, never improving, getting dull—like the knives in my kitchen drawer. When I'm getting ready to cook, I always go for the same knife—the sharp one. It doesn't matter that there are ten other knives to choose from; I go looking for the best one. When it gets dull, I get out my iron rod and sharpen the knife again.

That's what Samantha and Laura are—they are the iron rods that sharpen me.

The people in our lives who help us improve—whether they are friends, teachers, coaches, or parents—are the iron rods in our lives. **They work to make us better, sharper, wiser.** It's time for us to see that and thank them.

> **START THE REVOLUTION**
> Today, thank the "iron rods" in your life for all they do each day to make you a sharper girl.

Lord, thank you for those in my life who sharpen me, making me a godlier girl. Use me to lovingly sharpen others. Amen.

352: Out in the Open

Better is open rebuke than hidden love.
—Proverbs 27:5

•••●●••

Covert tweets. Undercover Facebook posts. Technology takes away the need for courage. Posting a slamming status takes no guts. There's no honor in using technology as a way to hide from facing relationship troubles.

When you are experiencing pain with a friend, take the hard road. Get it over with and give her a call. Meet for coffee. **Don't use texting as a screen.** Do the brave thing and bring the issue out in the open. Instead of dragging it on for hours, doing *anti*social networking, get the trouble corrected quickly by talking it out.

Scared? Who isn't? Embarrassed? You'll live.

Take the first step: begin with a humble apology.

"But I didn't do anything wrong!" you say. You can apologize for possibly misunderstanding her, for not thinking the best of her, or for assuming the worst in her.

Learning to talk things out now will give you a step up when it comes to building long-term relationships, such as a marriage, one day. Practice being a girl who is up-front and honest. Discover the peace that comes from doing relationships God's way.

START THE REVOLUTION
Take stock of your online relationship status. Do the things you say online bring glory to God?

Lord, your way is entirely different from the way of those around me. Give me the guts I need to do relationships your way, up-front and honest. Amen.

353: Look at Me

My command is this: Love each other as I have loved you.
—John 15:12

•••●••••

When it comes to being a good friend, Jesus says, "Look at me." He says, "Love each other as I have loved you."

This is how he's loved us:

- Rescuing us, unselfishly leaving perfect Heaven (John 6:38).
- Serving those around him (Philippians 2:7).
- Defending the weak (John 12:7).
- Telling the truth (Luke 10:41, 42).

Tough list, I know!

He is the best place to start when evaluating if you truly love your friends. Think about it:

- Am I unselfish—putting my friends' needs above my own?
- Do I serve my friends or look to be served?
- Am I on the lookout for those who need to be protected? Do I speak up for others?
- Am I always straight with people? Am I honest?

Maybe, like me, you wish you could say yes to all these questions, but you're just not there yet! Jesus can help us get there.

START THE REVOLUTION

Start with just one of Jesus' love traits and begin to live it out today. Pick one friend and go out of your way to show love the way Jesus did.

Jesus, thank you that I don't have to figure out what loving my friend looks like, I just need to look to you. Remind me today to _____. Amen.

354: Throw Off the Darkness

Anyone who claims to be in the light but hates a brother or sister is still in the darkness. Anyone who loves their brother and sister lives in the light, and there is nothing in them to make them stumble.

—1 John 2:9, 10

•••●●••

"**I** just can't stand him! He's done so much to hurt our family!" Jackie raged as she spoke of her deep resentment toward her dad. Since he had left, she figured there was no reason why she should want to have a relationship with him, let alone try. He didn't deserve it.

I've never experienced divorce like Jackie, but I do know the heartache of family pain. We expect our families to be there for us. When our expectations are crushed, we feel we have the right to hold it against them.

Every time Jesus gives us what seems to be a crazy command, we can count on it being for our good. He tells us that if we claim to be his, yet we hate our brother or sister (or plug in the name of anyone you are struggling to forgive), we're still in the darkness. He commands us to love.

You might say, "I don't care. I'll choose to still be in the darkness. I'm not forgiving them!"

Darkness is never a good place to be. When you can't see what's happening, it's the perfect time for the enemy to infiltrate every crevice of your heart, leaving you broken and ruined. When we choose not to forgive, **the real person we are hurting is us.**

START THE REVOLUTION
If you've been angry with someone for a long time, forgiving them could take a long time too. Be patient and diligent. Wake up every day and make up your mind to forgive.

For your sake and for the honor of the one who died to love you, forgive the one who has broken your heart, just as Jesus has forgiven you. I know you might not feel it. That's OK—forgiveness is not a feeling. It's an act of obedience. Find peace and comfort in a healing heart and let Jesus work on your feelings.

Jesus, I forgive _____. I don't feel it—in fact, I feel very angry. Set me free. Put me back in the light of your peace and love. Amen.

355: Prejudiced

This is how we know who the children of God are and who the children of the devil are: Anyone who does not do what is right is not God's child, nor is anyone who does not love their brother and sister.

—1 John 3:10

••●●●••

START THE REVOLUTION

What you say reveals what is in your heart. If you often point out others' differences in a negative way, just based on surface factors, you may be prejudging people. Correct yourself today.

Stacey believed in Jesus; she accepted him into her heart when she was a little girl. She read her Bible, knew it was true. Attending church and youth group were the norm for her. In fact, she pretty much had it all together. So why, when the youth pastor read 1 John 3:10, did she feel so bad?

Her youth pastor said everyone was considered her brother. *Everyone?* There were some kids at her school who were *really* different. Different colors. Strange cultures. The way they dressed, talked, and even walked was just plain weird!

Even her parents thought these people were strange. Were they missing something too?

As the sermon went on, it was as if Jesus were drawing a line. *If you are for me, if you are mine, you will love who I love!*

All of them?

All of them! Jesus doesn't say:

• You don't have to love those who are not the same color as you.

• You don't have to love those who believe differently than you.

• You don't have to love those who talk, dress, or act weird (according to you).

Nope. No exceptions. **If we are his, we love.** Period.

Lord, I am yours; my life has to reflect that. Change my prejudiced heart and mind, Jesus. Forgive me and teach me to love the way that you love. Amen.

356: Speaking in Love

A time to tear and a time to mend,
a time to be silent and a time to speak.
—Ecclesiastes 3:7

•••●●●•••

When you don't know what to say, it's not bad to say nothing at all. Love doesn't always have to talk.

Sometimes love holds—wrapping arms of comfort. Other times it serves—bringing a meal or a cup of coffee.

Often, love supports. Just being near says, "You're not alone."

Yes, there are times when love speaks words of encouragement or hope. But when the right words just aren't there, don't feel like a failure. Offer what you do have.

Actions speak love when words won't come.

Show love to someone near you today. Each person has her own love language and not everyone's includes words. Your loved one might hear love through a gift, an act of service, a hug, or time just being together.

START THE REVOLUTION

Identify how the people you care about receive love best. Love them their way.

Jesus, it takes time to learn how to love in the way others receive it best. Help me to be unselfish enough to learn to love the way others need. Amen.

357: Be a Big Girl

Fools show their annoyance at once, but the prudent overlook an insult.
—Proverbs 12:16

••••••

arely able to get through her story because of laughing so hard, my girl relived her hilarious meeting that night for all of us. Pushing Skittles into piles with their noses, races in the hallway with scooters—the tales went on and on and so did her energy. "Calm down," I told her. Squash! My tired self, annoyed with her energy, smashed her happy mood. Like air escaping from a balloon, the fun left the room.

"She's so annoying!" *Annoying*—definitely a word that is way overused. The word is generally used to put down someone, and to elevate the one who uses it. But does it?

According to Dictionary.com *annoying* means "irritatingly bothersome." *Irritating* and *bothersome* by whose description? Yours?

Those things you think are annoying, someone else may see as amusing. What drives you crazy may be the exact thing that draws a new friend. **Maybe the problem isn't that everyone is so annoying**, but that you are just too easily annoyed.

START THE REVOLUTION
Pledge to remove the word *annoying* from your vocabulary today.

The book of Proverbs says the person who is annoyed easily is the one who is really the fool. "Fools have short fuses and explode all too quickly; the prudent quietly shrug off insults" (12:16, *The Message*). The wise person, the one who really has it all together, is the one who blows off annoying comments. She doesn't let the small stuff get to her.

Show your maturity by ignoring the things you find annoying. If someone bugs you, let her alone. Allow her to be herself, and you worry about being you.

Jesus, I don't want to be foolish. Help me to worry less about others' actions and be more concerned about my own. Amen.

358: Quick and Slow

My dear brothers and sisters, take note of this: Everyone should be
quick to listen, slow to speak and slow to become angry.
—James 1:19

•••••••

*D*o you have a clothes stealer in your house? I've got one in mine. When I find my new shirt in her laundry, my teeth tend to grind. If I've misplaced my favorite pair of jeans, I might find them under her bed.

You know what this makes me want to do? SCREAM!

James 1:19, 20 nails me: "Post this at all the intersections, dear friends: Lead with your ears, follow up with your tongue, and let anger straggle along in the rear. God's righteousness doesn't grow from human anger" (*The Message*). I'm feeling like God put this one in the Bible just for me.

Pay close attention to the order of those ways that everyone should be:

- **Quick to listen.** (Maybe there is a good reason they did what made me so angry.)
- Slow to speak. (Or text! I need to give my words time to run past God's Word for approval.)
- Slow to become angry. (I can still speak my feelings without blowing a gasket!)

START THE REVOLUTION

If you often let angry words fly, find a place to catch them. Journal, go for a walk, count to ten.

Today, if you feel your blood starting to boil because she did *it* again (whatever it is), breathe deeply and make a choice. Listen, talk less, and refuse to become angry.

Jesus, love is patient and kind, but I don't always feel that way! I need you! Amen.

359: Do the Small Things

Finally, all of you, be like-minded, be sympathetic, love one another,
be compassionate and humble.

—1 Peter 3:8

••●●••

*H*umility is a word that is really misunderstood. Many people think it sounds wimpy—a humble person is someone who lets everyone run all over her. But if that were the case, why would Jesus tell us we should be humble? He is anything but wimpy! In 1 Peter 3:22 we read that Jesus has "angels, authorities and powers in submission to him."

Jesus is also all about love. This is what Peter was writing about in his letter to the Jesus followers scattered throughout the provinces. He was hoping they were living in community with one another, loving "one another deeply, from the heart" (1:22). **Love drives us to think of others before ourselves.** Love makes us concerned with other people's needs. Love makes us aware of how our actions affect others.

> **START THE REVOLUTION**
> Be humble. Do small things to show big love.

When you leave your shoes in the middle of the room, your actions say, "My time is more valuable than yours." How about your choice not to clean the car? Soft drink spills and ground-up French fries devalue it. If you didn't pay for the car, your choices yell, "I don't value your money." What about leaving your computer plugged in or the TV on? The utility bill reflects your choice of self over others.

These seemingly small decisions actually say something big. When you take the time to make good choices, you are really saying, "I love the person this decision will impact." Your actions communicate, "I value you more than I value me."

Think about it. What do you do over and over that shows a lack of concern for others? Do you leave your dirty clothes on the bathroom floor? forget your homework? play your music too loudly? Pay attention to the small things, so you can show love in a big way.

Holy Spirit, please remind me to think of myself less and others more. Amen.

360: Mean Girls?

Mean people spread mean gossip; their words smart and burn.
—Proverbs 16:27 (*The Message*)

•••●•••

*D*o you consider yourself a mean girl? I doubt it. But just to be sure, I've got a challenge for you. Ready? Go this entire day without saying anything bad about anyone. The entire day.

Will it be hard?

Today's verse says, "Mean people spread mean gossip." Notice it doesn't say "Mean people spread *untrue* gossip." What you are saying about that girl in the lunch room could very well be true. The real question is: does it make others want to know her, or does it cause them to run from her? Do your words "smart and burn"? **Would you say them to her face?**

A revolutionary Jesus girl has a reputation as the girl who snuffs out gossip. Others know better than to try to tell her stuff—she just won't listen to it. Rumors end at her door.

I hope that's you!

Go today without one mean word passing your lips, and when you crawl in bed tonight, you can tell the Maker of every girl and guy, "Thank you for helping me love others today."

START THE REVOLUTION

Take the challenge. No mean words all day long. Go!

Jesus, sharpen my conscience. Make me aware of every little word I say, and whether or not it honors you. Amen.

361: Junk Food

Listening to gossip is like eating cheap candy;
do you really want junk like that in your belly?
—Proverbs 18:8 (*The Message*)

Why did I feel so gross? I hadn't *said* anything wrong. My friends hadn't even said the name of the person they were talking about, but we all knew who it was. It was as if not saying the name made the cutting words OK. The way I felt, though, made it obvious—it wasn't OK.

Maybe you're like me, as long as *you* don't say the words, you think you're OK. We're wrong. The Bible says that listening to gossip is just as bad.

The *New Living Translation* gives this version of Proverbs 18:8: "Rumors are dainty morsels that sink deep into one's heart."

Participating in gossip by listening to gossip hurts us. Our hearts were not made to take in words that cut and tear down. Letting mean words sink down into your heart will just pull your spirit down as well.

Don't do it. Don't stand by while someone devalues and defames one of God's creations.

Whether the words are true or not, be true to the one who loves her. Call people out. Make them stop. At the very least, walk away. Don't get sick on junk food.

START THE REVOLUTION

Eat a piece of high-quality chocolate. Let your words be rich and sweet, not bitter and cheap.

Jesus, gossip is a common language.
Help me speak your language. Amen.

362: Secrets

Gossips can't keep secrets, so never confide in blabbermouths.
—Proverbs 20:19 (*The Message*)

She had a reputation—a really good one! "When you tell her, it's like putting it in a safe; nothing's going to get it out," Colleen told me. Not only is that the type of friend I want, it's the kind I want to be!

Everybody needs a person she can share the depths of her heart with and know the information is not going anywhere. What makes it so hard to keep a secret?

Secrets make us feel important—knowing something no one else knows! Burning in our hearts, the urge to tell boils, threatening to run over. But if it erupts, all kinds of damage and destruction could be the result.

Before you give in to the temptation to tell all, take a walk down the path this thing could take:

- A friendship destroyed.
- A reputation tainted.
- A wound created.

All so you can have the rush of sharing the latest news. **Is it worth it?** Think it through. Turn the story around. This time imagine it's your secret being shared:

- You feel betrayed.
- Your reputation's ruined.
- Your heart's broken.

Don't spread a scandal; speak to the Savior. Pray and sow seeds of revolutionary love. Be a secret keeper.

START THE REVOLUTION
Next time you feel like telling a secret, hold onto something tightly. Think before you let anything loose, including your tongue.

Lord, when temptation seems too hard to avoid, help me to tell you instead, and pray for my friend. Amen.

363: Sway

Walk with the wise and become wise;
associate with fools and get in trouble.
—Proverbs 13:20 (*NLT*)

•••●●•••

*E*very time Marie had a new friend, she would start talking just like her. When her friend was from the Northeast, she started having a New England accent. A friend from the South got her using the term *y'all*. It just seemed to happen naturally; the more time she spent with other people, the more she talked like them.

When you're hanging out with someone, **it is inevitable you'll influence each other.**

When this person is God-honoring, this is a great way to grow in your spiritual maturity. Together you can sharpen each other—challenging and encouraging one another to become more like Christ.

START THE REVOLUTION
Open your closet door and check your style. Is it looking wise or foolish?

But what happens if this person is not godly? As today's verse warns, "Associate with fools and get in trouble."

The girl who says "I can hang out with these guys and not become like them" is only fooling herself. It just doesn't work that way. The clothes you wear, the way you talk, the music you like . . . all of these choices are influenced by someone. It might be your sister, the star of your softball team, your mom, or your best friend—but don't kid yourself. Your likes and habits have a lot more to do with those around you than you might think.

Let's take your music: Who else do you know who likes the music you like?

Your hairstyle: Is it popular at your school?

Your wardrobe: I bet your style looks a lot like what your friends or your favorite celebrities wear.

Walk with the wise, become wise. It's your choice; make a good one.

Jesus, please help me find friends who love you and show it. Help me to be a wise friend too! Amen.

364: Sunny Side Up

A cheerful disposition is good for your health;
gloom and doom leave you bone-tired.
—Proverbs 17:22 (*The Message*)

••●●•••

*A*t first I thought she was fake. The first time I met Bonnie, I thought, *Nobody can be that happy. It's just not possible; can't be real.* Then I hung out with her for a while. A while became a few months; a few months turned into a few years. Thirteen years later, I know more than ever that Bonnie's joy is real. You see, I've seen her under the worst possible conditions, and you know what? **Her joy is still there.**

START THE REVOLUTION
Spread some joy today. Give someone a compliment.

This year, Bonnie has battled cancer, and through her fight, I have listened to her. Yes, I have heard her struggle. But more than the struggle, I have heard and seen a heart that trusts her Jesus and is looking for his best even in her worst.

Bonnie gets the secret of Proverbs 17:22. Even if she's not walking around quoting the verse, her life reflects that her hope in the goodness of her God is literally good for her body. Reflecting on sickness and fearing the future would only make Bonnie's battle harder.

How's your disposition? Do you see the glass as being half-full or half-empty? Is your sky blue or gray? How you see life doesn't affect just you; your joyful or jaded heart influences those around you.

Be a joy bringer. When others look at you, may they say, "Here comes Sunshine!"

Jesus, it's hard not to complain. Open my eyes to see all I have to be thankful for. Make me joyful, not jaded. Amen.

365: Give It Away

LORD, I have heard of your fame; I stand in awe of your deeds, LORD.
Repeat them in our day, in our time make them known;
in wrath remember mercy.
—Habakkuk 3:2

•••●•●••

If you've never read some of the great things that God has done in the past, I encourage you to read biographies of some of his servants. Read books about Elisabeth Elliot, Hudson Taylor, Amy Carmichael, and Billy Graham. Spend time digging into the Bible, reading miracles that Jesus did when he was on the earth. Dive into the book of Acts, soaking in the supernatural things that happened in the lives of the disciples in those early days after Christ died and rose again.

You are called not to just soak in this truth, but to give it away. Jesus wants to see your life, the lives of your friends, and the lives of those in your school **radically changed**. He wants it so bad, he died so it might happen. You are the one who can carry revolutionary love to your generation. What are you going to do about it?

START THE REVOLUTION

Spread radical love today. Give this book away!

Jesus, it's time. Time for me to let your radical love transform me into a girl who can start a revolution for you. Help me do it! Amen.

Author Chat

Want to find out more about the author, Lynn Cowell?
Lynn took some time to answer a few questions for us.

Hi, Lynn! Tell us a little about how you became an author.

My neighborhood had some cool teen girls I really wanted to hang out with. I invited them to come over one night for pizza and brownies and I shared with them how I came to know Jesus. The night was an absolute disaster—everything that could go wrong did. As I cleaned up, I was telling God how mad I was that I did this for him, and it turned out so bad! Then, one of the girls, Rachel, asked me if we could start hanging out often. That one girl invited another, and soon it became seven girls. We called our group L.I.G.H.T. (Love Ignited Girls Hang Tight). Each week I would send them stuff from the Bible. They would study the verses, answer the questions, and we'd talk about it when we got together. After a year or so, I felt that if these girls needed to know Jesus was crazy about them and was the only one who could fill the love gap in their hearts, other girls did too! That's when I began my five-year, nineteen-rejection journey to finding a publisher. (I'm so glad God didn't tell me in the beginning how hard it was going to be!)

Where/when is your favorite place/time to write, and why?

I LOVE to write in the mountains, but that can't always happen since I don't live there. Being in the middle of some of God's best work is so peaceful and inspiring. I always write in the morning. My body and brain shut off at 9:00 pm each night, so I have to take advantage of the daylight hours when I can. I usually start with reading my Bible and praying, and then it seems to naturally lead to writing.

What gives you inspiration?

Young people. We have two teen girls, plus a son in college. I also have a small group of high school girls I meet with each week. All these students give me TONS of inspiration. I hear the things that make them happy, the stuff that bums them out, and it makes me want to help them see that Jesus is the center of it all.

Lynn, we know you're not just a writer, but a speaker, youth worker, wife, and mother too. Tell us a little about why you have such a heart for teen girls.

First, I was one. Yeah it was a while ago, but the people in my life and the choices I made had such a huge impact on me, I recall the events and feelings like it happened last year. I absolutely love doing His Revolutionary Love conferences. When girls come up and tell me that my words have helped them to understand Jesus better, or that they get now just how wild he is about them, it pumps me up to write and speak more. Since each day I am surrounded by the highs and lows of young women, I am reminded of all that is at stake, and it empowers me to invest more and more!

This is a 365-day devotional. Do you mean to tell me, in your very busy world, you still find time to sit down with God every single day? How do you do that?

OK . . . every single day? I have to admit . . . I often miss Saturdays. Weird, I know—that should be the time I am there for sure! So, besides that day, I'm making sure that Jesus and I connect each morning. Here's just one reason why . . .

Two weeks ago, I had a really busy day ahead of me, so I decided to go slim on my time with Jesus. A quick two-minute devo with prayers in the car was going to be the way it was happening. So, there I am, music cranking, hair blowing in the wind, as I am flying down a mountain, when something took my breath away . . .

It was the police headlights in my rearview mirror! See, when I don't slow down and give Jesus the day ahead of me, I just plain mess it up! (I mess it up enough, even when I do give him the day!) I really need the awareness of his presence with me and in me the whole day long! His Word and my prayer time fill me with the strength and peace I need each day to honor him and live a fulfilled and purposeful life!

What Christian authors or speakers have been a help to you on your faith journey?

Lysa TerKeurst is the president of Proverbs 31 Ministries; she has really poured into me both through her books and as a friend. My pastor, Steven Furtick, is an amazing man of God. *Sun Stand Still* and *Greater* are two of his books that are life-changing. Right now I'm reading *The Cause Within You,* by Matthew Barnett. It is reminding me of what gives my life purpose and passion: giving to others. When I was younger, *Passion and Purity,* by Elisabeth Elliot, solidified my decision to live a life of purity. A. W. Tozer also nailed me when I was young.

You've mentioned this in your writing, but if you could go back and be a teenager again, would you do it? Why or why not?

No way. It was super hard the first time and would be even harder now. Thanks to the Holy Spirit's power living in me and through me, I am grateful to have lived a life that honored Christ then. No regrets.

What are your favorite memories from your teen years? What's your most embarrassing memory?

Cruising up and down our main road, looking for my friends. (We would have

LOVED to have cell phones back then!) Hanging out in parks after dark—it is so much more fun on the swings and slides when it is pitch-black!

My most embarrassing moment was when my zipper broke and my skirt fell off in the hall of my school. Of course there was this gorgeous senior guy at the end of the hall right then!

Can we see a picture of you from high school? Pretty please?

If you go on Facebook, my old friends have posted PLENTY of high school pics of me. You know the look, big hair . . .

We know you have teens of your own now. What's it like looking at teenage-land from the other side?

I know this doesn't sound very "mom-ish," but it is easier for me to look at it than to live it. I am so confident that my girls will make wise choices and for those times when they don't, Jesus is there to forgive, pick them up, and keep them pursuing him. He is faithful even when we aren't!

What do your teen girls think of what you say in your books?

I love it when they tell me! Mostly they say that they have never thought of Jesus this way before; that not only is he their best friend, Shepherd, and Savior, but he is the one who is crazy about them. I am so glad that they are getting this, because it is so important to know that no guy, whether it is your dad, your boyfriend, or your husband one day, can ever fill the love gap in your heart. Only amazing Jesus—he's the One!

What Bible verses give you comfort or encouragement or motivation? Do you have a favorite verse? If so, what is it, and why?

My favorite verse is Psalm 45:11: "The king is enthralled by your beauty." As girls, we were made to be loved and adored. This verse reminds me that I am just that! It fills the empty places in my heart and makes me feel wanted. Then there are all the good verses like John 3:16, which show that not only does he adore me, but he came and rescued me. You just will never find a better man than Jesus!

How would you say God helped you get through the teen years into adulthood? How does he help you today?

He gave me the reason to make wise choices. So often when I talk to students about important decisions, they say "Why not?" The reason we make good decisions has to be about more than pleasing our parents, not getting pregnant or an STD, or avoiding getting caught and doing jail time (because of course we all think we'll never get caught). You need to have a reason that is bigger. I did. His name was Jesus. Pleasing him and returning to him just a bit of the love he gave to me gave me joy and power. He is what motivates me today. When you are in love, you just want to make the other person happy. I hope that the things I do and the way I live makes him smile every day. I hope you want that too!

Thanks, Lynn!

Read more about Lynn and her Revolutionary Love ministry at www.lynncowell.com!

And if you haven't read it yet, be sure to check out

His Revolutionary Love

ISBN 978-0-7847-2981-6

Also check out the Leader's Guide and other free resources to help you go deeper in your study of his love.
These are available at
www.lynncowell.com
and also
www.standardpub.com/hisrevolutionarylove

ABOUT PROVERBS 31 MINISTRIES

If you were inspired by *His Revolutionary Love* and want to deepen your own personal relationship with Jesus Christ, I encourage you to connect with Proverbs 31 Ministries. Proverbs 31 Ministries exists to be a trusted friend who will take you by the hand and walk by your side, no matter what your age! We help lead you one step closer to the heart of God through:

- Encouragement for Today, online daily devotions
- The P31 Woman monthly magazine
- Daily radio program
- Books and resources
- Dynamic speakers with life-changing messages
- Online communities
- Gather and Grow groups

If you are a teen, check out RadRevolution.com. You'll find inspirational entries, vlogs, conference information, RadRev groups, and fun tips on fashion too!

Maybe you're past that stage; you're a twenty-something. Check out our ministry just for you at www.SheSeeks.org.

To learn more about Proverbs 31 Ministries or to inquire about having Lynn Cowell speak at your event, call 877-731-4663 or visit www.Proverbs31.org.

Proverbs 31 Ministries

616-G Matthews-Mint Hill Road • Matthews, NC 28105 • www.Proverbs31.org